TELOS

NUMBER 143   **SUMMER 2008**

40TH ANNIVERSARY ISSUE

NOTES AND COMMENTARY

REVIEWS

Introduction

With this issue, *Telos* marks forty years as an independent journal of critical thought. Founded amidst the events of 1968, *Telos* has remained true to its origins, maintaining a tradition of independent thinking, while also evolving through the change of four decades. What began as an effort to think philosophically about the political questions of the day continues with the same agenda: our reflections on various thinkers—to take examples from this issue: Alasdair MacIntyre, Walter Benjamin, Gillian Rose, or G. K. Chesterton—are not driven by antiquarianism or academic intellectual history. Rather, we have culled through philosophical traditions, modern and ancient, in order to address the changing character of society and the protean cultural expressions that have emerged from it. This constant redefinition of the critical project informs the teleology, a constant orientation toward the North Star of emancipation, as we navigate the shifting currents of circumstance.

The journal's initial investigation of the phenomenological tradition represented an effort to insert continental philosophy into the overwhelmingly quantitative and positivist terrains of American social science. That methodological critique of the established disciplines (it was 1968, after all) quickly turned however into a political critique: not only of the "establishment" but, with increasing emphasis, of the New Left, as it ossified into multiple but equally noxious forms of dogmatic thinking and mutilated lives. So it was that the phenomenological critique of scientism led to a recovery of the tradition of the democratic and, as we gradually came to recognize, anti-communist Left. During the 1970s and 1980s, this trajectory continued through readings of the Frankfurt School, and *Telos* became the primary venue for the introduction of Adorno, Horkheimer, Benjamin, and others, in the United States, long before their radicalism was recuperated into the normalizing scholarship of university presses. Yet just as Adorno had faced hostility from the student movement in Germany, the New Left similarly did its best to attack this journal for wandering into the forbidden realms of non-orthodox thinking. This is not to say that *Telos* blindly adulated Adorno. On the contrary, careful reconstructions led to similarly careful dismantlings, excavating the unreformed Marxism that still pervaded Critical Theory, its own protestations notwithstanding. The journal began to explore the potential compatibility between the Frankfurt School and our own older legacy of phenomenology: experience, intersubjectivity, and the life-world. Some of this played out through debates around second-generation Critical Theory, especially the work of

3

Jürgen Habermas, which led to heated debates and divisions. This also mapped onto the political disputes of the period, particularly the debate over the limits of détente with Communism or, more precisely, over the NATO program to place medium-range nuclear missiles in Europe to counter the Soviet threat. Like today, public opinion was divided over the estimation of the external threat. Liberals downplayed the Soviets and argued for demilitarization, while others, including many around this journal, understood the telos of emancipation to demand a more muscular response to danger. That policy led directly to the world-historical turn of 1989.

While the captains of ideology were still popping champagne bottles to toast the end of history, *Telos* turned to the undercurrents that would soon spoil the party. The journal's engagement with the political theory of the German jurist Carl Schmitt had elicited controversial responses: less because of his dubious politics in the Nazi era than because of the perspicacity of his critique of liberalism. Just at the moment when liberal democracy prided itself on its imminent universal realization, why bother with one of its severest critics? Yet Schmitt was also a keen diagnostician of the fissures within democracy. If one enemy, the Soviet empire, had disappeared, it was not long before another appeared, as if polarized enmity were itself a precondition for politics. The 1990s were just a bridge between two eras of historical combat. Moreover, Schmitt's critique of premature claims of universalism, pointing to a recognition (which Arendt would have endorsed) of the ineradicable plurality of political communities, indicated a recovery of the priority of particularity: this is the point, characteristic of *Telos*, where Schmitt and Adorno intersect. Particularity, however, is tradition, which in turn is inextricably tied to religion. Our turn toward questions of religion and, especially, the ongoing discussion with the British school of Radical Orthodoxy, was (like the turn to Schmitt) viewed skeptically in the liberal academy. For the institutionalized Enlightenment in universities, any validation of religion was an affront to secularism, just as considerations of enmity sinned against the promise of perpetual peace. The vacuity of that promise became apparent on 9/11, which definitively ended the end of history. Enmity and tradition, indeed enmity and religion, converged.

Telos had flourished thanks to the indefatigable perseverance of its founder and long-term editor, Paul Piccone, who set the agenda of a philosophical thinking of the contemporary condition. In this issue we honor that agenda by continuing the philosophical project itself: hence, the rich array of essays collected here bears witness to the vitality of the journal. We are concurrently releasing an important new book publication, *Confronting the Crisis: Writings of Paul Piccone*, which collects essays that trace the trajectory of his thinking and the evolution of the journal. It is an indispensable companion to *Telos*, documenting its history with choice selections, while also providing an insightful narrative to political and intellectual history since 1968.

In addition, we are also marking our anniversary by putting the journal online. As many readers know, we have been operating a website for the past few years, with active debates on current issues in our blog space. We are now placing current issues as well as the back archive of the journal online: after an initial trial period, full access will be available only to individuals associated with subscribing institutions. Our anniversary present to our readers is this greatly enhanced web presence at http://journal.telospress.com. Needless to say, we will continue to produce the classic, hard-copy *Telos* for years to come, as long as there is demand to warrant it. And right now, demand is growing.

This issue presents a dialectical tale of two cities, human and divine, community and communion. The philosophical project and its religious companion resonate with 1968 in terms of aspirations and failures: the search for the good life in the *polis* side by side with a redemptive aspiration to overcome a degraded world through the pursuit of new, post-material values. The proximity of rejuvenated political community and religious traditions might be read, wrongly, only in terms of a reactionary fundamentalism and traditionalist politics, except that it is equally reminiscent of Benedict XVI's rationalist insistence on the compatibility of faith and philosophy: enlightened religion.

In the special section on "Philosophy and Community," four articles explore how philosophy can theorize community. Is the sheer impact of such rationalization inimical to the organic lineages that keep social groups together? Thaddeus Kozinski begins this debate through an examination of Alasdair MacIntyre's critique of liberalism. He convincingly demonstrates how MacIntyre's alternative to liberal individualism, a Thomist traditionalism, cannot be proven superior (or inferior) to a pragmatic liberalism. Tradition and rationality find themselves in an irresolvable stalemate. Is there an alternative relation to the past that could provide a greater rationality? Yet rational consistency may be more an ideological projection than a compelling description of social forms, if, as Aniruddha Chowdhury argues, life is tied up more with incoherence and ruins than with wholeness and integration. He traces this problem in Benjamin's *Arcades Project* with regard to memory, which is the single dimension in which past members of a community remain present, but they do so only in a shattered condition. Chowdhury describes Benjamin's rejection of restorationist readings of his mystical "now-time," leading him to describe an alternative "destructive historiography," which "presents the present as an impossible spacing of ruins of time itself." This is surely more than a revisionist historiography of anti-triumphalism, indicating instead the value of incompleteness, which leaves the future open and therefore allows room for the other as well as the opportunity to pursue the ever-redefined telos.

Vincent Lloyd explores the (Hegelian) phenomenology of love in Gillian Rose's philosophical memoir, *Love's Work*. The reading of the Arthurian utopia of Camelot stages a conflict between love and law in Launcelot's betrayal, which bears comparison to *Antigone*. Here, the tragedy is unavoidable, which renders Arthur, the King, sad: philosophy is fundamentally the study of this sadness, which is to say, the indelible flaw of community. Meanwhile, Ralph Shain works through Hegel, Bourdieu, and especially Charles Taylor to interrogate the constitutive role of recognition in community. While the desire for recognition is satisfied, formally, by obedience to the law and, especially, to property law, this only leads to the reciprocal recognition as "persons" or "persons who are property owners." This bond, however, is far too abstract to be operative: it has none of Rose's love nor MacIntyre's tradition with which to counteract the secular alienation that undermines the very possibility of community.

The special section on Christianity groups together three distinct pieces, all concerned with the viability of Christianity as tradition. James Schall reflects on Chesterton on the centenary of the publication of *Orthodoxy*; Aryeh Botwinick reads Paul within the Rabbinic tradition and with regard to the immanent dialectics of monotheism; and Mary-Jane Rubenstein reports and analyzes the tensions within contemporary Anglicanism regarding gay clergy, the role of women, and the dynamic between Africa and the developed world.

In the Notes section, Zoltán Balázs comments on post-1968 temporality, a transformed sense of time marked by the disappearance of past and future. The modernist destruction of tradition generates the "no future" despair, a step forward in the bad progress of secularization. Kenneth Marcus, in contrast, turns to the venue of summer pastimes, the baseball stadium, and its recent redesign: by analyzing changes in the space of athletic performance, he identifies important social and cultural changes, as working-class tradition is recycled into a higher-end consumer good for a new public.

Finally, Klaus Berghahn provides a detailed review essay of Russell Jacoby's seminal treatment of the resistance to utopia. Anti-utopianism gained renewed currency after 1989, but now, after post-history, utopia may recover some of its erstwhile standing, if not as a blueprint than as an iconoclastic corrective to administered societies. François Debrix presents Jean-Claude Paye's *Global War on Liberty*, concerned with the contemporary erosion of freedom through the expansion of police powers. A fundamental transformation of law is under way; Debrix highlights Paye's meticulous account of the process. That this process in some ways began in Europe and before 9/11 indicates that we are facing a profound and disturbing metamorphosis of politics everywhere.

Russell A. Berman

Alasdair MacIntyre vs. Pragmatic Liberalism

Thaddeus J. Kozinski

Alasdair MacIntyre is one of the foremost critics of liberalism. As an alternative to the abstract utilitarianism and emotivist relativism of liberal moral theory, he has proposed virtue-ethics and "tradition-constituted rationality." As an alternative to the individualism and bureaucratization of liberal moral practice, he has proposed the practices and politics of local community. He has presented his anti-liberal moral and political vision in his great trilogy, *After Virtue, Whose Justice? Which Rationality?* and *Three Rival Versions of Moral Enquiry*, in later works such as *Dependent Rational Animals*, and in numerous articles, lectures, and interviews, and he has done so with a brilliance, erudition, and sophistication unmatched by his liberal opponents. Nonetheless, MacIntyre's philosophical vision does not ultimately overcome the *strongest* of his liberal adversaries. To show this, I will contrast his anti-liberal project with the "pragmatic liberalism" of Jeffrey Stout. Neither project can successfully refute the other, and I conclude by suggesting a reason for the stalemate.

I. Tradition-Constituted Liberalism: A Fourth Rival Version?

As anyone who has studied the work of MacIntyre knows, the differences between his project and liberalism, of whatever variety, both in theory and in practice, are radical. One of the most radical differences is how each understands the relation of tradition to rationality and the necessary conditions for human flourishing. While MacIntyre considers participation in teleologically ordered, hierarchical, and authoritative traditions to be the *sine qua non* of rational and moral activity and human flourishing, the liberal sees such traditions as obstacles to these and a threat to human flourishing. For MacIntyre, this false perception is the fundamental defect of liberalism, and because of it, liberalism is essentially one giant contradiction. Liberalism purports to be a rationally transparent, culturally and religiously neutral account of objective reality, accessible to all men in terms of their shared universal reason; however, in truth, it is merely one particular, debatable account among others, stemming from a particular debatable tradition of rationality. Showing that liberalism is, indeed, a tradition has been the linchpin of MacIntyre's strategy to defeat liberalism, for it diffuses its primary rhetorical strategy of preempting any debate as to the debatable character of its own premises.

However, a non-MacIntyrean attitude toward tradition is not necessarily definitive of liberalism. Consider the possibility of a form of liberalism that accepts MacIntyre's overall understanding of tradition-constituted rationality, that is, one not in denial, as it were, about the its tradition-constituted character. Such a liberalism might transcend MacIntyre's three-fold categorization of rival traditions: encyclopedia (Enlightenment liberalism), genealogy (post-Enlightenment Nietzscheanism), and Thomism. A MacIntyrean critique of this "fourth rival version," then, would have to go beyond the basic incoherence of standard liberalism, as a tradition that pretends it is not a tradition, and deal with *substantive differences* between Thomism and liberalism. MacIntyre would have to contend with, for example, this liberalism's radically different conception of human nature, the human good, God, the relationship of faith and reason, virtue, and the supernatural. The "pragmatic liberalism" of Jeffrey Stout would seem to successfully sidestep MacIntyre's critique of liberalism by agreeing with it. Tom Bridges summarizes the project: "If liberalism is to survive the collapse of Enlightenment culture, liberals must now attempt to de-universalize or contextualize their political language, to learn to explain and advocate liberal democratic moral ideals in a vocabulary that can express the particularism of liberal political norms without thereby invalidating them."[1] What would a confrontation between MacIntyreanism and this renovated, "particularist" liberalism look like?

Stout summarizes his project as follows:

> There is much to be gained by abandoning the image of democracy as essentially opposed to tradition, as a negative force that tends by its nature to undermine culture and the cultivation of virtue. Democracy is a

1. Thomas Bridges, *Culture of Citizenship: Inventing Postmodern Civic Culture* (Albany, NY: SUNY Press, 1994), p. 15.

culture, a tradition, in its own right. It has an ethical life of its own, which philosophers would do well to articulate. Pragmatism is best viewed as an attempt to bring the notions of democratic deliberation and tradition together in a single philosophical vision. To put the point aphoristically and paradoxically, *pragmatism is democratic traditionalism.*[2]

Stout takes MacIntyre to task for his characterization of modern liberal democracy, its philosophy, politics, and culture, as inherently anti-traditional and thereby defective. To prove his point, he enacts his own competition of rival moral traditions in which the "old" liberalism of Rawls and the "new traditionalism" of MacIntyre lose to the new "pragmatic liberalism" of Whitman, Emerson, and, of course, Stout. Enlightenment, modernist liberalism presented itself as empty of substantive moral content, neutral with respect to any particular conception of the good, and independent of history, culture, and tradition. Due to the devastating postmodern critique of the Enlightenment's facile foundationalism and universalism, liberalism could no longer rely upon its previous epistemological and ontological privileges. Enlightenment "reason" now seemed to be only empty rhetoric, being just one narrative of one particular culture's self-understanding among many, and a deeply problematic narrative at that. In order to defend itself in the present intellectual climate, liberalism must adopt a postmodernist, narrative approach to its own origins and history, accepting the a priori characterization of all philosophical systems as culturally and historically particularistic. If it does not reconfigure itself in this way, it remains vulnerable to the critiques of both the antimodern traditionalist and the postmodern genealogist.

Stout adopts such a narrative approach to liberalism in the attempt to render democratic traditionalism immune to MacIntyre's critique. For Stout, liberalism succeeds as a version of moral enquiry because it possesses all the required elements that MacIntyre ascribes to a tradition in good working order: virtues, rules, internal goods, and a coherent narrative that justifies these goods and orients them to an ultimate good. Liberalism has nothing against teleology, as long as it is of a certain type, and liberalism certainly does, and should, endorse a particular conception of the good for man. Like Aristotelianism and Thomism, Stout's liberalism possesses both a conception of man-as-he-is and man-as-he-could-be-if-he-realized-his-*telos*. It is, in short, a full-fledged tradition: "Democracy, I shall argue,

2. Jeffrey Stout, *Democracy and Tradition* (Princeton, NJ: Princeton UP, 2004), p. 13.

is a tradition. It inculcates certain habits of reasoning, certain attitudes toward deference and authority in political discussion, and love for certain goods and virtues,...This tradition is anything but empty....The notion of state neutrality and the reason-tradition dichotomy should not be seen as its defining marks."[3] For Stout, there is no incoherence or sign of an imminent epistemological crisis in this revamped liberalism.

"We can say that the liberal project was simply to tailor the political institutions and moral discourse of modern societies to the facts of plural-ism."[4] Instead of conceiving modern liberal democracy as the embodiment of an anti-Aristotelian, theoretical philosophical system, the end result of an ideologically driven movement of anti-traditional secularists, Stout sees it as a reasonable and pragmatic response to a sociological fact, the fact that citizens no longer freely agree (if they ever did) upon a particu-lar, religiously based philosophy of life: "Ethical discourse in religiously plural modern democracies is secularized, according to my account, only in the sense that it does not take for granted a set of agreed-upon assump-tions about the nature and existence of God."[5] Secularization, in politics and public discourse, then, is a non-ideological, purely pragmatic process; it is simply what happens naturally to a political order when the fact of worldview pluralism is recognized without resentment. This ideologically neutral process is the correct explanation for the "secularization" of dis-course and institutions, and railing against it only renders one politically ineffective and divisive: "Nobody currently knows how to bring about by acceptable means what the theological opponents of secularized discourse are suggesting. Their proposals are unrealistic if pursued without recourse to coercion and morally harmful if pursued collectively."[6]

Contra MacIntyre, "we" democratic traditionalists *do* agree upon fun-damental moral matters, as evidenced by, in spite of all its present faults and past injustices, the robust and thriving political order of the United States. Our present political order is based upon the fundamental ethical practices of "giving and asking for ethical reasons," and "holding each other accountable." In a democratic society, these play the role of meta-norms upon which all other particular norms are to be based: "The norm user is anyone who possesses the expressive resources to exchange reasons

3. Ibid., p. 3.
4. Ibid., p. 129.
5. Ibid., p. 99.
6. Ibid., p. 100.

for and against explicit normative claims."[7] Democratic culture is not, of course, based upon any particular religious or philosophical norm. Instead, it is, as Stout identifies it, based upon *pragmatic* norms, what he calls "moral bricolage," defined by Stout as the "selective retrieval and eclectic reconfiguration of traditional linguistic elements in hope of solving problems at hand."[8] Pragmatism is not a philosophical system that purports to explain and justify the ideological basis of the liberal political order, for liberalism has no ideological basis. Indeed, pragmatism is precisely recognition of the necessity of abandoning both ideology and fundamental doubts as to moral convictions:

> Our fellow citizens are not nervously awaiting vindications of philo-sophical pictures before proceeding to hold each other valuable. A modest pragmatism, fully understood, would encourage us to view most of our first-order beliefs as more certain, and most of our dispositions as more worthy of confidence, than any of the pictures philosophers have introduced in the hope of explaining and grounding them.[9]

The specific norms of democratic society include such virtues as piety, deference to others, and perfectionism. Thus, Stout sees in liberal culture none of the community-corrosive individualism that MacIntyre describes. It is not based upon an atomistic, individualist ideology, for it is not based upon any ideology. Nor are the norms of liberal society inherently anti-tra-ditional and anti-theological: "[Democratic traditionalism] entails neither the denial of theological assumptions nor the expulsion of theological expression from the public sphere. And it leaves believers free to view both the state and democratic political culture as domains standing ulti-mately under divine judgment and authority."[10]

Ironically, it is MacIntyre's ability as a non-Thomist and non-Aristo-telian, indeed, as a citizen living within the tradition of a non-Thomistic and non-Aristotelian liberal democracy, to discern the superiority of the Aristotelian-Thomistic tradition and then convert to it, that suggests the resources of the liberal tradition alone are adequate for coherent ratio-nal and moral activity. Moreover, MacIntyre's notion of the individual as

---

7. Ibid., p. 197.
8. Jeffrey Stout, *Ethics After Babel* (Princeton, NJ: Princeton UP, 1988), p. 293.
9. Ibid., p. 253.
10. Stout, *Democracy and Tradition*, p. 93.

"deeply formed by social forces but not thereby committed to a substantive conception of the human good,"[11] with the capacity to move freely from one tradition to another, is an eminently modern attitude. Finally, the inherent historicity of his conception of rationality is thoroughly modernist as well, apparently irreconcilable with the eminently non-modernist doctrinal authority of the institution that is central in the tradition to which he has committed himself, the Roman Catholic Church.

II. Pragmatic Liberalism: Neither Pragmatic nor Liberal

MacIntyre does not deal in particular with pragmatic liberalism, but his overall critique of liberalism appertains to it. This becomes apparent if we analyze pragmatic liberalism (PL) in terms of its encyclopedic and genealogical components. It can be argued that PL is not a fourth rival version at all, but rather a sophisticated hybrid of Encyclopedia and Genealogy. PL is encyclopedic in the particular values it upholds and its attitude toward non-liberal traditions. Like encyclopedic liberalism, it values above all the freedom of self-creation, or personal autonomy, and identifies it as the only possible candidate for a publicly authoritative value. Thus, the value of personal autonomy would be as publicly authoritative in the pragmatically liberal political order as it is in the encyclopedic liberal order. Since pragmatic liberalism admits the truth of MacIntyre's understanding of rationality as tradition-constituted and accepts itself as a tradition, the meaning of "person," "autonomy," "freedom," "self-creation," as well as any of the particularist norms that serve as *de facto* moral authorities for liberal social practices, can only be accurately understood from the perspective gained by personal participation in these practices, that is, in the tradition of pragmatic liberalism. Stout is careful not to give any particular content to these norms, for the *raison d'être* of the pragmatic liberal order is the individual's right to inform and ground the norms he deems authoritative with a meaningful content and philosophical explanation of his own choosing, whether liberal or non-liberal in character. However, the question arises: are citizens *actually* free to impose, even if only upon themselves, *non-liberal* meanings and explanations upon the ostensibly meaning-and-explanation-free norms of pragmatic liberal society? The answer would be "yes" under the *philosophical* liberal order, because, being tradition-*independent*, its norms are not constitutively determined

11. Ibid., p. 106.

by the meaning and explanation given to them by any particular tradition. However, the answer would seem to be "no" under *pragmatic* liberalism in virtue of its peculiar norms.

By simply asserting that non-pragmatic philosophy has failed in itself and as a grounding for contemporary democratic political order, pragmatic liberalism attempts to position itself as the only possible grounding. But a theory that cannot be subjected to rational scrutiny by others, that is unwilling or incapable of undergoing dialectical challenge, is rendered incapable of rational vindication, as MacIntyre points out:

> It may seem to be, but it is not paradoxical, to conclude that the discovery that it is possible for our own particular moral standpoint to be rationally defeated by some rival standpoint is a necessary condition for arriving at a rational vindication of our own point of view. For the strongest vindication that any point of view can receive is that it has so far survived encounters with as wide as possible a variety of other and rival standpoints without suffering such defeat.

Stout claims that "exchange of reasons" is the essence of democratic traditionalism. But can there be a fruitful exchange of reasons between the traditionalist who sees theological truth as a publicly authoritative divine communication to all men, and indispensable for the objectivity of ethical evaluation, and the "traditionalist" who sees theological truth as primarily a creation of individuals and an expression of subjective desire? If such exchange cannot take place between PL and other traditions, and if PL is publicly authoritative anyway, then is not this a clear example of the unjust imposition of one belief upon another—not the "expressivist discourse" that Stout recommends? PL undemocratically and non-pragmatically excludes non-pragmatic philosophical and theological viewpoints that claim to possess more than merely private significance.

Stout writes: "It is an aspect of our substantive commitment to the ethical life of democracy, because it coheres with the widely (but not unanimously) held conviction that no merely human perspective has a monopoly on the truth."[12] And: "The need for some sort of cultural covering may belong to human nature, but once we think of this covering as the product of our artifice, we are in a position to take responsibility for it."[13] Ironically, by discounting the legitimacy of any other grounding

12. Stout, *Democracy and Tradition*, p. 197.
13. Ibid., p. 224.

but its own, pragmatic liberalism asserts a "monopoly on the truth"—an eminently undemocratic assertion; and by refusing both to engage other traditions on their own terms and to engage its own tradition on theirs, pragmatic liberalism shows itself to be eminently "irresponsible." The irony is that the pragmatic liberal, more than anyone else, undermines the "expressive discourse" of "giving and receiving reasons" that supposedly serves as the lifeblood sustaining the pragmatic liberal society. He refuses both to give and to receive a reason in defense, not simply of any particular moral value, cultural practice, or political policy of the pragmatic liberal order, but of the pragmatic liberal order itself.

III. A More Honest Liberalism?

We have shown that the pragmatic liberalism of Stout is essentially a hybridization of the encyclopaedic and genealogical traditions, and as such is vulnerable to MacIntyre's critique of these traditions. Nonetheless, a successful defense of pragmatic liberalism still remains possible. Suppose that PL were explicitly to defend its anti-theological conceptualization of truth, its theologically intolerant political application of this conceptualization, and its refusal to provide any rational grounding for itself, denying any self-contradiction in these elements. How would MacIntyre's theory assess this "tradition-constituted, exclusivist liberalism"? Would a liberalism that *defended* its theoretical and practical exclusion of non-liberal theories and citizens be as vulnerable to a MacIntyrean critique?

A more *honest* tradition-constituted liberalism could accept this politically exclusive dynamic—and even endorse it—in accordance with its particular conception of the good. For the honest pragmatic liberal (HPL), the liberal tradition is self-contained and absolute, with personal autonomy an "internal good" of a practice, whose meaning is itself a constitutive element of the liberal tradition; thus, to attain personal autonomy one must adopt the meaning given to it by the liberal tradition. The attainment of personal autonomy, at least for those living within this tradition—and that means every "non-separatist" citizen living within North Atlantic nation-states—requires the citizen's acceptance that public agnosticism toward transcendent reality is, for all intents and purposes, the "truth." With MacIntyre, the HPL recognizes that to preserve the integrity of the liberal tradition, "fundamental dissent must be excluded." Thus, anyone with an understanding of personal autonomy incompatible with the liberal tradition is subversive to the intergrity of the tradition. Such people *should* be excluded to some extent from active participation in the practices that constitute the liberal tradition, for as "unbelievers" they are incapable of benefiting from and can only damage the integrity of the tradition, which must be safeguarded at all costs to facilitate the attainment of personal autonomy for those capable of it. In short, a fully honest pragmatic liberalism would freely and happily admit that it is that which its predecessor liberalism defined itself by rejecting: an ideologically homogenous, exclusivist, and authoritarian—yet liberal—community.

IV. An Unresolved Rivalry

Pragmatic liberalism maintains that a MacIntyrean conception of tradition, one with an inherited culture integrated and oriented to some transcendent being through authoritative texts, rituals, personages, and institutions, is less facilitative of individual rationality and the common good than its own non-authoritarian and non-theistic tradition. MacIntyre, of course, denies this, depicting pragmatic liberalism as a radically defective project. Can MacIntyre and the liberal traditionalist settle the matter? Can either recognize the superiority of the other? When we contrast PL's purely rhetorical, ultra-conservative, and descriptivist conception of the nature and role of philosophy to MacIntyre's speculative, critical, and realist view, it is apparent that the possibility of rational adjudication between them, by which both could recognize the superiority of one over the other, is highly improbable if not impossible.

In MacIntyrean Thomism, the purpose of philosophical activity is not simply to provide a rational articulation of one's tradition, but to discover the *right* tradition, to access and express, from within the tradition, supra-traditional *truth*. Philosophical activity should serve not only the cultural function of rendering a tradition intelligible, and the rhetorical function of making it attractive, but also the speculative function of describing the *truth* insofar as human reason can describe it. And it is this more important speculative function that is rejected by the pragmatic liberal. Consider this characterization of philosophy by Gary Gutting, an avowed pragmatic liberal: "We have renounced the traditional philosophical goal of rationally established fundamental truths about what the world is like and how we ought to live.... Philosophy does, then, have a distinct subject matter (the development and explication of fundamental concepts) and a distinctive set of techniques (conceptual analysis, historical critique, and creative redescription)."[14] In light of Gutting's definition of philosophy, how would one characterize a *defense* of the pragmatic liberal tradition? Since PL rejects the possibility of knowing whether words are descriptive of "what the world is like and how we ought to live," its words must serve some other purpose. As Gutting puts it, the job of the philosopher is to "creatively redescribe" the liberal democratic tradition to make it *desirable*.

MacIntyre claims that what is essential to good philosophy is vulnerability to radical self-criticism, whereby adherents of a tradition may "identify the difference between how things in fact are and how they have hitherto taken them to be." This attitude "presupposes that truth is a good, independently of one's own particular moral standpoint," for "to fail to make explicit this recognition of truth as a good is to deprive claims on behalf of one's moral standpoint of the only authority that can successfully legitimate them."[15] Although PL defends the validity of claims to truth, whether the claim be metaphysical, moral, or theological, it rejects the validity in principle of any claim to *know* that one's assertions of truth are true. If this weren't enough, it refuses to expose *this* epistemological claim, one that is the very foundation of the liberal democratic tradition, to rational verification or refutation! However, as MacIntyre rightly points out, exposing one's claims to the possibility of dialectical refutation is an indispensable requirement for being able to claim that one's claims are true. And the claim to know the truth of one's claims applies not just for those in one's own tradition, but for *all* people and for *all* time: "To claim that some thesis is true is not only to claim for all possible times and places that it cannot be shown to fail to correspond to reality in the sense of 'correspond' elucidated earlier but also that the mind which expresses its thought in that thesis is in fact adequate to its object."[16] According to MacIntyre's criteria for justifiable truth-claims, PL proponents cannot justifiably claim that the pragmatic liberal tradition is true. However, for a pragmatic liberal to recognize and accept this would require that he share with the MacIntyrean Thomist a common notion of the nature of truth and shared criteria for justifiable truth claims, and this would presuppose

14. Gary Gutting, *Pragmatic Liberalism and the Critique of Modernity* (Cambridge: Cambridge UP, 1999), pp. 190, 193.

15. Alasdair MacIntyre, "Moral Pluralism without Moral Relativism," in Klaus Brinkmann, ed., *Proceedings of the Twentieth World Congress of Philosophy*, vol. 1, *Ethics* (Bowling Green, OH: Philosophy Documentation Center, 1999), p. 4.

16. Alasdair MacIntyre, *Whose Justice? Which Rationality?* (Notre Dame, IN: Univ. of Notre Dame Press, 1988), p. 363.

a common identification of the nature of philosophical work in general. Since the nature of philosophy is theoretical for the MacIntyrean and rhetorical for the pragmatist, the MacIntyrean requirements for truth-claiming would not be pertinent for the liberal pragmatist—for claims of truth are not even an issue for him.

If there are no shared standards of rationality by which otherwise incompatible traditions could evaluate each other, then there is no rational reason for choosing one tradition over another. We would be left with only fideism. As Micah Lott points out, MacIntyre does admit the existence of common rational standards, but he makes a distinction between "weak" and "strong" standards. Weak standards are "trans-traditional" and include such purely formal matters as consistency and comprehensiveness. In these areas, pragmatic liberalism (but not, I have argued, a more honest pragmatic liberalism) fails in rationality. Strong standards, however, are entirely tradition-specific, and include substantive matters, such as particular conceptions of the good, truth, human nature, and God. MacIntyre maintains that while all traditions hold similarly weak standards of rationality, these are not sufficient to settle inter-traditional rivalries.[17] Pragmatic liberalism and MacIntyreanism differ quite radically in *strong* standards of rationality, and for this reason I think that MacIntyre's critique of liberalism, which utilizes only the weak standards of rationality, is ineffective to deal with the "honest pragmatic liberalism" that we have described, a tradition with a rhetorical conception of philosophy and a non-apologetic attitude toward its exclusion of non-pragmatist views from public political authority and full participation in the authoritative liberal democratic tradition.

To be successful, MacIntyre's argument against Honest Pragmatic Liberalism would not only have to refute the "strong" standards of rationality inherent in and specific to the HPL tradition, such as its rhetorical conception of philosophy, its pragmatic conception of truth, its agnosticism toward the truth of any particular religious belief, and its rejection of any claim to public, political authority for such a belief. But HPL would also have to admit this refutation according to these very same strong standards. Such a result seems very unlikely. HPL's invulnerability to MacIntyre's critique exposes a significant weakness in his theory. A MacIntyrean Thomist must judge HPL to be a defective tradition, for philosophy is not rhetoric.

17. Alasdair MacIntyre, *Three Rival Versions of Moral Enquiry: Encyclopaedia, Genealogy, and Tradition* (Notre Dame, IN: Univ. of Notre Dame Press, 1990), p. 101.

In Thomism, one can justify one's claims to truth, and to know that one knows the truth, through intellectual contact with a tradition-transcendent reality. MacIntyre would be the first to admit, however, that the honest pragmatic liberal is obliged to accept the Thomist's judgment against HPL only if perceived *from within his own tradition* as being an accurate judgment, according to its particular rational criteria. And, even though an epistemological crisis may exist within the pragmatic liberal tradition, it does not exist, for all intents and purposes, unless those within the tradition recognize it. As MacIntyre admits, sometimes such recognition never takes place, and when it does, it is rare.[18] HPL could possibly recognize defectiveness in its own tradition—for example, if as a practical matter it lost popular support and the ability to make decisions peacefully—but to articulate the problem and its solution it has to inhabit imaginatively some other tradition in order to observe how HPL looks from the outside, and might well resist doing so. Neil Levy points out the problem:

> Tradition A encounters tradition B, or develops out of it. In retrospect, A claims that B was in crisis, and that it provided the resources for the solution of that crisis. A Nietzschean genealogist might be forgiven for seeing in this claim a retrospective justification for the fundamentally unjustifiable exercise of the will-to-power [in the case of the pragmatic liberal, the unjustified exercise of rhetoric], especially when it is recognized that the defects of the earlier position may only be perceived from the perspective of the latter.[19]

A basic problem with MacIntyre's theory regarding the comparative evaluation of the rationality of traditions is that it presupposes a certain level of *abstraction* from any strong standards of rationality, from any peculiar epistemological, metaphysical, theological, and morally substantive claims or groundings: "Like other procedural approaches, MacIntyre's theory of rational conflict resolution between traditions cannot be stated without abstracting from the particular epistemological crises, concrete claims, and internal standards at issue."[20] Abstraction from matters of particular substantive commitment is, of course, an earmark of Enlightenment

18. MacIntyre, *Whose Justice? Which Rationality?* p. 366.

19. Neil Levy, "Stepping into the Present: MacIntyre's Modernity," *Social Theory and Practice* 25, no. 3 (Fall 1999): 490n9.

20. Ibid., p. 536.

liberalism.[21] Why expect the Enlightenment liberal approach to work better in this case than in others? For there to be any chance of resolution of the conflict between MacIntyreanism and HPL, absent utter collapse of one or the other as a going concern, it would not be sufficient for the participants to follow a general methodology for such resolution, one sufficiently abstract to allow agreement between the parties. They would have to address the *concrete* claims of each tradition and grapple with concrete, tradition-specific philosophical questions such as: Can one *know* that he knows the truth? Is religious truth ultimately a cultural creation of man, or is it revealed to us by a culture-transcending God? Can the truth about God be known, and if so, is it something that is to be publicly authoritative? Has God revealed the ideal political order, and is this revelation publicly accessible? Should such a revelation be given communal obedience and political recognition on a large scale? Can political theology have political authority in a democratic society? Of course, HPL and Catholicism provide entirely different answers to these questions. It is in dealing with these sorts of questions, and showing that there either are or are not definitive and knowable answers to them, that the relative superiority of traditions as radically incompatible as pragmatic liberalism and MacIntyrean Thomism could be assessed. Consider, though, that these are not strictly philosophical questions, but theological ones. In short, a competition between two traditions as radically incompatible as HPL and MacIntyrean Thomism, if it is to result in a definitive judgment of relative superiority, cannot be restricted to philosophical discourse. A theological argument is required.

V. Tradition-Constituted Theological Rationality

For a Roman Catholic, the Church exists as a public institution claiming to be the embodiment and spokesman of a publicly authoritative divine revelation bearing directly on morality and politics. Therefore, the Church should be seen as at least a *possible* candidate for a publicly authoritative, politically relevant institution. In articulating an ideal political order, the political philosopher must therefore deal in some way with the Church's claim to have the authority to define the ultimate meaning of goodness, by either accepting or denying that claim. Ignoring the claim or claiming

---

21. Jennifer A. Herdt, "Alasdair MacIntyre's 'Rationality of Traditions' and Tradition-Transcendental Standards of Justification," *The Journal of Religion* 78, no. 4 (October 1998): 535.

that it only applies to private life would be an implicit, practical denial of the Church's *actual* authority. To do so is to make a theological judgment *against* the Church's authority. When such a judgment becomes part of a lived social tradition, and becomes embodied in its social structure, one can justifiably call such a tradition a religion. As D. Stephen Long points out: "Ethics cannot be the province of a philosophical discourse that brackets out theological consideration, unless philosophers assume a being greater than God giving access to goodness."[22]

In a dialectical confrontation between HPL and MacIntyrean Thomism, then, theological questions such as God's existence, man's knowledge of God, and the political ramifications of this knowledge are paramount. But considering the standards of rationality involved in adjudicating theological claims, this leads to what is perhaps the most vital theological question: as Flett puts it, "Why should an inquirer commit to a particular contingent tradition in the first place?"[23] Does MacIntyre provide a convincing reason to embrace Thomism over liberalism, pragmatic liberalism, or honest pragmatic liberalism, other than their purported internal contradictions and his contention that only Thomism can survive sustained dialectical philosophical questioning? We have seen that the former argument does not apply to HPL, and the latter is unconvincing to anyone but the Thomist. HPL is not, of course, justifiable according to Thomistic rational standards, but this doesn't settle matters, because Thomism itself is unjustifiable according to PL's standards.

The conclusion one can draw from the preceding discussion is that since MacIntyre confines himself to answering strictly philosophical questions, he is ultimately unable to argue effectively against the theological judgments we have shown to be implicit in the tradition of pragmatic liberalism. Indeed, within this stricture, MacIntyre is unable to argue effectively against any tradition with prescriptions for the ideal political order, because these prescriptions must involve theological judgments, whether they be implicit or explicit. In conclusion, the methodological refusal to consider theological judgments is the primary weakness in MacIntyre's project, for it precludes both the effective vindication of his own theologically based

---

22. D. Stephen Long, *The Goodness of God: Theology, The Church, and Social Order* (Grand Rapids, MI: Brazos Press, 2001), p. 300.

23. John Flett, "Alasdair MacIntyre's Tradition-Constituted Enquiry in Polanyian Perspective," *The Polanyi Society Periodical* 24, no. 2 (1999): 1. Flett argues that MacIntyre, unlike Polanyi, does not address this question adequately. For Polanyi, "commitment, belief, and faith are viewed as the inescapable ground of all knowing."

and informed Thomistic tradition, and the possibility of its being refuted by other rival traditions. As we have attempted to show, any intellectual tradition articulating an ideal political order must necessarily include a judgment as to whether God has communicated His will to man regarding the political order. Neither MacIntyre nor pragmatic liberalism makes any explicit judgment on this question, but the refusal to make a judgment on this matter is already a judgment. By not prescribing an authoritative role for political theology, both MacIntyrean Thomism and pragmatic liberalism effectively deny that God has spoken authoritatively regarding the proper construction of the political order. In sum, both deny the authority of revealed political theology.

Memory, Modernity, Repetition: Walter Benjamin's History

Aniruddha Chowdhury

In an important fragment in *The Arcades Project*, Walter Benjamin points to two perspectives on the present. The present is defined either as catastrophe or as triumph.[1] Two perspectives, Benjamin seems to suggest, constitute two *modes* of temporality. Whereas for a triumphant history, the present is located in the duration of time that Benjamin famously calls "homogeneous, empty time,"[2] in the movement of the same, for the historiography of the oppressed, on the other hand—and that is how Benjamin sees the position of historical materialism—the present is located in a temporal disjuncture "in which time stands still and has come to a stop" (Thesis XVI). What is progress for a triumphant history is catastrophe for the historian of the oppressed. "The concept of progress must be grounded in the idea of catastrophe. That things are 'status quo' (that things just go on) *is* catastrophe" (N9a, 1). The historical materialist conception of the present as *site* of catastrophe will serve as a guiding thread of the paper.

---

1. Walter Benjamin, *The Arcades Project*, trans. Howard Eiland and Kevin McLaughlin (Cambridge, MA: Belknap Press, 1999), convolute N9a, 8. All future references to convolute N of *The Arcades Project* will be cited parenthetically in the text as "N" followed by the fragment number.

2. Walter Benjamin, "Theses on the Philosophy of History," in *Illuminations*, ed. Hannah Arendt, trans. Harry Zohn (New York: Schocken Books, 1968), thesis XIV, p. 261. Hereafter all references to the individual theses of "Theses on the Philosophy of History" will be cited parenthetically as "Thesis" along with the corresponding thesis number. References to the other essays collected in *Illuminations* will be cited in the text as "I" followed by the page number.

"The modern is a principal accent" of Benjamin's thought.[3] An important aspect of our reading of Benjamin is to situate his literary-historiographic thought in the context of his theoretical articulation of the experience of the modern. It will be crucial to think of Benjamin's articulation of the modern as designating a structure of experience *and* its distinctive temporality, rather than a historical period. Experience of the modern, for Benjamin, is "devoid of substance" (I 177); its time is homogeneous and empty. In several places Benjamin mentions that the aim of his book on the Baroque plays is partly to "expose the seventeenth century to the light of the present day" (i.e., the nineteenth century) (N1a, 2). There is a certain originary technicity in the experience of the modern. Similarly, script rather than language, death's head rather than face, citation rather than mimesis—these are the allegorical emblems in which the baroque world is "expressed," or better, shattered.[4] Benjamin's historical materialism is a response to, and a match for, the modern experience. One of the arguments of this paper, to be developed through a reading of Benjamin's reflections on Marcel Proust, as well as of Benjamin's theses and fragments, is that memory that characterizes historical materialism is a *temporal experience of image.* A certain temporal asymmetry, a determinate non-identity (between image and experience, between *Gedächtnis* and *eingedenken*, between repetition and the new) structures the dialectical image, which is the enigmatic core of Benjamin's historical thinking. Benjamin's conception of "actualization," to which *repetition* belongs as a strategy without finality, has to be grounded, I will argue, in the non-identity and asymmetry between the messianic and the historical. Crucial in this context will be the idea that repetition, as a theatrical concept in Benjamin, is a *relation* of difference (non-semblance) between the "fore-history" and "after-history," the relation that constructs the interiority of the event *of* repetition or historical event. This construction of the "inside" of an event from a certain "outside" is the work of repetition. It will be my argument that actualization/repetition, in Benjamin, is in-finitely negational.

I. Death and the Aura of Memory

In "The Image of Proust," Benjamin speaks of Proustean time as "convoluted," as opposed to "boundless" time. Proust's true interest, Benjamin

---

3. Benjamin, *The Arcades Project*, p. 10.
4. Fredric Jameson, *Marxism and Form: Twentieth-Century Dialectical Theories of Literature* (Princeton, NJ: Princeton UP, 1971), p. 72.

says, lies in "the passage of time in its most real—that is, space-bound—form" (I 211). The Proustean experience of time is a retroactive experience of time that has passed. Time of the present, lived time, is a time under the sign and shadow of death. Infinite effort of *mémoire involontaire* consists in rescuing the un-lived time from death. "On a larger scale, however," Benjamin writes, "the threatening, suffocating crisis was death, which he was constantly aware of, most of all while he was writing" (I 214). Benjamin describes memory as "a match for the inexorable process of aging" (I 211). In a fascinating paragraph, Benjamin describes the death as manifested in aging, to which Proust responds by "letting the whole world age by a lifetime in an instant":

> [Proust] is filled with the insight that none of us has time to live the true dramas of the life that we are destined for. This is what ages us—this and nothing else. The wrinkles and creases on our faces are the registration of the great passions, vices, insights that called on us; but we, the masters, were not home. (I 211–12)

Our unhomeliness, our oblivion is precisely the sign of the domination of death. It is the work of death, Benjamin would argue. In "The Storyteller," Benjamin returns to the idea of the work of death that is presupposed and matched by remembrance: "Death is the sanction of everything that the storyteller can tell. He has borrowed his authority from death. In other words, it is natural history to which his stories refer back" (I 94).

The paradigmatic theme of natural history in Benjamin's extraordinary study of the seventeenth-century German baroque dramas, *The Origin of the German Mourning Plays*, conveys the idea of history as "petrified nature," and nature as "petrified history." The popular baroque emblems of human skeletons and skulls signify the idea of history as constant mortification and transience. In the baroque image of the fossil is embodied the idea of the survival of the past in the present. It is Theodor Adorno who, in the remarkably complex essay "The Idea of Natural History," offers a philosophical interpretation of Benjamin's idea of natural history. A brief discussion of some of the crucial themes of Adorno's essay might give us an important perspective on the broader historiographic dimensions of Benjamin's thinking, to which we will return later.

In "The Idea of Natural History," Adorno compares Benjamin's concept of natural history with Lukácsian idea of "second nature." This term designates, for Lukács, the reified world of capitalism, the alienated world, the world of convention. Adorno quotes from Lukács's *Theory of the Novel*: "This (second) nature is not mute, corporeal, and foreign to the senses like first nature: it is a petrified, estranged, complex of meaning that is no longer able to awaken inwardness, it is a charnel-house of rotted interiorities."[5] The charnel-house, Adorno suggests, is the cipher, the signifier. For Lukács, the petrified history is nature, or the petrified life of nature is an effect of historical "development." But Lukács, in keeping with the German idealist tradition, "can only think of this charnel-house" within the horizon of eschato-theological totalization. For Adorno, Benjamin represents "the decisive turning-point in the formulation of the problem of natural history."[6] The emblem of natural history is "a cipher to be read." Natural history is the "original-history of signification."[7] Natural history appears as a sign language of transience. History and nature meet deeply in the elemental transience. Adorno thus articulates the essential difference between Lukács and Benjamin:

> If Lukács demonstrates the retransformation of the historical, as that which has been, into nature, then here is other side of the phenomenon: nature itself is seen as transitory nature, as history.[8]

Here, Benjamin's concept of allegory and its difference from symbol is of crucial importance. What marks their difference is "the decisive category of time."[9] As Adorno quotes Benjamin:

> Whereas in the symbol, with the glorification of death and destruction, the transfigured face of nature reveals itself fleetingly in light of redemption, in allegory the observer is confronted with the *facies hippocratia* of history, a petrified primordial landscape.[10]

Allegory "expresses" the original-historical relationship between nature—as what appears—and its signification, i.e., transience. Nature never appears alone as simply present; it appears with its double, its

---

5. Theodor Adorno, "The Idea of Natural History," trans. Bob Hullot-Kentor, *Telos* 60 (Summer 1984): 120.

6. Ibid., p. 119.

7. Walter Benjamin, *Origin of German Tragic Drama*, quoted in ibid., p. 119.

8. Ibid., p. 119.

9. Benjamin, *Origin*, quoted in ibid., p. 120.

10. Ibid., p. 120

destructive double, i.e., with death. Allegory expresses this original doubling of nature (life) and history (death).

According to Adorno's reading, the structure of Benjamin's natural history is a constellation, "namely those of transience, signification, the idea of nature and the idea of history."[11] Nature and history are not simply fused with each other; "rather, they break apart and interweave at the same time in such a fashion that nature appears as a sign for history and history, wherever it seems to be most historical, appears as a sign for nature."[12] The essential point that Benjamin and Adorno make is that natural history as constellation, as signification, illuminates the original-history of signification. Original-history cannot mean an original presence from which history is a fall. Rather, origin is *already* transience; decay is the origin. Original-history, in this sense, is originary historicity. Historicity here is not an abstraction from historic experiences, which would then amount to another hypostatization, to a divination of history (second nature) as immutably given. In the chapter "World Spirit and Natural History" of *Negative Dialectics*, Adorno takes Hegel to task for hypostatizing the "spirit" (second nature) into world spirit, thereby absolutizing domination and projecting it on Being itself.[13] "In the midst of history, Hegel sides with its immutable element, with the ever-same identity of the process whose totality is said to bring salvation."[14] On the other hand, in Benjamin's reading of the baroque, the historicity that natural history signifies does not require identity of the nonidentical, does not return to a suprahistorical, or, which is the same thing, ahistorical reconciliation of chance and necessity. Rather, historicity signifies an originary passing, an unrecoverable diachrony. If nature and history form a constellation as signification of transience, then the constellation can only be momentary. As Adorno writes in *Negative Dialectics*: "The moment in which nature and history become commensurable with each other is the moment of passing."[15] For Adorno, as for Benjamin, that moment of passing is precisely present as a ruin.[16] "As transience all original-history is absolutely present. It is present

---

11. Ibid.

12. Ibid., p. 121.

13. Theodor Adorno, *Negative Dialectics*, trans. E. B. Ashton (New York: Continuum, 1973), p. 356.

14. Ibid., p. 357.

15. Ibid., p. 359.

16. Ibid.

in the form of signification."[17] In other words, the present is the *site* of original-history. But as a site, the present is also a *return* of original-history. The latter, as Adorno comments, is "signified in allegory, *returns* in the allegorical."[18] The apparently paradoxical concept of the present as a site of passing, and of the return of what is passed, offers us a proper angle and perspective on the Benjaminian idea of the present as a critical or an interruptive moment of history, and thereby provides us an entry into Benjamin's broader notion of historiography as a record and articulation of memory. We will have occasion to return to this idea in the context of Benjamin's historiographic response to what he calls modernity.

The present as a site of passing and of return is, Benjamin would argue, endowed with the *claim* that he describes as "a *weak* messianic power" (Thesis II). The messianic is weak because the moment that is the temporal space of the constellation of the past and the present is the moment of passing. The messianic has a structure of haunting in that it returns at the moment of passing. Benjamin calls this haunting "the unforgettable."

The unforgettable receives several redemptive descriptions throughout Benjamin's writings. The unforgettable, in Benjamin's writings, is not a naïve antithesis of what is forgotten. Rather, as we will see later in the context of Benjamin's reflections on Proust, the unforgettable is situated in a dialectic of forgetting and remembering. Something becomes unforgettable when it threatens to be irretrievably lost. In both "The Task of The Translator" and "The Storyteller," the unforgettable appears—or, to be more precise, returns—as a *claim*.

In "The Task of The Translator," Benjamin states his central point at the very beginning: "The translation is a mode" (I 70). Translation is not simply derivative of, or secondary to, the original. Rather, as a mode, translation issues from the original itself. The original itself "contains the law governing the translation: its translatability" (I 70). Translatability is the essential feature of the original. Benjamin explains his contention by introducing the crucial idea of the "afterlife" of art and of language as such: "A translation issues from the original—not so much from its life as from its afterlife" (I 71). A work of art, or, for that matter, language as such, according to Benjamin, is characterized by a beyond. Its significance and its truth lie beyond its natural presence, beyond its "organic

17. Adorno, "The Idea of Natural History," p. 121.
18. Ibid. (emphasis added).

corporeality" (I 71). But Benjamin distinguishes the idea of the afterlife of truth from theological notions like "scepter of the soul" (I 71). On the contrary, "in the final analysis, the range of life must be determined by history rather than by nature. . . . The philosopher's task consists in comprehending all of natural life through the more encompassing life of history" (I 71). We will misunderstand Benjamin fundamentally if we regard his view of the determination of nature by history in properly historicist terms. Rather, the historicity of art and language should be understood, Benjamin suggests, beyond the category of natural growth, ripening, and unfolding, and thus beyond the category of organic corporeality.[19] Historicity signifies a movement of constant mortification *and*—this is Benjamin's most crucial argument—"the course of its survival" (I 72). So, it is not so much life as *after*-life that determines the translatability and reproducibility of linguistic art work. The original itself attains its truth, its actuality, in its reproduction, which also means that the life of the original is already marked by death. The original lives on, as it were, *after* its death.[20] The unforgettable is precisely that which lives on and makes its anachronic claim. It is the task of the translator (and analogously, of the historiographer) to respond to this claim.

It is not my intent here to discuss in detail Benjamin's enigmatic "The Task of the Translator." What we are trying to see, rather, is how in that essay, as in "The Storyteller," Benjamin articulates the historiographic dimension as a movement not so much of life as of mortification and of living-on (neither simply life nor simply death), and also as a space of remembrance and bereavement. In "The Task of The Translator," the idea of the after-life allows Benjamin to speak, in metaphysical terms, of the essential relation between the law of translation (and, by extension, language as such) and of remembrance. Benjamin writes:

> It should be pointed out that certain correlative concepts retain their meaning, and possibly their foremost significance, if they are not referred exclusively to man. One might, for example, speak of an unforgettable life or moment even if all men had forgotten it. If the nature of such life or moment required that it be unforgotten, that predicate would not

---

19. I owe this point to Paul de Man's reading of Benjamin, in his essay "Walter Benjamin's 'The Task of The Translator,'" in *The Resistance to Theory* (Minneapolis: Univ. of Minnesota Press, 1986).
   20. Ibid.

imply a falsehood but merely a claim not fulfilled by men, and probably also a reference to a realm in which it *is* fulfilled: God's remembrance. Analogously, the translatability of linguistic creations ought to be considered even if men should prove unable to translate them. (I 70)

"God's remembrance" is perhaps an analogue for the messianic end of what Benjamin calls pure language. In "The Storyteller," epic memory serves as a model of that holistic remembrance. But in Benjamin's thinking, that holistic memory is not accessible to man as it does not belong to historical time proper. In his "Theologico-Political Fragment,"[21] Benjamin draws the distinction between messianic temporality and the temporality of history. The messianic does not unfold from within history; rather, the messianic represents a cessation, a termination of historical time. The Messiah, Benjamin seems to suggests, comes from *outside* of history and "himself consummates all history."[22] More importantly, as we will see later, the messianic end of remembering the unforgettable is available to *us* (in history) only as an instantaneous image. That image is a concern of the present because, as a *site* of passing and of return, the present itself is the unforgettable. As Benjamin writes in Thesis V:

> The true picture of the past flits by. The past can be seized only as an image which flashes up at the instant when it can be recognized and is never seen again.... For every image of the past that is not recognized by the present as one of its own concern threatens to disappear irretrievably. (Thesis V)

The only instant in which the image of memory flashes up, as we read in next thesis, is the "moment of danger" (Thesis VI). Elsewhere, Benjamin refers to that image as the straw for the drowning man: "The smallest guarantee, the straw at the drowning man grasps....*Eingedenken* as the straw."[23]

And that moment of danger is, as we read in "The Storyteller," the moment of dying. This brings us back to the point we started with: the

---

21. Walter Benjamin, "Theologico-Political Fragment," in *Reflections: Essays, Aphorisms, and Autobiographical Writings*, trans. Edmund Jephcott (New York: Schocken Books, 1978), pp. 312–13.

22. Ibid., p. 312.

23. Quoted in Wohlfarth Irving, "On the Messianic Structure of Walter Benjamin's Last Reflections," *Glyph* 3 (1978): 148.

relation between dying and the form of memory that we know as storytelling. Let me quote an important passage from "The Storyteller," where, just after giving an historical account—account that already blurs the conventional distinction between history and story—of the epochal change in man's perception of death, Benjamin writes about the relation of dying and the unforgettable:

> It is, however, characteristic that not only a man's knowledge or wisdom, but above all his real life—and this is the stuff that stories are made of—first assumes transmissible form at the moment of his death. Just as a sequence of images is set in motion inside a man as his life comes to an end—unfolding the views of himself under which he has encountered himself without being aware of it—suddenly in his expressions and looks the unforgettable emerges and imparts to everything that concerned him that authority which even the poorest wretch in dying possesses for the living around him. This authority is at the very source of the story. (I 94)

II. Storytelling, Modernity, and Proustean Non-Identity

In "The Storyteller," Benjamin looks at another world, another time, which is "remote from us" and "is getting even more distant" (I 83). There is pathos, but no revivalist nostalgia, in this looking back. Story is no longer a "present force" in its "living immediacy" (I 83). Storytelling embodied a structure of experience whose ground has been permanently eroded by what Benjamin calls modernity. So, to reflect on "someone like Leskov as a storyteller does not mean bringing him closer to us but, rather, increasing our distance from him" (I 83). The word "reflection" in the title of the essay involves a "proper distance and angle of vision" (I 83) on the part of the observer.

Why does Benjamin reflect on the story, then? What is precisely at stake in this retroactive reflection? What is at stake is not simply the story and its vanishing beauty, but the historiographic dimension to which story belongs as one of its forms.[24] Story involves a specific form of memory that Benjamin still wishes to retain in his own version of historical materialism. So, the proper angle of vision, in the context of our reading, can be achieved when Benjamin's reflections on story are read together with his "Theses On The Philosophy of History" and with his reflections on another

---

24. In my discussion of the historiographic dimension of the storytelling and the novel, I am indebted to Irving Wohlfarth's important essay mentioned above.

"storyteller" of modern times, Marcel Proust. For both in the "Theses" and in his reflections on Proust, Benjamin seeks to retain a certain messianic traits (in his word, "utopia") that the storyteller's remembering involves while at the same time canceling its historicist legacy.

Benjamin opens up this historiographic dimension in sections XII and XIII of "The Storyteller." It is evident that in these two crucial sections, as well as later in the essay, he keeps faith with Lukácsian triadic structure of the development of literary forms in the West, as it is articulated in *The Theory of The Novel.* Storytelling as an essentially oral literary form can only originate in a space where experience is shared and transmitted from one to another. In contrast to the novel, the story presupposes a collective sharing of experience, a space of community based upon tradition: "[T]he listener's naïve relationship to the storyteller is controlled by his interest in retaining what he is told. The cardinal point for the unaffected listener is to assure himself of the possibility of reproducing the story" (I 97). Thus, the story, by virtue of its structural possibility, belongs to the epic dimension of memory. As Benjamin writes: "Memory is epic faculty *par excellence.* Only by virtue of a comprehensive memory can epic writing absorb the course of events on the one hand and, with the passing of these, makes its peace with the power of death on the other" (I 97). It is memory that "creates the chain of tradition" (I 98). And it is in this context that Benjamin relates the literary forms of the story and the novel to the broader question of historiography. The important and distinctive aspect of Benjamin's analysis is that he relates the development of the western literary forms to the question of the *temporalization* of memory itself. According to Benjamin, it is historiography that forms the common ground of all forms of the epic. Benjamin uses the term "historiography" in the broadest possible sense, that is, as "the record kept by memory" and which "constitutes the creative matrix of the various epic forms" (I 97). The epic is the oldest form of historiography, its original and undivided form. Epic art has "Mnemosyne, the rememberer" as its muse and contains within itself the germs of two distinct and partial literary forms of memory: the story and the novel. The emergence of two distinct literary forms of memory and of historiography signifies "a parting of the ways in world history" (I 97). The passages of occasional invocations of the Muse in the Homeric epics contain within themselves the unity of two distinct forms of memory: "the perpetuating remembrance of the novelist as contrasted with the short-lived reminiscences of the storyteller. The first is dedicated to *one* hero, *one* odyssey, *one* battle; the second to *many* diffuse occurrences. It is, in other words, *remembrance* [*Eingedenken*] which, as the Muse-derived element of the novel, is added to reminiscences [*Gedächtnisse*], the corresponding element of the story" (I 98). The historiographic counterpart of the story is the chronicle. "The chronicler is the history-teller" (I 95). The chronicler, unlike the historian or writer of history, whose task it is to explain the happenings with which he deals, has from the outset lifted the load of explanation from his shoulder and only shows how his tales "are embedded in the great inscrutable course of the world" (I 96). The storyteller, Benjamin says, is the secularized chronicler. His remembrance rescues the events of the past from history. What Benjamin writes of the chronicler in Thesis III is true of the storyteller, too:

> A chronicler who recites events without distinguishing between major and minor ones acts in accordance with the following truth: nothing that has ever happened should be regarded as lost for history. To be sure, only redeemed mankind receives the fullness of its past. (Thesis III)

The novelistic memory (*Eingedenken*) is messianic, too, in that it bears testimony to the cessation of happening and to the founding moment of history. A new calendar that is introduced by the revolution is an exemplary form of such *Eingedenken.* We read in Thesis XV:

> The great revolution introduced a new calendar. The initial date of the initial day of calendar serves as a historical time-lapse camera. And, basically, it is the same day that keeps recurring in the guise of holidays, which are days of remembrance. (Thesis XV)

But after the fragmentation of the epic unity, if we follow Benjamin's Lukácsian narrative, *Gedächtnis* and *Eingedenken* remain in sharp contrast. Only a redeemed humanity will get them in their unity. The past will become "citable in all its moments." That day is Judgement Day. Judgement Day, then, is a messianic end of history when *Gedächtnisse*, reminiscences of *many*, will appear at a flash of an instant in *Eingedenken*, memory of the *one*. Such is Benjamin's utopia. The peculiar form of memory that Benjamin calls historical materialism will be a unity of both or, as Irving Wohlfarth reminds us, a remembrance of that unity.[25] But it is not simply utopian hope that is in question in Benjamin's articulation of such

---

25. Wohlfarth, "On the Messianic Structure," p. 151.

unity in historical materialism. Rather, this rearticulation is a response to the present that we know as the modern. Modernity designates a structure of experience and of temporality that has already eroded the basis of storytelling. Whereas the story is based on transmissibility of experience that makes possible the authentic continuity of tradition, modernity represents "a tremendous shattering of tradition," a historical shock.

Before moving on it is important to assert that for Benjamin, unlike much of sociological tradition, modernity is no mere name for a historical period and the specific social forms that belong to it. Rather, it designates a structure of experience and its distinctive temporality.[26]

In "The Storyteller," Benjamin notes the distinctive characteristic of storytelling as "an artisan form of communication" (I 91). "It does not aim to convey the pure essence of the thing, like information or a report. It sinks the thing into the life of the storyteller, in order to bring it out of him again. Thus traces of the storyteller cling to the story the way the handprints of the potter cling to the clay vessel" (I 92). Modernity, Benjamin suggests, marks an epochal shift from the mode of production based on artisan manufacture to that based on industrial machine. Crucial, in the context of machine, is the decline of practice. With practice as the basis, Benjamin writes quoting Marx, "each particular area of production finds its appropriate technical form in *experience* and *slowly* perfects it" (I 176). The cumulative experience of practice provides the ground for "the process of assimilation which takes place in depth" (I 91), which is the defining characteristic of storytelling. In contrast, machine production "requires early drilling of the worker" (I 176). "His work has been sealed off from experience; practice counts for nothing there" (I 176). Each segment of work at the machine is without any connection with the preceding operation for the very reason that it is its exact repetition. The work at the industrial machine, Benjamin concludes, is "devoid of substance" (I 177). It is the voiding of substance, the experience of *being voided*, that characterizes the experience of not only the industrial worker, but the modern as such. As Benjamin reflects in "On Some Motifs in Baudelaire," modernity designates the structure of experience "for which shock experience

---

26. Peter Osborne has already described Benjamin's conception of the modern as "a kind of phenomenology of structure of consciousness" rather than a period term. See Peter Osborne, "Small-scale Victories, Large-scale Defeats: Walter Benjamin's Politics of Time," in *Walter Benjamin's Philosophy: Destruction and Experience*, ed. Andrew Benjamin (London: Routledge, 1994), p. 83.

has become the norm" (I 162). The shock experience of the passerby in a crowded city, the worker's experience at the industrial machine, the film actor's sense of exile in front of the camera, and the mass reception of films are all metonyms of the "same" shock experience. In his essay on Baudelaire, Benjamin employs the Freudian interpretive model to explain the paradoxical situation of consciousness without experience. In Freud's term, a living organism confronted with a traumatic shock uses its protective shield against stimuli by readily registering in consciousness such "external" threat without retaining them in memory. The latter becomes the repository of what is repressed, of unconscious traces. Consciousness becomes empty space of memory, of memories without memory. True memories become involuntary, becomes heavier with *traces* of "what [the subject] has not experienced explicitly and consciously, what has not happened to the subject as an experience" (I 160–63).

In the empty space of modern experience, what is new always appears as "ever-always-the-same"; new as eternal recurrence of the same. Such, according to Benjamin, is also the fetish character of commodities, whose privileged example is fashion. The thorough impoverishment of experience has its menacing impact on human communication as such. Communicability of experience is replaced by a new form of communication: information. The latter "reflects the increasing atrophy of experience" (I 159). It is one of the features of information (a news item, for example) that it conveys the happenings without connecting them with the experiential realm of the reader. The brevity of information means that it does not survive the moment when it is fresh for consumption. It does not enter the tradition.

Modernity, as it appears in Benjamin's phenomenological description, is that temporal space where experience is characterized by a loss of what is experienced. The experience is marked by time lag. Temporality of the modern is without *duration*. The modern experience, if we follow Benjamin's employment of Freud, is a *retroactive* experience. In this precise sense, the modern is a temporal space *already* marked by a certain *post*. The prefix "post" *before* the modern means that modern as a beginning is a beginning *after*, an after-beginning. "Post" expresses the *mode* of existing of the modern.

Now it is the task of the historical materialist to (re)articulate a historiographic *form* that can be adequate to the experiential structure of the modern. To return to the story will be a pure nostalgia. Worse still, storytelling *after* modernity will amount to the empty chronology characteristic of historicism that tells "the sequence of events like beads of rosary" (Thesis XVIII). In historicist chronicle, epic continuity is transformed into a homogeneous empty time of "tradition" and into the narrative of infinite progress. The empty continuum of "tradition" and of boundless progress is precisely what Benjamin calls catastrophe. Thus, "historical materialism must renounce the epic element of history" (N9a, 6).

And yet, historical materialism has the task of articulating a unity of the two forms of memory. To be sure, this projected unity would not be a simple fusion of the story and the novel; neither of them would remain the same in this unity. Rather, it would appear as constellation in the form of an image. The model of messianic remembrance in contemporary modernity, Benjamin asserts, is neither the story nor even the novel, but the image. One of the elementary doctrine(s) of historical materialism is, Benjamin reflects generally, that "[h]istory decays into images, not into stories" (N11, 4). The remembering thinker gathers his energy to seize hold of the image that "in the next moment is irretrievably lost" (N9, 7). The literary model of this historiographic form Benjamin finds in the work of Proust.

The time lag, the lateness, that characterizes the structure of experience and of temporality of modernity also structures the remembering work of Proust. In "The Image of Proust," Benjamin quotes Jacques Rivière's enigmatic observation that "Proust died of the same inexperience which permitted him to write his works" (I 213). The word "inexperience" in this quotation does not so much mean a simple lack of experience as, rather, a time-lag *in* experience. Experience itself is structured by this lag. In "the inhospitable, blinding age of big-scale industrialism" (I 157), experience means the empty message of information that we can recollect at will. This empty (in)experience is the basis of what Proust calls *voluntary memory*, "one that is in the service of the intellect" (I 158). But the true dramas and experiences of existence that call on us, but which "we the masters" "never (have) time to live," *become* experience only in the instant of spontaneous remembrance. This is the domain of Proustean *involuntary memory*. What lies at the bottom of Proust's frenetic, infinite, efforts is the desire to "rejuvenate," in a flash of involuntary memory, things that have always already been past, the past that he has never experienced, the past that, in this precise sense, never existed as such. This desire—Benjamin describes it as "elegiac idea of happiness" (I 204)—to rejuvenate the past and pull it together with the present in an instant "transforms existence into a preserve of memory" (I 204). This is the *other* side of the "inexperience" to which Rivière refers. The inexperience that "had begun to crush him" (I 213) also becomes, for the *writer*, the enabling condition of the involuntary memory to which the writer's enormous work of remembrance is dedicated.

The time of involuntary memory is convoluted, interwined time, as opposed to historicism's boundless time. It is a constellation of a particular past and a particular present in a space-bound form. In this constellation, the particular past becomes recognized, for the first time, as a mark, a trace, in an instant. "This concept [of involuntary memory] bears the marks of a situation which gave rise to it" (I 159). The past that never had a chance to live, if we follow Benjamin's reading of Proust, lives on as traces in the fragile density of some material objects or in the sensation that it arouses in us "though we have no idea which one it is . . . it depends entirely on chance whether we come upon it before we die or whether we never encounter it" (I 158). The chance of involuntary memory that Proust refers to here in a tone of private despair is, in Benjamin's language, the messianic instant that arrests the empty continuum of voluntary memory, "a revolutionary chance in the fight for the oppressed past" (Thesis XVII).

The astounding weight of Proust's work consists in the fact that it is not so much a remembrance of the past as it was lived and experienced as, rather, a weaving of memory. This is what Benjamin says in "The Image of Proust." Proust's work, as Benjamin reads it, is a dialectical "web"—"the Latin word *textum* means "web" (I 202)—of remembering and forgetting. "Is not the involuntary recollection," asks Benjamin, "Proust's *mémoire involontaire*, much closer to forgetting than what is usually called memory?" (I 202). In Benjamin's fascinating expression, the Proustean weaving of memory is "a Penelope work of forgetting" (I 202). But it is also a counterpart to Penelope's work rather than its likeness: "For here the day unravels what the night has woven" (I 202). With the night comes not the events of life, but "an everyday hour." With the night unfolds the most banal, most fleeting, "weakest hour" of lost time. This is what joins Proust to the art of storytelling. We read in "The Storyteller": "The more *self-forgetful* the listener is, the more deeply is what he listens to impressed upon his memory. When the rhythm of work has seized him, he listens to the tales in such a way that the gift of retelling them comes to him all by itself. This, then, is the nature of the web in which the gift of storytelling is cradled" (I 91). In the nighttime of "listening," then, the self (the "dummy" of purposiveness, of day time) is loosened and forgotten in the passivity (web of weakest hour) of immemorial. What emerges in the night is the web of "memory" of the immemorial woven by forgetting. In such a Proustean web, Benjamin has discovered "the bridge to the dream." "No synthetic interpretation of Proust can disregard it" (I 204).

Let us follow Benjamin's "synthesis" more closely. Involuntary memory has the structure of dream, and, like dream, it is a world of opaque resemblances. The experience of similarity that we have in our wakeful state, the domain of voluntary memory, reflects only superficially "the deeper resemblance of the dream world in which everything that happens appears not in identical but in similar guise, opaquely similar one to another" (I 204). This should suggest, let us note, a crucial, yet only initial, similarity between involuntary memory and Benjamin's historical materialism. If "historiography in the strict sense is thus an image taken from involuntary memory,"[27] then a historiographic image shows the past in its non-identity with the present. Whereas "historicism gives the 'eternal' image of the past," the image of eternal identity of things, "historical materialism supplies a unique experience with the past" (Thesis XVI), a unique experience of non-identity. But this is only the first move of Benjamin's articulation of the *dialectic* of remembering and forgetting, of waking and dreaming. Whereas our purposive recollection of daytime, of "waking consciousness," offers us only images of empty (in)experience, the "forgetting" of night time, of "dream consciousness," weaves a web of images of deeper resemblances. In the "forgetting" *of* spontaneous recollection, "the eye perceives an experience of a complementary nature in the form of a spontaneous afterimage as it were" (I 157). In the second move, however, Benjamin makes a second crucial reversal of the earlier reversal. "Proust," Benjamin reminds us, "finally turned his days into night, devoting all his hours to undisturbed work in his darkened room with artificial illumination so that none of those intricate arabesques might escape him" (I 202). "Proust," writes Benjamin, "did not give in to sleep" (I 203). The work of involuntary memory—and historical materialism—cannot be the self-forgetfulness that once characterized the community of listeners to stories in the days of weaving and spinning. With alert *attentiveness* (the mark of voluntary memory), Proust actualized the element of dream consciousness in an*other* waking consciousness. The actualization is dialectical, because here the "presence of mind" is predicated on its initial

27. Wohlfarth, "On the Messianic Structure," p. 163.

absence and the time lag in which memories interact in the unconscious. We read in *The Arcades Project*:

> Realization of dream element in the course of waking up is the canon of dialectics. It is paradigmatic for the thinker and binding for the historian. (N4, 4)

But actualization is dialectical, as it is less akin to "daydreaming" than to the consciousness of an insomniac. For actualization, strictly speaking, is not only a realization of "what has been from time immemorial" in an instant, but, more critically, it is a recognition of image *as* particular image, in and *for* the instant. "Proust," Benjamin writes, "could not get his fill of emptying the dummy, his self, at one stroke in order to keep garnering that third thing, the image" (I 205). Actualization, Benjamin seems to suggest, is no longer a dream moment of non-identity, but rather the actual recognition of non-identity, which we can properly call a *determinate* non-identity, "the one in which humanity, rubbing its eyes, recognizes just this particular dream image as such" (N4, 1). The double, split recognition of the immemorial in the "flash" of an image *and* of image *as* (particular) image introduces *asymmetry* to the core of actualization and brings the moment of recognition to a "standstill." In this sense, "the image is dialectics at a standstill" (N3, 1). "For while the relation of the present to the past is a purely temporal, continuous one, the relation of what-has-been to the now is dialectical: is not progression, but image, suddenly emergent" (N2a, 3).

In crucial passages in *The Arcades Project*, Benjamin deploys the term "awakening" to describe this moment of non-identity. Awakening, according to Benjamin, is "the synthesis of dream consciousness (as thesis) and waking consciousness (as antithesis)" (N3a, 3). But then, the dialectical synthesis does not amount to a supra-identity of identity (waking consciousness) and non-identity (dream consciousness). Rather, as determinate non-identity, it constitutes, in Benjamin's description, "life's supremely dialectical point of rupture" (N3a 3). "Thus, in Proust, the importance of staking an entire life on life's supremely dialectical point of rupture: awakening. Proust begins with an evocation of the space of someone waking up" (N3a, 3). In our reading, awakening is a constellation of double, asymmetric recognition that makes the moment both a realization of "dream" and waking up *from* dream. In other words, awakening is a realization of dream *as* dream *image*.

The double, split recognition introduce *historicity* into the moment of actualization. Distinguishing his project from Louis Aragon's, Benjamin writes: "Whereas Aragon persists within the realm of dream, here the concern is to find the constellation of awakening. While in Aragon there remains an impressionistic element, namely the 'mythology'...here it is a question of the dissolution of 'mythology' into the space of history" (N1, 9). In several important passages in *The Arcades Project*, the synthetic moment of awakening is identified with the "'now of recognizability,' in which things put on their true—surrealist—face" (N3a, 3). The "now of awakening," insofar as it is a realization *and* a recognition of dream *as* dream *image*, is a pregnant constellation or configuration of the two forms of temporalities, the messianic and the historical, in that the now condenses into the space of the instant the "presence" of the immemorial, as a *whole*, mediated by a historically *specific* present (the *specific* image). The dual, dialectical character of the now of awakening—constellation of immemorial and the specific image—brings the moment to a standstill, crystallizes it into what Benjamin most ambiguously calls a "dialectical image." The dialectical image is an image in which is constellated, differentially, the vision of the image and the image *as* image. A certain "internal" resistance to image is what is constitutive for dialectical image. In dialectical image, image tears itself away from itself. An internal dispersion belongs to the constitution of dialectical image. Benjamin writes:

> Where thinking comes to a standstill in a constellation saturated with tensions—there the dialectical image appears. It is the caesura in the movement of thought. Its position is naturally not an arbitrary one. It is to be found, in a word, where the tension between dialectical opposites is greatest. (N10a, 3)

The dialectical image, Benjamin writes, is "genuinely historical—that is, not archaic—image" (N3, 1). It is important to reflect on the nature of the historicity of the dialectical image. What constitutes the historicity of the image is *not* any essential "semblance" or identity between the past and the present. The image must be strictly distinguished from "essences" and, Benjamin asserts, must be thought of entirely apart from the categories of habitus (N3, 1). "It is the inherent tendency of dialectical experience to dissipate the semblance of eternal sameness...in history" (N9, 5). Rather, historicity of image lies in its indexicality. Image functions as a *temporal* index only when there exists non-identity between the past and the present.

(Does not Combray in Proust represent difference in-itself?) Image is not an index for the past "the way it really was," i.e., its identity, but for the past's essential difference. In this precise sense, "the past carries with it a temporal index by which it is referred to redemption" (Thesis II). On the other hand, and more critically, image as a temporal index is synchronic with every present (N3, 1). Image, so to speak, releases the non-identity of the present. Dialectical image is an imagistic—thus determinate—*spacing* of non-identity itself. As an index, image is a repetition. But whereas in the modern experience, new is always the recurrence of the same, the dialectical image, in as much as it is synchronic with the present, produces the new in its repetition. As a figure of non-identity (repetition *and* the new), the image is dialectical and genuinely historical. The dialectical image can thus be conceived as a dialectical counterpart to the empty identity of the modern experience.

"The Image of Proust," Benjamin writes, "is the highest physiognomic expression which the irresistibly growing discrepancy between literature and life was able to assume" (I 202). The image of Proust does not reconcile, but synchronizes, the "discrepancy" between poetry and life, between image and experience. As synchronization of the non-synchronous, of the non-identical, the image of Proust is a dialectical match for the modern.

III. Toward a Destructive Historiography

It was our contention that in Proust, Benjamin finds the historiographic form that is adequate to the temporal structure of the experience of the modern. Materialist historiography responds to the time lag that structures modernity precisely by dialectically transfiguring that retroactivity into the "afterimage" of the past. And this transfiguration that the history writer sets as his task constitutes the present as what Benjamin calls the now-time.

In a brief reflection on Benjamin in *The Sublime Object of Ideology*, Slavoj Žižek points to the distinction between the method of hermeneutics and Benjamin's historical materialism. Whereas the fundamental guidance of hermeneutics is to situate a text or event in the totality of the historical epoch, Benjamin's historical materialism, in contrast, *isolates* a specific work from the totality and continuity of history.[28] But the distinction in method can only be explained by the broader asymmetry between the

28. Slavoj Žižek, *The Sublime Object of Ideology* (London: Verso, 1989), pp. 137–38.

two different modes of temporality: homogeneous, empty time proper to historicism; and the now-time of historical materialism. What marks the difference is the decisive *articulation* of the present. From the perspective of historicism, the present is an empty point, a moment, in the infinite, boundless perfectibility of mankind, which it calls progress. Time of progressive history, as Benjamin famously describes, is "a homogeneous, empty time" (Thesis XIII), whether conceived of as an empty sequence of instants, or a homogeneous, even ecstatic, duration of past, present, and future. "Historicism [which] rightly culminates in universal history" (Thesis XVII) is accumulative; it accumulates, as its data, the spoils of past successes and triumphs. In this continuous and progressive time frame, the present is always a transition. It is a hollowed-out space or, more properly, a non-space. But, for a materialist history writer, as for the writer of involuntary memory, authentic historical time is a time "in its most real—that is, space-bound—form" (I 211). This is the crucial point of distinction that Benjamin draws between historicism and materialist historiography. Whereas the former places every event within an ideal time frame of history, and thereby empties out the singular spatiality of happening, the latter spatializes time, presents a spacing of time. There is thus a fundamental asymmetry between historiographic evolutionism and historical materialism:

> A historical materialist cannot do without the notion of a present which is not a transition, but in which time stands still and has come to a stop. For this notion defines the present in which he himself is writing history. (Thesis XVI)

Is the present of historical materialism to be conceived of in utterly ahistorical terms? If not, then to what kind of temporality and historicity is Benjamin pointing?

A present not as transition and progression, but as disjuncture, defines the temporality of now-time. To be sure, now-time is not the present in any simple sense of the term. Rather, it is a certain historical *presentation* of the present. The historian finds now-time as what Benjamin calls a "historical object."

Strictly speaking, as we have suggested above, now-time (now of awakening) is a configuration of two different dynamics of time, the messianic and the historical. In it, the now condenses into the space of the instant the immemorial as a *whole*, mediated by a specific historical present

(i.e., a specific image). It is messianic because, as an allegorical signification, it "transubstantiates" the immemorial as a whole into "one single
catastrophe" (original-history), in order to redeem history as a *whole*. It is
historical as it always remains the now of particular (historical) recognizability. The configuration of two temporalities thus remains asymmetric
and non-identical. The asymmetry is evident in the asymmetry of optics
depicted in the famous Thesis IX: "Where we perceive a chain of events,
he [the angel of history] sees one single catastrophe which keeps piling
wreckage upon wreckage and hurls it in front of his feet" (Thesis IX).
But it is the present instant as *site* of catastrophe that joins the messianic
and the historical, since the chain of events itself *is* catastrophe. By the
same token, the very transient nature of the present instant also disjoins
the historical and the messianic. We may also recall, in this context, that,
for Benjamin, the messianic remains radically exterior to history. From
the standpoint of history, the messianic is not the goal but the termination. Redemptive remembrance of the fullness of the past will be possible
only on the Judgment Day: the end of history. The now-time, in spite of
being a paradigmatic constellation of now and then, remains transient and
incomplete. If now-time is the time of rescue, as Benjamin believes, then
the rescue "can operate solely for the sake of what in the next moment is
irretrievably lost" (N9, 7). It is for this reason that Benjamin can think of
the now-time as the site of the *weak* messianic, a messianic without the
Messiah.

It is tempting to see the "angel of history" (Klee's *Angelus Novus*) as
the Messiah, as "a prophet looking backwards" (Friedrich Schlegel): "His
face is turned toward the past," and he sees one single catastrophe. But
there is no futural prophecy in Benjamin's description.[29] The angel wants
to be the Messiah. He "would like to stay, awaken the dead, and make
whole what has been smashed." But there remains a temporal asymmetry, a time lag between the motion of the angel and *this* profane historical
world. The storm blowing from Paradise "has got caught in his wings
with such violence that the angel can no longer close them. This storm
irresistibly propels him into the future to which his back is turned, while
the pile of debris before him grows skyward" (Thesis IX). And yet the
time lag is *determinate*, for in the space of the time lag is located the historian himself, whose task, in the absence of the Messiah, it is to *actualize*

29. For an insightful discussion of prophecy in Benjamin's thought, see chap. 1 of
Ian Balfour, *The Rhetoric of Romantic Prophecy* (Stanford, CA: Stanford UP, 2002).

the immemorial in the specific living present. The struggling, oppressed class itself, "as the avenger that completes the task of liberation in the name of generations of the downtrodden" (Thesis XII), is located in the interface of the messianic and the historical. Prior to the coming of the Messiah, the now-time is the time of historical actualization. The task of the historian of the oppressed is to disrupt the "chain of events." Historical actualization, as opposed to progression (in homogeneous time), Benjamin reminds us, is the founding concept of historical materialism (N2, 2). Actualization signifies genuine progress insofar as progress means, in Benjamin's radical definition, interference in the "continuity of elapsing time" (N9a, 7).

Actualization is the *work* of repetition. But for the historian of the oppressed, there cannot be such a thing as repetition or retrieval (*Wiederholung*) of the essence of the past. Empathetic "reconstruction" of the past, "which despairs of grasping and holding the genuine historical image as it flares up briefly," Benjamin critically reminds us, always ends up empathizing with the victor (Thesis VII). Repetition that defines the materialist historiography is a repetition *and* the first time, a repetition sundered from the notion of empty progression of the same. In "Theses on the Philosophy of History," Benjamin describes repetition as "a tiger's leap into the past" (Thesis XIV). As a *leap*, repetition terminates the temporal continuity between the past and the present. Repetition, thus, has to be strictly distinguished from gazing *purely* into the past "without involving in this retrospective glance anything that has taken place in the meantime" (N7, 5). An event becomes historical, attains its historical actuality posthumously, as Benjamin writes, "[b]ut no fact that is a cause is for that very reason historical. It becomes historical posthumously as it were, through events that may be separated from it by thousands of years" (Thesis add. A). Time of actualization/repetition is thus a convoluted time, as opposed to an *identical*, boundless line of time. Rather than being a retrieval of the essence of the past, repetition, if we may assert it once again, synchronizes a particular past and a particular present in their non-synchronous and non-identical constellation. Not only ancient Rome became charged with "the time of the now" (French Revolution), and thus became something entirely different from "the way it really was," but also the French Revolutionaries saw themselves as resurrected Romans when they created something entirely new. Repetition *relates* the "past" and the "present" through *difference*. Revolutionary repetition, Benjamin would have argued, following Marx or Blanqui, is a theater, a costume drama. But, more importantly perhaps, underneath the theatrical masks, the event *of* repetition, the historical event, *really* becomes a "force field in which the confrontation between its fore-history and after-history is played out" (N7a, 1).

"Force field" is another term for what we have called a non-synchronous constellation. The distinction and confrontation between "fore-history" and "after-history" appears in important passages of *The Arcades Project*. Thus we read:

> For the materialist historian, every epoch with which he occupies himself is only prehistory for the epoch he himself must live in. And so, for him, there can be no appearance of repetition [*Wiederholung*] in history, since precisely those moments in the course of history which matter most to him, by virtue of their index as "fore-history," become moments of the present day and change their character according to the catastrophic or triumphant nature of that day. (N9a, 8)

But repetition, repeatability, belongs to the "original" as the original itself is marked with an *after*. The *claim* of fore-history is fulfilled only when it is *recognized* by after-history:

> Historical "understanding" is to be grasped, in principle, as an afterlife of that which is understood; and what has been recognized in the analysis of the "after-life of works," in the analysis of "fame," is therefore to be considered the foundation of history in general. (N2, 3)

The event *of* repetition in which the "historical confrontation" between the claim of fore-history and its recognition by after-history takes place turns the (remembered) event into a *monadic* historical object which the historian blasts out of the historical succession. And with this act of repetition, with the blasting of historical continuity, Benjamin argues, the historical object first constitutes itself (N10, 3). The historical confrontation "makes up the *interior* (and, as it were, the bowels) of the (monadic) historical object, and into which all the forces and interests of history enter on a *reduced* scale" (N10, 3, emphasis mine). There is consequently no *transhistorical* foundation of history (and thus no History with capital "H"). Foundation is located, as we read, in the event of repetition itself, in the event of acceding "to legibility" of the claim of the particular past in the particular present in the form of an image: "Every present day is determined by the images that are synchronic with it: each 'now' is the now of particular recognizability" (N3, 1). But Benjamin distinguishes historical actualization from historical relativism. Although constellation is something entirely different from "timeless truth," "truth is not—as Marxism would have it—a merely contingent function of knowing, but is bound to a nucleus of time lying hidden within the knower and the known" (N3, 2). And yet, as we have already noted, it is the present, as site of catastrophe, which joins the messianic and the historical. The dialectically presented historical circumstance becomes the force field "insofar as the present instant interpenetrates it" (N7a, 1). It is the singularity of the present instant that "determines where, in the object from the past, that object's fore-history and after-history diverge so as to circumscribe its nucleus" (N11, 5). Thus, since the present is the site of repetition, the repetition takes place "always anew, never in the same way" (N7a, 1). If we may attempt to articulate it more rigorously, *each* "now" is actualization and articulation of "what has been" (the same) *as* new, as opposed to new as the same. In this precise sense, the now-time is a non-synchronous constellation.

It is in this context that we may return to Benjamin's historiographic project of rearticulating the unity of two forms of memory: unity of reminiscences of *many,* and the remembrance of *one.* One might be tempted to read Benjamin's couching of the monadic now, as a modern form of *Eingedenken*, as another attempt to salvage the whole through its embodiment in part itself; a dialectical fusion of eternity and time—a holistic recollection (*Erinnerung*). Our discussion above points to the opposite conclusion. If now-time, as a *model* of messianic time, "comprises the entire history of mankind in an enormous abridgement" (Thesis XVIII), then that cannot mean that now-time *preserves* the whole of the past in the present, as Benjamin seems to suggest in Thesis XVII. *Eingedenken* will bespeak an uncritical hypostatization "as soon as it becomes the signature of historical process *as a whole*" (N13, 1). Benjaminian *Eingedenken* marks a progress not because it represents tradition as a whole, but because it, as avant-garde, *isolates* the monadic, and necessarily non-synchronous, constellation ("where the tension between the dialectical opposites is greatest") from the whole. Ultimately, the now is "the fissure" within the tradition (N9, 4). Benjaminian historiography, as *Eingedenken*, can only be an infinite act of destruction (negation):

Historical materialism must renounce the epic element in history. It blasts the epoch out of the reified "continuity of history." But it also explodes the homogeneity of the epoch, interspersing it with ruins—that is, with the present. (N9a, 6)

The now-time *presents* the present as an impossible spacing of ruins of time itself. The destructive historian and the rememberer places himself in the time filled with the now—that is, with ruins. He gathers his power to situate himself in a spaced-time that remains, in this precise sense, *blank*:

No vision inspires the destructive character. He has few needs, and the least of them is to know what will replace what has been destroyed. First of all, for a moment at least, empty space, the place where the thing stood or the victim lived. Someone is sure to be found who needs this space without its being filled.[30]

---

30. Walter Benjamin, "The Destructive Character," in *Reflections*, p. 302.

On Gillian Rose and Love

Vincent Lloyd

The contemporary American philosopher David Velleman recently noted, "Love is a moral emotion precisely in the sense that its spirit is closely akin to that of morality."[1] Although their kindred spirits are manifest, it is the tension between love and morality that at first glance is striking. Love seems to be supremely personal, unique to one individual and directed at another for highly contingent and possibly mysterious reasons. Even if Kantian or Utilitarian fantasies of objective morality are dismissed, the common alternatives that put emphasis on community values or obligation to the Other are still distant from an affect directed at a concrete individual. Not even Nietzschean or Foucauldian ethics of self-creation seem to share a kindred spirit with love. Love has an anomic quality; it seems to reside in a different register than any project of imposing a regimen on oneself.

Perhaps Velleman's observation of the similarities between love and morality sounds plausible just because it represents a slightly veiled secularization of elementary Christian ethics: from the maxim "love thy neighbor" to its theorization by Augustine through Aquinas through Niebuhr. Perhaps Velleman has not taken a sufficient dosage of Nietzschean medicine to recognize a "love ethic" as the ethic of the weak, instituted by slave revolt and then disguised and naturalized.

But perhaps in the phenomenology of love, in the lived experience of lover and beloved, in the tension and teasing, in the fulfillment and frustration, perhaps in the sorrow and in the confrontation with another

---

1. David Velleman, "Love as a Moral Emotion," *Ethics* 109 (January 1999): 341.

being, distinct yet demanding—perhaps this is where the similar spirits of love and morality reside. This is where Gillian Rose turns in *Love's Work*, her philosophical memoir, which is at once a work of autobiography and an ethical-political polemic.[2] The culmination of two decades of investigation of Hegel, Marx, the Frankfurt School, post-structuralism, Christian theology, and the Jewish tradition, as well as four decades of living a life as sensually suffused as it was intellectually robust, *Love's Work* offers a (Hegelian, not Husserlian) phenomenology of love that explicates and concretizes Rose's prescient and incisive views on morality and politics.

After first exploring Rose's retelling of the Arthurian legend, which encapsulates the issues she wants to raise for love, morality, and politics, we will suggest thesis and antithesis positions concerning the phenomenology of love that Rose puts in tension. Then, we will turn to an examination of what Rose says about love and morality in *Love's Work* and to a consideration of its implications.

The question of the relationship between love and morality is posed by Rose allegorically through her narration of the story of Camelot. The question is posed but not resolved—the resolution, or rather the work of resolution, is the project of *Love's Work* as a whole. The story Rose retells is this: in a time of endless feuding and bloodshed, King Arthur has a vision. He wanted to create a kingdom that was based on justice and equality. There would not be favoritism, the rule of law would be respected, and knights would sit at a Round Table to participate in the governance of the regime on equal footing. A regime founded on justice and equality, Arthur believed, would be an island of peace and prosperity in a sea of chaos and violence.

King Arthur recruited knights to Camelot who shared his aspirations. The French knight Launcelot, emotional and idealistic, befriended King Arthur and joined the Round Table. But Launcelot fell in love with King Arthur's wife, Guinevere. According to the laws of Camelot, Launcelot must be banished and Guinevere must die. But King Arthur deeply loved his wife and his friend. King Arthur is faced with a choice. If he follows Camelot's laws, he will stay true to his ideal of ruling a kingdom based on justice and equality. However, he will lose those individuals who are closest to him. If King Arthur makes an exception to Camelot's laws, he will

---

2. Gillian Rose, *Love's Work: A Reckoning with Life* (New York: Schocken Books, 1995). Page references will be documented parenthetically within the text.

be able to save his wife and friend but Camelot will be tainted. The people will know that the laws are not always applied fairly, that exceptions are made for those whom the King favors.

The choice that King Arthur must make is a choice between his two loves: between his love for the ideal of Camelot and his love for his wife and friend. It is the tension between these two sorts of loves as allegorized in the story of King Arthur, and the way that this tension might be resolved, that frames Rose's understanding of the phenomenology of love. But the choice that King Arthur must make is also, clearly, an issue of morality and of politics. To what extent should his allegiance be to his nation (better: to the ideals for which it stands) and to what extent should it be to his family and friends?

King Arthur decides to follow the law, but Launcelot manages to rescue Guinevere before she is executed. The banished Launcelot and King Arthur fight a war that King Arthur wins. But Camelot is no longer a peaceful kingdom, and King Arthur has lost his wife and his friend. Rose concludes that, regardless of what choice King Arthur would have made, "the King must now be sad." And, more generally, "sadness is the condition of the King" (123). When law is understood as an ideal, whether imposed by a King or a sovereign people, "humanity is forgotten, and so will be the law" (124). This is because the focus on a distant ideal allows the lawmakers to forget their personal vulnerability and power, with inevitably tragic results. But tragic results would have just as surely followed had King Arthur favored his family and friends and forgotten his ideal.

When philosophy is done right, Rose thinks, philosophy is about the sadness of the King. When philosophy is done wrong, it is about finding an easy way out, accepting one of the King's options as obvious, ignoring (but actually suppressing) this sadness. The result is melancholy: interminable fixation on suppressed sadness (Rose names neo-Kantianism, post-structuralism, and neo-pragmatism as victims of this melancholy). Philosophy done the right way acknowledges that, regardless of the choice that is made, there will inevitably be regret. Philosophy done the right way does not dwell on this regret but is propelled by it back into the fray to try again at justice. Metaphysics is "the perception of the difficulty of the law," and ethics is "the development of it…being at a loss yet exploring various routes, different ways towards the good enough justices, which recognizes the intrinsic and contingent limitations in its exercise" (124).

Rose concretely develops this philosophical prospectus by building on the Hegelian notion of "speculative identity." As Rose explains it, a speculative identity simultaneously acknowledges identity and non-identity.[3] Instead of understanding Hegel as a teleological thinker, collapsing difference into totalizing identity, Rose argues that we should understand Hegel as allowing difference and identity to persist together, in tension, one never triumphing over the other.[4] "A is B" and "A is not B" at once. The apparent contradiction does not make the statement vacuous. Rather, the identity "must be understood as a result to be achieved."[5] It is through experience, historical and social, that the identity is achieved. It is thus only through a thorough examination of social and historical context, minding the winds of the actual existing world, that one is able to explicate a speculative identity.

The elements of a speculative identity are this-worldly and otherworldly, immanent and transcendent. For example, Rose examines the development of jurisprudence, witnessing the evolving tension between positive law and natural law through the ancient world into modernity.[6] Natural law supposes a transcendent foundation for law; positive law supposes law to be posited by humans. Rose does not align herself with one position or the other. Instead, she charts the tension as the two develop in relation to each other. She bears witness to their speculative identity.

The speculative identity with which Rose appears to be concerned in regard to love is similarly the identity of an immanent option and a transcendent option. Rose does not explicitly examine these options: *Love's Work* is, first of all, a memoir, not a philosophical treatise. But by filling out this identity in a manner that parallels Rose's method regarding law, we will try to shed light on what Rose might have in mind regarding her own positive account of love. These immanent and transcendent conceptions of love will be filled out by turning to their formulation in ancient Greece. The immanent understanding of love exemplified by Homer will be contrasted with the transcendent understanding of love exemplified by

3. Gillian Rose, *Judaism and Modernity: Philosophical Essays* (Oxford: Basil Blackwell, 1993), p. ix.

4. See, for instance, Gillian Rose, *Dialectic of Nihilism: Post-Structuralism and Law* (New York: Basil Blackwell, 1984), p. 139, and Rose, *Hegel contra Sociology* (London: Athlone, 1981).

5. Rose, *Hegel contra Sociology*, p. 49.

6. This is one level of the project of Rose's *Dialectic of Nihilism*.

Plato. In both cases, these conceptions of love have clear ethical and political implications.

The difference between the immanent and the transcendent conceptions of love, as their labels imply, is that the former conception takes love to be a natural, worldly phenomenon while the latter conception takes love to be somehow other-worldly. In Homer's *Iliad*, forms of the verb *philein* are used for a broad variety of contexts, ranging from friendship to spousal love to quite different uses. For instance, *philos* is used reflexively to indicate a special bond with something rather like the English word "dear." A soul, heart, life, or breath could be *philos*, as could a body part like a knee. In addition to the reflexive "dear" usage, *philos* was used to describe bonds of friendship. When there was some sort of reciprocal agreement between two parties, an agreement creating what might be called a friendship, the individuals became *philoi*. Gods could have *philoi* among humans, those whom they favored and who did them favors. The word also applied to less formal arrangements, such as between comrades in war. The verb *philein* also took on the meaning "to kiss," as a kiss was an action that signified a reciprocal agreement between friends.[7]

To make sense of these varying uses and their evolution, Émile Benveniste suggests that *philein* began meaning a formal, reciprocal agreement but later evolved to mean a relationship with "emotional color" involving a "sentimental attitude" beyond the formal institution of friendship. *Philos* described things that were, broadly, mine: things relating to my household and my family, for instance, as well as my physical body and spirit. *Philos* described "'a scale of affection' involving 'a fixed gradation of friends and relations,'" where a wife was situated at the top of the scale.[8] Affection for one's wife was not qualitatively different from affection for servants or colleagues or even one's own soul. Rather, affection for a wife was different only in quantity, in the special degree to which she was close to oneself.

In sum, love in the Homeric, pre-Platonic sense was a special quantity of affect, where affect attached to objects and people because of their

---

7. Émile Benveniste, *Indo-European Language and Society*, trans. Elizabeth Palmer (Coral Gables, FL: Univ. of Miami Press, 1973), pp. 273–88. Cf. Henry Staten, *Eros in Mourning: Homer to Lacan* (Baltimore, MD: Johns Hopkins UP, 1995).

8. Henry Staten, *Eros in Mourning*, p. 28, citing J. T. Kakridis, *Homeric Researches* (Lund: C. W. K. Gleerup, 1949), p. 20.

"closeness," in a rather existential sense, to oneself.[9] Closeness here does not refer to physical proximity but rather to the amount of comfort and attachment that one has to the object or person in question. The more comfort and attachment, the closer it is. What one loves, on the Homeric view, is that with which one is most comfortable, that to which one is most attached. Love is entirely this-worldly, immanent. It simply describes a fact about human existence. Everyone loves just as everyone eats, just as everyone has parents.

In the Socratic dialogues we occasionally see the implications of this immanent conception of love. In the *Gorgias* and the *Republic*, for example, the naïve understanding of justice is helping friends (*philoi*) and hurting enemies. What one *should* do is to benefit those who are closest to oneself, those whom one loves. A further implication of this conception of love is that there is no need to change one's self because of one's love. On the contrary, one becomes more entrenched in one's self (one's body, the people one likes, the things one has) as one acts to advance the interests of those whom one loves.

This, of course, is exactly what Plato's Socrates argues against. He argues that one might have to change one's behavior, to alter one's self, based on love for something which is other-worldly, transcendent. To be good is not to benefit one's friends. It might take strenuous physical or intellectual effort. It might make one uncomfortable. Through his persistent questioning, Socrates pushes his interlocutors to abandon their comforting beliefs and practices; he forces them to part with those things that they love in the Homeric sense.

On Plato's view, the world is full of deception, of mere images. But Plato is concerned with reality, and he thinks reality is what everyone ought to be concerned with. For Plato, love (*eros* now, not *philia*) has to do with desire.[10] But desire can be deceptive. We desire to go to the doctor for the sake of our health, but we desire health for the sake of being able to do activities we enjoy and we desire activities we enjoy because...into

---

9. Compare Jean-Yves Lacoste's discussion of "place" at the start of his *Experience and the Absolute: Disputed Questions on the Humanity of Man*, trans. Mark Raftery-Skehan (New York: Fordham UP, 2004).

10. The slippage from *philos* to *eros* here might seem suspicious, but it is useful and not unprecedented. Catherine Pickstock allows the same slippage in her "The Problem of Reported Speech: Friendship and Philosophy in Plato's *Lysis* and *Symposium*," *Telos* 123 (2002): 35–64.

an infinite regress, or so it seems. But, Plato argues, these worldly things we desire are mere images, the equivalent of shadows in the *Republic*'s allegory of the cave. The question that interests Plato is: what is the "first object of love, for whose sake we say all other objects are loved?"[11]

This question is elaborated, among other ways, through the ascent from worldly love to other-worldly love described in Plato's *Symposium* (especially 210b–211b). Although readings of this passage are contentious, for the ideal-type presentation needed here we can simply note the ascent from the material to the transcendent. Diotima instructs Socrates on the ways of love. First, the young man should love just one physical body. Then, he advances to loving all beautiful bodies, now finding his fixation on just one body petty. He then advances to love for mental beauty. He can now love someone without attractive physical attributes but with an attractive mind. He penultimately advances to love for what makes minds attractive: knowledge. And, finally, he ascends to love for something eternal and purely attractive, the form of beauty in which all other instances of beauty participate. The young lover has advanced from the state of a "small-minded slave," focusing on individual, material instances of beauty, to one who gazes on "the vast sea of beauty" (210d). This transcendent conception of love functions as an escalator out of the material world to something higher.

If we were to continue following Rose's methodology, examining the speculative identity of immanent and transcendent conceptions of love, we might note how the Homeric conception of love is refined in Aristotle's discussion of friendship and virtue, and we might note more distant echoes in Aquinas and recent communitarians. Nietzsche vividly described the avatars of the Platonic conception of love in Christianity, Kant, and beyond. Further, we would trouble these conceptions, noting their longings for sufficiency frustrated by their interdependence.

Both the immanent and the transcendent conceptions of love are closely tied to value. On both views, what one loves is what one values. What one values is what one will organize one's life around or, less abstractly, what one will change one's behavior in response to. On the immanent conception of love, the conception on which love is reaffirming what one already cares about, one both loves and values what is close to one's self.

11. Lysis 219d; cf, Gregory Vlastos, "The Individual as an Object of Love in Plato," in *Platonic Studies* (Princeton, NJ: Princeton UP, 1973), pp. 3–34.

Moreover, one works to advance the interests of those one loves (helping friends, hurting enemies). On the transcendent conception of love, it may seem less clear how one can value something like "the beautiful" or "the good." But there certainly is a sense in which one's life can be organized around a transcendent love. One's daily practices and beliefs are changed on the basis of the transcendent object of one's love for the committed Platonist—and, of course, for the committed Christian.

What does Rose herself have to say about love and its relationship to morality and politics? Recall how the problem was stated in her narration of the story of King Arthur. Torn between two loves, King Arthur would inevitably be sad. However, the King's sadness was magnified because his imagination was limited to two options, and he wanted both. He imagined an ideal kingdom of peace based on justice and equality as well as ever-lasting love for his wife and for his friend, Launcelot. The acuteness of King Arthur's sadness was due to his dedication to ideals rather than to the hard work of real life and real love, the hard work of what Rose calls the "middle," the space where the tension between identity and non-identity plays out.[12]

Rose's autobiographical "first love," as she describes it, was the same sort of love that she attributes to King Arthur. As a child, Rose was infatuated with Roy Rogers. As she writes, "it caused me acute physical pain just to think of him, and the high point of every week was watching his programme on television" (61). Rose wore cowboy clothing, played with plastic pistols, and taught herself to urinate standing up. In short, she had an "unshakeable desire *to be* him" (61).

Rose's love for Roy Rogers appears at first to be of the transcendent variety. Roy Rogers was not a real person, not a material entity with whom Rose had become comfortable, used to, attached to. Certainly one could describe Roy Rogers; his name did attach to some definite characteristics. But most of Roy Rogers was mystique. Rose's behavior certainly did change because of Rogers: she started to imitate his behavior, to change her life to more closely resemble his.

Despite these clear affinities with the transcendent conception of love, Rose very quickly reminds us of the ubiquitous but often hidden link between the transcendent and immanent conceptions of love. Roy Rogers

---

12. The theme of the "middle" is developed in greater theoretical depth in Rose's *The Broken Middle: Out of Our Ancient Society* (Oxford: Blackwell, 1992).

was on television at the exact time that she was supposed to leave her mother's house to visit her father—her parents having been involved in an especially messy divorce. Despite the appearance of distance, of abstraction from her material surroundings, Rose's love for Roy Rogers was very much rooted in those things and people around her about which she cared and to whom she was attached. Like the sophists' rhetorical techniques, Rose's love for Roy Rogers was a means by which Rose could help her friends and hurt her enemies, could attach herself to her mother's house and could resent her distant father's intrusion.

The sort of love that Rose had for Roy Rogers, like the sort of love that King Arthur has, is the wrong sort of love, the sort of love that is personally and politically problematic. It involved elements of both immanent and transcendent conceptions of love. But it did not synthesize them; it did not put them in dynamic tension. It allowed for a seemingly easy choice—a choice for one (Roy Rogers) that was really the other (her mother): just the sort of easy choice which all of Rose's oeuvre condemned. But Rose offers an alternative. She offers a phenomenology of love without idealization as either immanent or transcendent.

In her description of writing, an activity Rose describes as a less intense form of loving, the characteristics of her positive account of love begin to unfold. Writing is a "mix of discipline and miracle, which leaves you in control, even when what appears on the page has emerged from regions beyond your control" (59). Here, we find, first, the opposition between immanent and transcendent, between law (discipline) and grace (miracle), which forms of the core of Rose's thought. Instead of standing in confrontation, "discipline and miracle" mix, they are somehow (through speculative identity) both present in writing. Indeed, writing is the product of the fecundity of their tension. Discipline, the this-worldly, immanent ingredient, "leaves you in control." You feel as if you are determining the outcome. You have created the regime, you have set pen to paper for this hour, you have created this outline, you are addressing these topics. So what you write is yours. Yet somehow what you say—that is, what appears on the page to yourself and to your readers—is always something different. It "emerged from regions beyond your control," it includes an element of miracle. Perhaps more familiarly, the concert pianist who rehearses hours each day for a performance practices a highly disciplined regime, yet the product that the concert-goers—and the pianist—hear at the performance is somehow not reducible to that disciplinary regime.

In the space between presenting oneself in words on a page and that self being represented as those written words are read, there is an unbridgeable gap, the entry point of miracle.[13] As the author is confronted with the words that she wrote, she is forced to change herself to accommodate the different person who she now sees that she is. In the case of writing, the words written remain static, engraved in ink, as it were. But in loving, when the relationship is between two individuals, there is a dynamic feedback process in which each presentation and representation is constantly forcing alterations in the parties. The lover and the beloved, as they interact with each other, are constantly forced outside of themselves by the miracle of love, by the miracle enacted in the space between them. Neither party remains who they were before the interaction; each, through the interaction, is forced to become a new person. Loving involves greater intensity than writing; it is punctuated by "joy" and "agony" to a degree that writing is not.

In this process we can see how the speculative identity of immanent and transcendent conceptions of love plays itself out. Like the immanent conception of love, Rose's understanding of love takes the beloved to be a concrete individual: the object of love wears a tight semantic belt. But, unlike the immanent conception of love as articulated in the Homeric tradition, the clarity and concreteness of objects of love do not result in any sort of stasis. The lovers must change themselves because of their love. Their objects of love, though concrete and this-worldly, force the same sort of change that results from other-worldly beloveds on the transcendent conception of love.

This reconstruction of Rose's view of love makes sense of otherwise opaque passages in *Love's Work*. Rose describes the experience of love as being one in which there is "someone who loves *and* desires you, and he glories in his love and desire, and you glory in his ever-strange being, which comes up against you, and disappears, again and again, surprising you with difficulties and with bounty" (60). When Rose writes of one who "loves *and* desires," we can quickly think of *philos* and *eros*, the immanent and transcendent conceptions of love in Homer and in Plato. The conjunction is crucial because it reaffirms the distinctness of the two conceptions of love while also linking them in the new formulation that Rose offers. The "ever-strange being" is equally crucial, for it reminds us of the

---

13. For the "presented" and "represented" terminology, see Alain Badiou, *Being and Event*, trans. Oliver Feltham (London: Continuum, 2005).

mechanism by which Rose seeks to synthesize and surpass the immanent and transcendent conceptions of love. In the immanent conception of love, those who are loved are never strange. Indeed, they are the opposite of strange: they are as familiar as possible, for that is precisely the reason that they are loved. Yet it is them, those very specific "beings," who are loved. They are not loved because they are representatives of something else, because of the bit of beauty or good (or God) in them.

The precise mechanism of love, as Rose describes it, is a pushing and pulling, an ever-present tension that performs what love is. The lover "comes up against you, and disappears, again and again." The lover challenges you, surprises you, makes you uncomfortable. In reacting to the advances of the lover, one changes oneself, grows in response, and through response, pushes back at the lover, forcing the lover to respond—"again and again." This process is not an easy one but it is a rewarding one—it is characterized by "difficulties" and "bounty." It is painful to be pushed, to be ill at ease, to be forced to respond in ever novel ways. But this is where the magic of love in its true sense, neither immanent nor transcendent but the speculative identity of the two, resides.

The intensity of love, greater than that of other relationships in life, is due in part to the absolute vulnerability that love entails, according to Rose. Colleagues have roles to play. They interact with each other as colleagues, following the script assigned to their positions. Their interactions are mutually beneficial, but they are like trains on a track: they may be able to travel far and in varied directions, but their interactions are always closely guided by pre-laid rails. In contrast, lovers interact with each other not as people putting on a performance, not as people playing a role, but as what is most essentially human in them. You do not see your lover as a postman, a brunette, or a golfer; you see your lover as a human being stripped of all social roles.[14]

Because of this nudity in which we interact with our lovers, because of this lack of rails, anything is possible. They are under no obligation to act toward us in a predetermined way, in a manner that we can anticipate. As Rose writes, lovers "have absolute power over each other" (60). Because there is no "contract," no agreed rails to guide the interaction, "one party may initiate a unilateral and fundamental change in the terms of relating without renegotiating them" (60). In sum, "There is no democracy in any

14. Cf. Emmanuel Levinas, *Time and the Other: And Additional Essays*, trans. Richard A. Cohen (Pittsburgh, PA: Duquesne UP, 1987).

love relation: only mercy" (60). This is what so greatly intensifies the relationship of love over life. Although the push and pull that characterize love also characterize life in the world more generally for Rose—as a version of the struggle for recognition, perhaps—in love this struggle is magnified because it starts *ex nihilo*, it cannot rely on previously acknowledged customs as a starting point. The miracle of love, in other words, is that lovers walk together over a cliff, on thin air. Occasionally, they may experience vertigo, but they continue walking, all that they can do, together.

As a lover, one must understand not only one's "absolute vulnerability" but also one's "absolute power" (60), in sum, one's "riskful engagement" (71). It is not only you who are at the mercy of your lover, but your lover who is at your mercy. You, too, can take advantage of the lack of rails, can take advantage of your lover. At any moment, you have the ability to radically alter the relationship between the two of you, just as the relationship can be radically altered by your lover.

"Happy love is happy after its own fashion," while "[a]ll unhappy loves are alike," writes Rose (62). This conclusion straightforwardly follows from Rose's positive account of love. Happy love is no more than the performance of the give and take between lovers. This is a dynamic performance, ever changing, involving different pulls, different pushes, as the personalities, and the persons, of the lovers differ and develop. Unhappy love, in contrast, always follows the same structure. Unhappy love has an effectively empty content: either it is solipsistic (on the immanent conception) or it refers to an effectively empty signifier (on the transcendent conception), both of which collapse into one and the same thing—as Rose showed with her example of Roy Rogers. In unhappy love, one elevates an opaque object to the position of most loved, one structures one's life around that object—which, it turns out, is really just a reflection of one's own self, one's own desires exteriorized into an object.

But the story is more complex still. "The unhappiest love is a happy love that has now become unhappy" (62). In such cases, there was once the dynamism of happy love, performed in the space of the "middle," between the two lovers and between immanence and transcendence. But, for whatever reason, the love has been lost; its dynamism has been stilled. It has become a memory, incorporated into the being of each lover, part of them in love's immanent form and projected as a broken hope in love's transcendent form. The pain of happy love turned unhappy is especially acute because of the loss involved, because of the personal knowledge that it was once animated. It is a taxidermied pet rather than a taxidermied animal in a museum diorama.

Rose's first love, her love of Roy Rogers, was a story of failed love, of loving the wrong way. If King Arthur had loved rightly, he would have loved according to Rose's account of love, an account that she exemplifies with her description of her relationship with Father Dr. Patrick Gorman (Rose's pseudonym for the priest-scholar). Their relationship begins with exchanged notes and mystery: Gorman claims to have seen Rose; Rose searches her memory to recall on what occasion this might have been. At a meeting, Rose senses "an intense aura emanating from someone whom I had never seen before, an intense, sexual aura, aimed precisely and accurately at my vacant being" (65). She is introduced to Gorman and realizes that he is the same man she earlier encountered at the faculty meeting. She is invited to dine with Gorman, and, as she enters, "he gripped my hand and, looking straight in the eye, did not release the tension between our clasped hands and locked eyes" (66). It is in this tension, this exchange of advances in which each party's desire manifests itself in various modalities as the love progresses, as the future lovers become closer, that love is performed.

"We knew we wanted each other in the way those who become lovers do—with simultaneously a supernatural conviction of unexpressed mutual desire and a mortal unsureness concerning declaration and consummation" (68). Here again, in yet another form, the transcendent and the immanent meet. The practical realities of growing closer, of physical proximity, the material manifestations of love as deep bodily, sexual, attachment are set in tension with desire, *eros*, the "supernatural," the transcendent conception of love in which the object is purely desired but only vaguely defined. As Rose points out, in her particular circumstances this tension was magnified: there was a material obstacle (the priestly vocation of Gorman) as well as a supernatural supplement (again, the priestly vocation of Gorman).

Rose and Gorman finally consummate their love. In her graphic yet delicate description of their physical intimacy, Rose again exemplifies the phenomenology of love which she offers. "The sexual exchange will be as complicated as the relationship in general—even more so. Kiss, caress and penetration are the relation of the relation, body and soul in touch..." (69). Each touch, in love, is a push, at once eliciting a response, at once transforming the lovers and propelling the performance of love forward. In bed together, the nudity of the lovers is literalized: their vulnerability and their power magnified. The immanent (body) and the transcendent (soul) are put in dynamic tension, "in touch." The lover "succumbs so readily and with more joy than I could claim" (69), with an excess that is reducible neither to the immanence of the material bodies of the lovers nor to the transcendence of their desire for their ideal images of each other.

Rose characterizes a night spent together as a "shared journey," "unsure yet close" (70). The immanent conception of love is "close," that is its defining feature. But it is also sure of itself, it is characterized by certainty, predictability, lack of surprise. In the immanent conception of love, one loves what one is most used to, what is closest to one's self and so is most well understood, not what one is "unsure" of. Yet the "unsure" character of the love, and its nature as a "journey," does not unequivocally point to the transcendent conception of love. Although the transcendent conception of love involves a movement forward, an alteration of one's own conduct and life based on an underdetermined object, the transcendent conception of love takes love to be an individual phenomenon. Rose most definitely considers love "shared" and "close." In her phenomenology of love, love is definitively between two material beings; yet the two beings move beyond themselves through their interactions with each other.

In an opinionated aside, Rose articulates her opposition to "sex manuals" and "feminist tracts which imply the infinite plasticity of position and pleasure" (69). Her opposition arises from the same roots as her opposition to the stark choices that King Arthur sees. To imagine countless varieties of pleasure is to settle for an ideal, to imagine—and to seek to create—a Camelot. Such a project is inevitably doomed. But, more importantly, even the consideration of such a project is problematic. It is an easy solution, a way out of the difficult work of negotiating the push and pull of life and love. Sex manuals are "dangerously destructive of imagination, of erotic and of spiritual ingenuity" (69). It is against the stasis implied by both immanence and transcendence and in favor of the dynamism of negotiating their synthesis that Rose's phenomenology is positioned.

Lovers walking together without rails, walking together over a cliff—this is how Rose links love and faith. In the morning, after a night spent with a lover, Rose writes, "There can be no preparation or protection for this moment of rootless exposure" (70). The lovers have opened themselves to each other; love has been performed. They have walked over the cliff and they now, in the morning light, realize where each stands, together, walking on thin air—this "holy terror," this "rootless exposure."

At this moment, Rose writes, love is replaced by faith. It is only faith that keeps them together, keeps them walking on thin air, prevents them from falling—against all odds.

What can Rose's phenomenology of love tell us about morality and politics? First, it becomes clear that Rose understands love and morality to be kindred spirits. "To spend the whole night with someone is…ethical. For you must move with him and with yourself" (70). It is an experience that twins love and faith. She describes love as "sacramental even without the benefit of sacraments"; she describes love as offering the possibility that lovers can "achieve the mundane" (71). So it seems as though Rose is suggesting that somehow the experience of love alters one's experience of the world. Somehow, love offers a conduit of the holy (in an unconventional sense) into the ordinary.

On the immanent conception of love, love reinforces the way one already lives. On the transcendent conception of love, love forces one to change one's way of life in accordance with an underdetermined abstract object. In contrast, Rose's development of a speculative identity between the two conceptions turns love into an exemplary instance of how one should live. Rose wants to suggest that a life lived well is a life continually pushing and being pushed—by and against individuals, groups, and institutions. When we are in a true love relationship, we are taken into a corner of the world where life is lived more intensely and from which we can return to life all the more dedicated to continuing to participate in the difficult work of living, all the more committed to rejecting the easy options of falling into the stasis of pure immanence or the fantasy of pure transcendence.

One of the most profound elements of Rose's account of love—and morality, and politics—is her explicit acknowledgment of the pervasiveness of tragedy in a way that few others dare to suggest. "There are always auguries, not only of future difficulties but also of impossibility" (71). During the love affair, as the love is performed through the tension of push and pull between the lovers, the tragic nature of love is forgotten, elided. In Rose's own case, in her relationship with Gorman, this was particularly acute and explicit. He was, of course, a priest. In the performance of their love, the impossibilities inherent in the situation are easily overlooked. But Rose suggests that her relationship with Gorman is just a particularly acute instance of a much more general phenomenon. Love that is happy becomes unhappy; lovers change irreconcilably; lovers die.

Yet the inevitably tragic nature of love should not discourage us from participation—in love, such as in life. As the epigraph of *Love's Work* tells us, "Keep your mind in hell, and despair not." Rose offers the vivid image of the paradoxical circularity involved in learning to swim. Before one enters the water, one must know how to swim, yet one cannot know how to swim by being told how on dry land. One must enter the water. To think one knows how to swim before entering the water is to believe in Camelot, to believe in the immanent/transcendent ideal. In our short lives, in our few loves, we will never learn to swim well, Rose suggests. We will only flounder about, thrashing our arms and legs, pushing and pulling ourselves against the water as we try to begin to swim. Once in a while, we succeed, beginning to find a rhythm; but more often we thrash about again, gasping for breath. Yet there is something indisputably more desirable about the novice swimmer thrashing about in the water than the person who has never been in the water but believes she can swim because she read how in a book.

Again, Rose's view of love functions as a microcosm of her view of life. *Love's Work* is decorated with examples of decline and death, ranging from a friend dying of AIDS to an octogenarian cancer survivor to vivid descriptions of Rose's own terminal illness. In all of these cases, Rose admires and advocates persistence in the face of apparently insurmountable difficulties. King Arthur cannot remain silent. He must choose, and then he must move on to choose again. His weakness is that he imagines that he can avoid difficult choices, avoid the work of love, the work of ethics, the work of life. Rose concludes, on the final page of *Love's Work*, that she aspires "to be exactly as I am, decrepit nature yet supernature in one....I will stay in the fray, in the revel of ideas and risk; learning, failing, wooing, grieving, trusting, working, reposing—in this sin of language and lips" (144).

Is Recognition a Zero-Sum Game?

Ralph Shain

> For society people, *chic* emanates from a comparatively small
> number of individuals, who project it to a considerable dis-
> tance—more and more faintly the further one is from their
> intimate center.... But Odette was one of those persons... who
> do not share these notions, but imagine *chic* to be something
> quite other, which assumes different aspects according to the
> circle to which they themselves belong, but has the special
> characteristic... of being directly accessible to all.
>
> Marcel Proust, *Swann's Way*

I.

In the last two decades, a number of political theorists have published a
great deal of theory that argues for the centrality of the idea of recognition.
In the most prominent of these papers, Charles Taylor makes the claim
that "recognition is a human need."[1] The immediate spur for this flurry of
interest has been a discussion of multiculturalism and its attendant issues,
which are expressed in terms of "group recognition."[2] This work focuses
on the importance of group identity or social characteristics, as well as on
their relation to individualism and liberalism. These issues are important,

1. Charles Taylor, "The Politics of Recognition," in Amy Gutmann, ed., *Multiculturalism and "The Politics of Recognition"* (Princeton, NJ: Princeton UP, 1992), p. 26.
2. Other reasons for the prominence accorded to this idea, I believe, include the
lingering charisma of Alexandre Kojève's interpretation of Hegel and the failure of socio-
economic theories of human motivation of both the classical (profit-maximizing) and
Marxian (class-affiliation) varieties. The desire for recognition explains cases recalcitrant
to either theory, such as that of the starving artist, while subsuming the successes of both.

and there is much to be learned from this work; but what is lacking in these papers and books is an analysis of the concept that they purport to take as central: recognition. It is this concept that I will examine here, specifically by raising the question posed in the article's title.

By making "recognition" central to social theory—a move that I think is long overdue—these theorists face a serious risk if it should turn out that recognition is a zero-sum game. The prospect that social life is a zero-sum game is widely recognized as an obstacle to developing a political theory, especially by social contract theorists. John Rawls, in *A Theory of Justice*, recognizes that self-respect is a very important primary good, "perhaps the most important primary good," and that "our self-respect normally depends upon the respect of others."[3] Rawls's assumption that individuals are most concerned about their own life projects raised an enormous amount of well-justified criticism for presupposing a fundamental individualism; what was overlooked, though, was the necessity of this premise for avoiding what Rawls rightly perceived to be a serious threat to any social contract theory: the prospect of the zero-sum game, which would preclude one of the fundamental requirements of justice, i.e., that social life should be mutually advantageous.[4] Social contract theorists are not the only political theorists who worry about the prospect of the zero-sum game; egalitarian ideals in general are threatened by the hierarchical outcomes involved. It is in this broader horizon that I wish to pose the question: what happens to egalitarian ideals if recognition is—as it appears to be—a zero-sum game?

Zero-sum games, in the narrowest sense of the term, involve a situation in which no participant can gain unless someone loses. As such, they are inescapably competitive. Less narrowly, they are also thought of as situations that have dramatically hierarchical outcomes. It should be noted that zero-sum games do not necessarily have harsher outcomes than non-zero-sum games. "Running 100 meters in less than 10 seconds" is a non-zero-sum criterion, since the achievement by one person in no way precludes (or even hinders) its accomplishment by another,

---

3. John Rawls, *A Theory of Justice* (Cambridge, MA: Harvard UP, 1971), pp. 440, 178.

4. This basic individualism is not thought by Rawls to be sufficient to ensure self-confidence; people must also "avoid any assessment of the relative value of one another's way of life" (ibid., p. 442). Rawls does not discuss the possibility that the very structure of decision-making involves or implies such assessments.

whereas "winning a track meet" is a zero-sum criterion. It is easy to see that the harshness of the outcome is a function of the relative difficulty of achieving the goal, since far fewer people fall into the former category than the latter. If the bar is set low enough, a zero-sum game can have very egalitarian outcomes, with nearly all games ending in ties, such as tic-tac-toe. Furthermore, whether a game is zero-sum may depend on factors external to the criteria used to determine the winners. If a game has multiple identical prizes, it will be a zero-sum game if there are more applicants than prizes, but non-zero-sum if there are fewer applicants than prizes (as long as the rules specify that all of the prizes should be distributed). But this is all by the way. Zero-sum games typically have harshly hierarchical results, and theorists are correct to worry about them.

Without going through a thorough analysis of the full semantic potentials of the word "recognition," we can describe three types:

(1) *Recognition as identification or acknowledgement.* In this sense of the term, one can recognize a person, but also a plant, an animal, a fact, a pattern, or a situation. This sort of recognition can have a negative or neutral valence as easily as a positive one; the added specifications needed to bring this sort of recognition in line with a positive prestige—recognizing a celebrity or being acknowledged by one—would move those situations into one of the other categories. This category is not the sort of "recognition" with which I am concerned.

(2) *Non-zero-sum forms of recognition*, such as a high school diploma or a driver's license. Although the track example mentioned above shows that non-zero-sum criteria need not be so egalitarian, these examples are more typical. In fact, a category like "running 100 meters in less than 10 seconds" takes on the importance it does because of its exclusivity, which makes it the functional equivalent of a zero-sum criterion.

(3) *Zero-sum forms of recognition*, such as a competitive prize, a chess rating, or bridge points, as well as any sort of ranking or "best of" list.

It might be thought that recognition could not be a zero-sum game, because it is possible to achieve recognition in an entirely new category. These new categories might arise out of nowhere (e.g., inventing the Numa Numa dance, or any number of categories in the *Guinness Book of World Records*), or a particularly charismatic individual might achieve general recognition at a very high level from a field in which no one had yet done so (e.g., Muhammad Ali, Woodward and Bernstein). But it is not clear that the prestige in a new category is a gain made at no one's expense, or whether the prestige of others suffers. Certainly the enormous gain in prestige attached to playing the electric guitar during the British Invasion wiped out the prestige associated with playing the accordion.

In one way, I have already answered the question raised in the title: some forms of recognition are zero-sum, while others are not. But it would be premature to be satisfied with this answer, since non-zero-sum games may have zero-sum aspects or effects. This possibility arises from the reflexive aspect of forms of recognition: they compete with each other for recognition. It may be that achievements that are non-zero-sum are considered to be less important as more people attain them (and failure to attain them will carry more and more of a stigma). Non-zero-sum achievements may simply confer less prestige than zero-sum achievements. So, another way of putting the question might be: which kinds of recognition matter—zero-sum, non-zero-sum, or both? If theorists claim, as Taylor does, that recognition is a need, then which kind of recognition is needed—zero-sum or non-zero-sum? In the remainder of this article, I will use the term "zero-sum game" loosely, but in a way that captures the worries that political theorists have. To ask if recognition in this sense is a zero-sum game is to ask if recognition is necessarily hierarchical.

The specific question that I raise is not discussed in the literature. In the next section, I will examine Taylor's "The Politics of Recognition" in order to show how a number of problems arise from a failure to address the issue explicitly. But to say that the question is not discussed is not to say that it is not answered. There is an implicit assumption that recognition is not a zero-sum game. Sometimes this assumption is made explicit, as in the following footnote from a paper by Nancy Fraser:

> Here I am assuming the distinction, now fairly standard in moral philosophy, between respect and esteem. According to this distinction, respect is owed universally to every person in virtue of shared humanity; esteem, in contrast, is accorded differentially on the basis of persons' specific traits, accomplishments or contributions. Thus, while the injunction to respect everyone equally is perfectly sensible, the injunction to esteem everyone equally is oxymoronic.[5]

Although widely assumed, neither Fraser nor any of the other theorists argue for the possibility of a universal, equal recognition or respect. I think

5. Nancy Fraser, "Recognition without Ethics?" *Theory, Culture & Society* 18 (2003): 39n6.

this may be due to the general assumption that it has been proven by Hegel in the master-slave dialectic. I will return to this issue in the third part of the article.

II.

Taylor's argument proceeds through two phases. In the first phase, Taylor characterizes the shift in European history to democratic political systems as a shift from a politics of honor to a politics of recognition. According to Taylor, honor differs from recognition and, although supplanted as a basis for politics, continues in awards:

> I am using honor in the *ancien régime* sense in which it is intrinsically linked to inequalities. For some to have honor in this sense, it is essential that not everyone have it. This is the sense in which Montesquieu uses it in his description of monarchy. Honor is intrinsically a matter of "*prefer-ences*." It is also the sense in which we use the term when we speak of honoring someone by giving some public award, for example, the Order of Canada. Clearly, this award would be without worth if tomorrow we decided to give it to every adult Canadian.[6]

The key figures in his story are Rousseau, Kant, Herder, and Hegel. With Rousseau, the idea of individual authenticity becomes central, and the political ideal becomes one of mutual, equal recognition. Kant shifts the idea of individual dignity from emotion to rationality, and Herder estab-lishes that authenticity/dignity can be thought of as cultural as well as individual. Hegel establishes that human beings are "dialogical." Of these figures, Rousseau is central for Taylor's account, as he mediates between the old idea of honor and the Stoic/Christian discourse that condemned the seeking of honor. Rousseau's solution to the problem is equal honor: "The answer seems to be equality or, more exactly, the balanced reciprocity that underpins equality."[7]

In the second phase, Taylor deals with three examples: Quebec, Rush-die, and canon formation in universities. With the example of Quebec, we get to the central, twofold point of Taylor's essay, which is to provide an analysis of Québécois cultural separatism in which: (1) it is seen as a kind of liberalism rather than a kind of communitarianism;[8] and (2) this

---

6. Taylor, "The Politics of Recognition," p. 27.

7. Ibid., pp. 46–47.

8. There is a shift in the terms of discussion here. In phase one, Taylor speaks in terms of Kant and Rousseau and honor and recognition. In the second phase, Taylor speaks in

kind of (or interpretation of) liberalism is understood to be superior to the individual rights version, because it is more difference-friendly and more suited to multiculturalism. In discussing canon formation, Taylor wishes to distinguish himself from other multiculturalists by establishing his position as less extreme.

Not everything goes smoothly in the move from the first to the second phase of Taylor's argument. To begin with, Taylor never explains how Quebec separatism avoids the problems that he finds in Rousseau. The first phase ends with a discussion of the political problems that arise from Rousseau's theory. The flaw is that in order to achieve mutual, equal recognition, a community requires a common purpose. For Rousseau, "equality of esteem requires a tight unity of purpose that seems to be incompatible with any differentiation."[9] As Taylor points out, "This has been the formula for the most terrible forms of homogenizing tyranny, starting with the Jacobins and extending to the totalitarian regimes of our century."[10] The Quebec case of linguistic and cultural separatism is one of common purpose, so it would fall prey to Taylor's objection to Rousseau. Taylor's point would seem to be that, unlike the Rousseauian case, the common purpose of Quebec separatism is compatible with some differentiation. This leaves us with the unsatisfying conclusion that we should accept Quebec separatism because it is not one of "the most terrible forms of homogenizing tyranny."

Next, Taylor fails to address the issues raised by the concepts of potentiality and actuality. In the first phase, Taylor discusses the Kantian idea that respect for human individuality involves respect for rational *potentiality*, whereas some multiculturalists demand respect for cultural *actuality*. According to Taylor: "But at least in the intercultural context, a stronger demand has recently arisen: that one accord equal respect to actually evolved cultures."[11] A number of problems internal to Taylor's argument arise here, problems that touch on the heart of the issues involved in hierarchy and recognition.[12] First, Taylor fails to discuss the possibility that

terms of liberalism, and the theorists he refers to are Ronald Dworkin, John Rawls, Bruce Ackerman, and Michael Sandel. This shift does not affect my argument.

9. Taylor, "The Politics of Recognition," p. 50.

10. Ibid., p. 51.

11. Ibid., p. 42.

12. I am only raising internal criticisms. Excellent external criticisms have been provided by Jürgen Habermas and Anthony Appiah in their replies to Taylor. These are included in Gutmann, ed., *Multiculturalism and "The Politics of Recognition"*.

one could make a minor conceptual change in the canon-formation view by requiring respect for cultural potentiality, bringing it into line with the Kantian view. Of course, this may be a minor conceptual change, but it is doubtful that it would be considered to be a minor change in terms of the demands of multiculturalists for cultural respect. This suggests a second problem, which is that the Kantian idea of respecting rational potential cannot be accepted at face value and meets with crippling objections.

Any view that puts itself forward as a theory of equal, universal recognition faces two problems (obviously enough): (1) universality[13] and (2) gradation. The concept of "potentiality" is introduced to solve the problem of universality, as Taylor points out. But it fails to do so, since potentiality, as usually assessed, is something that some people do not have (for example, I have no potential to be a star in the World Cup). And potentiality, as usually considered, fails the second test as well: potential is something of which one can have more or less. These two problems will be central to the analysis that follows, since for any characteristic that is proposed as deserving of recognition, it would need to be established that it is universal and non-gradated.[14] This latter problem is elided through use of the phrase "mutual recognition," because mutuality is not the same as equality. A chess grandmaster and master recognize each other mutually through their respective rankings, but their recognition is not equal.

Rationality and autonomy both face problems of gradation. Some are more rational than others; some are more autonomous than others. Rousseau's "common purpose" does not escape this problem, since some contribute more than others to a common purpose. Of course, here we have left behind the Kantian use of "reason" and "autonomy" as non-empirical (i.e., noumenal) concepts. A Kantian can appeal to the noumenal nature of these concepts in order to say that they are universal and non-gradated, since one can say whatever one wants about non-empirical concepts. But this strikes me as a refutation of, rather than a support for, the Kantian view.

Leaving aside a priori thinking, we can note that potential plays an interesting role in the economy of recognition. Being judged according to

---

13. By "universality," I mean all human beings. Equal recognition for all citizens of one country is not sufficient, since it does not provide a concept of equal human rights. In fact, it is likely to be destructive of such a concept, since it is likely to result from, or result in, competitive and destructive nationalism.

14. Also, that it is of merit. Cases where people desire negatives exist, but I am leaving them aside to simplify matters.

potential when young (as opposed to being judged according to achievement) is a great privilege. But this only holds true when one is judged according to one's own self-image and one's own desires. If judged according to another's desires and self-image, as in the case of Kant's criticism of the South Sea Islanders in the *Groundwork of the Metaphysics of Morals*, such judgments denigrate rather than respect others.

Aside from these two criticisms, there is another that is more important for an analysis of recognition. This third problem is the way in which ideas relegated to the concept of "honor" reassert themselves as intrinsic to recognition in Taylor's analysis of canon formation. As Taylor points out in his discussion of canon formation, one needs to know about a culture in order to recognize it; not to know anything about it is not to recognize it but to condescend to it:

> Moreover, the giving of such a [favorable] judgment on demand is an act of breathtaking condescension. No one can really mean it as a genuine act of respect. It is more in the nature of a pretend act of respect given on the insistence of its supposed beneficiary.[15]

This would seem to contradict Taylor's discussion of the recognition of individuals in the first phase of his essay, where the concepts of rationality and potentiality are introduced to obviate the need to know anything about an individual. Stated more generally, in the first phase, Taylor treats honor as entirely separate from recognition; being lauded for excellence is a question of honor and is not a matter of recognition.[16] But in discussing canon formation, assessment of excellence is treated as part and parcel of cultural recognition.

This unresolved tension in Taylor's discussion is not due to his analysis; it is embedded in the political common sense of democratic politics. Although Taylor wants to direct our thinking about liberalism toward authenticity and away from individual rights, his main strategy is to appeal to political common sense in order to argue that Quebec linguistic separatism accords with liberal ideals. Looking too deeply into the presuppositions underlying this common sense is, therefore, not in Taylor's interest.

---

15. Taylor, "The Politics of Recognition," p. 70.
16. See the first quotation from Taylor in this section.

III.

As I noted earlier, I think that the assumption that politics can be based on mutual, equal, universal recognition is based on the idea that Hegel has established this as true. This assumption is made explicit in the interpretations of Hegel by Alexandre Kojève and Robert Williams.[17] They see Hegel as attempting to base a universal egalitarian political theory on the concept of recognition. I find this interpretative direction plausible and will work within its terms in this section of the paper. Other interpretations are also plausible, but I will not spend time trying to establish the truth of any particular interpretation, as my interest in this paper is recognition, not interpreting Hegel.[18] Those who find these interpretations implausible—either because they think it obvious that Hegel's political theory does not aim at universality (or equality), or because Hegel does not rely on the concept of recognition to achieve these ends—can skip to section IV.

Taking his cue from Fichte, Hegel relies on recognition as a condition for the emergence of self-consciousness. Hegel introduces this idea at a particular place in the *Phenomenology*: at the origin of self-consciousness. Leaving the stage of consciousness, the self has learned that it cannot take the external world (objects or forces) as "absolute," but that they are perceived through the self (transcendental apperception).[19] The self at this point is conceptually impoverished, thinking only "I," "I," "I," and, experiencing desire, wishes to internalize everything by devouring it. However, in devouring others (as one devours animals and plants), one fails to become certain of one's own value and to attain what one truly desires, which is recognition. Recognition, in Hegel's terminology, is a return of a self-consciousness out of another self-consciousness. In order for this return to be recognition, "the second consciousness must do 'in-itself' what the first consciousness is doing in it."[20] In other words, the master values himself as the master and is recognized as a master because

---

17. Alexandre Kojève, *Introduction to the Reading of Hegel* (Ithaca, NY: Cornell UP, 1969); Robert W. Williams, *Hegel's Ethics of Recognition* (Berkeley: Univ. of California Press, 1997).

18. For the same reason, I will not concern myself with the differences between Kojève's and Williams's interpretations.

19. See Robert Pippin, *Hegel's Idealism: The Satisfactions of Self-Consciousness* (Cambridge: Cambridge UP, 1989).

20. *Hegel's Phenomenology of Spirit: Selections*, trans. Howard Kainz (University Park, PA: Penn State UP, 1994), p. 52. See also pp. 60–61.

the slave also values him as the master.[21] Rather than run through all of the (well-known) details of the section, I will list a few important points: Two selves fight to the death for recognition. One must risk one's life. But if one dies, then recognition is not achieved.[22] If one surrenders, he becomes the slave of the other. The winner becomes the master. However, the master's victory is supposedly unsatisfying, because the recognition attained is unsatisfying. The master's life is one of pleasure, which perpetuates itself indefinitely. There is no dialectical continuation of the master's life; it is a phenomenological dead end. The slave, through work, continues the dialectic.

Let us consider how the problems of universality and gradation, raised earlier, apply to Hegel's scenario. The master/slave dialectic does nothing to confront the problem of universality. It suggests that one must recognize someone else, rather than simply thinking "I," "I," "I"; but that is a far cry from establishing that one must recognize everyone else.

The problem of gradation is not discussed explicitly here either. Instead, Hegel finesses the problem by limiting his scenario to two combatants. With enslavement, the value of the slave's desire is diminished. But it only reduces to zero because only two people (or two positions) are involved, allowing for a binary, non-gradated value of desire—all or nothing. If the scenario included others, then there could be degrees of value to the desire of others. For example, there could be masters with fewer or more slaves, and even the relative desire of different slaves could have greater or lesser value. This problem is an especially pointed one for Hegel, since he convincingly argues, in the *Science of Logic*, that mere quantitative change can, and frequently does, result in qualitative change. So the desire of three can differ qualitatively from the desire of two. Even if the desire of the slave can be unsatisfying for the master, the desire of a second slave can be relatively more satisfying.

Because Hegel's account is so sketchy, it is worth examining Kojève's and Williams's interpretations. Although these interpretations expand on

---

21. Kojève provides, as a definition of recognition, the felicitous phrase "the desire of the desire of the other" (Kojève, *Introduction*, p. 7). This may be a bit narrower than Hegel's view, but it fits quite well with the master/slave scenario, which Kojève treats as the education of desire.

22. Why couldn't killing the other satisfy the desire for recognition if the look in the eye of the one killed shows that he knows he is defeated? Couldn't the memory of this look satisfy the desire?

Hegel's account by saying more about what one is being recognized for, neither escapes these difficulties. In fact, they show only more clearly that Hegel's scenario faces these problems. Kojève's interpretation fleshes out Hegel's account, making it easier to see how the problem of gradation arises in the text. In terms of gradation, Kojève's account jumps from terms that are gradated to terms that are binary/non-gradated. On the one hand, the struggle is one for "pure prestige," and prestige is gradated.[23] (That Kojève is referring to our common concept of prestige here is illustrated by his examples of a medal or the enemy's flag.)[24] But he then switches to using binary, non-gradated terms of recognition between "autonomous" and "dependent" existences. Although Kojève does treat these terms as binary,[25] he never establishes that they are so. As I noted earlier, autonomy and dependence are matters of degree.

The same oscillation between gradation and non-gradation occurs in Williams's interpretation. Williams uses binary terms to describe recognition: whether one "counts" or "doesn't count" for another. Following Kojève, Williams treats the master/slave scenario as the transition from the non-human to the human—that is, as the transition to autonomy. Risking one's life allows one to realize one's autonomy in both senses of "realize": one comes to be autonomous and to know that one is autonomous.[26] Autonomous and non-autonomous existence are thus binary, non-gradated states, whereas respect and honor are both forms of recognition,[27] and thus recognition is gradated. Williams, however, has a solution to this problem: the concept of a "threshold of the ethical." In other words, there is a minimum of recognition that is necessary and satisfying; above this level, presumably, recognition is superfluous. In this way, recognition can be both binary and gradated, and the binary aspect is taken to be of greater significance. Whether or not this claim accurately reflects Hegel's views is of little consequence for my argument; of greater significance for my purposes here is the fact that Williams says nothing to establish the plausibility of this claim. Williams needs to demonstrate that the "threshold" is more important than the gradation in order to establish that recognition is non-hierarchical.

23. Kojève, *Introduction*, p. 7.
24. Ibid., p. 6.
25. See ibid., p. 20.
26. Williams, *Hegel's Ethics of Recognition*, p. 60.
27. Ibid., p. 90.

An analysis of Hegel's treatment of recognition must extend beyond the master/slave scenario. If we consider the immediately succeeding sections of the *Phenomenology of Spirit* and the later System, Hegel's view can be construed in the following way. The desire for recognition finds some sort of fulfillment in obedience to law (primarily, property law), whereby in obeying, one is "recognizing" others as law-abiding, since one would not obey if one thought others would not obey. This is what it means to recognize someone as a "person."[28] This "recognition" results in an equilibrium whereby all members of a society act in harmony without force, discussion, or other coordination. However, this sort of recognition is too abstract, since it is not granted on account of any particular characteristics of the individual. If we think of Hegel's recognition as granted for being a person, then his view is subject to his own criticism here. As Steven Smith has pointed out: "One difficulty with this right of recognition is that it is every bit as formal and abstract as the deontological ethic Hegel often claims to attack. The idea of personhood is itself based on an abstraction from all empirical characteristics and attachments we develop in the course of our lives and histories."[29]

Another problem with stopping at the concept of "personhood" for elucidating the concept of recognition would be the failure to take into account prestige or "honor," in Hegel's term. Honor falls within the definition of recognition in the *Phenomenology of Spirit*, to the extent that I have been able to reconstruct it above. And Hegel seems to treat these concepts as continuous in the *Philosophy of Subjective Spirit*.[30] Hegel's treatment is significant, because it shows that Hegel did not think that recognition based on personhood, the sort of recognition that might be achieved if the combatants in the master/slave scenario were sufficiently reflective about their experience, would be sufficient. In the *Philosophy of Right*, Hegel hoped to solve the problem of the need for recognition (here, "honor") through the guilds ("corporations") to which all workers would belong. Since different professions have different levels of prestige, the

---

28. In the *Phenomenology*, the world of the Roman Empire, in which the concept of a "person" arose, is a horror show. Nevertheless, the concept of personhood has some validity and thus is taken up into later institutions.

29. Steven Smith, *Hegel's Critique of Liberalism* (Chicago: Univ. of Chicago Press, 1989), p. 125.

30. *Hegel's Philosophy of Subjective Spirit*, ed. M. J. Petry (Dordt: D. Reidel, 1979), 3:71 (sec. 436).

problem of gradation is not addressed. And it seems to me implausible that the unemployed would achieve equal recognition merely through guild membership—even though the improvement of their economic circumstances would be a laudatory goal. Further, we can note that if problems from the inabilities of civil society to gratify citizens' desire for honor lead to unrest that can threaten social stability, then the equilibrium arrived at earlier in the dialectic involving personhood and obedience to the law is not really so "equilibrious." This sort of recognition cannot really be said to satisfy the desire for recognition, since honor is a form of recognition.

One way of attempting to save Hegel's position is by pointing to the distinction between vanity and recognition, putting all desire for prestige on the side of vanity. However, the texts do not support this interpretation. In the section of the *Philosophy of Subjective Spirit* on recognition (section 436), Hegel treats honor and fame as virtues in his clarifying "remark." In a qualifying sentence, which was (according to M. J. Petry) added to the remark for the 1830 edition, honor and fame may become separated from "what is substantial" when cultivated for their own sake.[31] So the desire for fame and honor are not matters of vanity per se. And this is what we would expect from the *Phenomenology of Spirit*, where Hegel scorns those who try to distinguish their own individual desires from the "way of the world." Society works through individual desires, and these are lauded, since they arise from the effective substance of spirit. In the section on the "Animal Kingdom of Spirit," which involves a struggle for recognition, Hegel could have condemned the search for prestige and distinguished it from the desire for recognition. But he does not do so. Instead, he refutes this position with an argument similar to the one that he uses against the "way of the world." In each section, the individual who is concerned with their own personal action/contribution must learn that when they act for themselves, they are acting for others as well. In the latter section, as in the former, those who condemn others for taking a proprietary interest in the results of their action are not vindicated, but instead they are refuted since their condemnations similarly make claims of proprietary interest.

Of course, one might claim that recognition is achieved only at the end of the chapter on *Geist*, when confession and forgiveness comes into play. This would seem to have been Hegel's thought on the matter, since he does specifically say that by confessing and forgiving, the "acting

---

31. Ibid., 3:71.

consciousness" and the "judging consciousness" come into a relation of equality and recognition, and absolute spirit is referred to as "a reciprocal recognition."[32] This section seems to have dropped out of the scholarly discussion of recognition, perhaps because it may be thought to be theologically grounded. These worries are, to some extent, well-founded, as Hegel introduces in this section the concepts of worship, religion, and God. I will venture some comments on this "enigmatic" section as if it does not have theological presuppositions, while still regarding its function as the transition to "Religion."[33]

The chapter on "Conscience" is clearly a culmination toward which the phenomenology has been heading since the master/slave dialectic. In that section, the concept of *Geist* is announced as "an I which is a We and a We which is an I," a sociality/community that is achieved in the section on Conscience. The struggle for recognition, which resulted in an unsatisfactory unequal recognition, here achieves a satisfying equal recognition. This equal recognition is, indeed, absolute spirit, the culmination of the entire book.

"Conscience" is introduced to resolve the antinomies of the earlier sections of the "Moral" worldview. In acting pursuant to one's conscience, one can be confident that one is doing the right thing, staying true to oneself at the same time that one connects with others. One is recognized for acting from conviction, and this recognition is the social glue that binds the community together. In order to secure one's actions, and thus also one's recognition, one needs to express in language that one is acting from conviction.[34] Although acting from conviction is the social glue, speech in which actors attest to their conviction is needed for this glue to set.[35]

32. G. W. F. Hegel, *Spirit: Chapter Six of Hegel's Phenomenology of Spirit*, ed. Daniel E. Shannon (Indianapolis, IN: Hackett Pub. Co., 2001), pp. 154, 157.

33. The epithet is Robert Pippin's, in his essay "Recognition and Reconciliation: Actualized Agency in Hegel's Jena Phenomenology," in Katerina Deligiorgi, ed., *Hegel: New Directions* (Montreal: McGill-Queen's UP, 2006), p. 139.

34. Hegel's justification is that speech is a special medium connecting people, because in speech one hears oneself speaking at the same moment that others hear one speaking. This is the point that Jacques Derrida takes to be the moment of atemporal univocity, the apogee of metaphysics. Following Derrida's idea that Hegel's point has to do with the univocity of speech, Hegel's argument would be that language cannot be interpreted in different ways by the participants, while their actions can. If one does not follow Derrida here, Hegel would seem to have no argument whatsoever. Hegel also argues that one cannot lie about acting from conviction, or that lying cannot be an issue.

35. Speaking also demonstrates one's awareness that acting from conviction is not a retreat inward but establishes a connection to others.

This type of recognition has three important characteristics. First, acting from conviction is treated as a simple either/or, so there is no gradation. Second, this recognition is a matter of seeing that someone else is like oneself. Third, in order for this recognition to be satisfactorily achieved, a problem called the "antithesis of singularity and universality that is involved in acting," which has popped up in earlier sections of the chapter on *Geist*, must be overcome. In overcoming this problem, there is a reconciliation between action and judgment involving confession and forgiveness. There is also, as one moves through the chapter, a shift away from the individualism of the concept of duty, as one is supposed to realize that the "spirit certain of itself" is as much the broader community as the individual.

The antithesis of singularity and universality is worked out through a dialectic involving an "acting consciousness" and a "judging consciousness." The problem is that thought, and thus purpose, is universal, but action is always singular. It arises through the engagement of a particular individual with particular desires and inclinations in a particular situation. There would seem to be a disproportion between one's purposes and one's actions in all cases. This disproportion allows the judging consciousness to refuse to recognize the acting consciousness, alleging that the act was not performed out of conviction but instead out of a particular interest, such as ambition or the pursuit of fame. This discussion of fame and ambition as motivations, cropping up as it does where equal recognition is achieved, is of great significance.

It might be claimed, because Hegel does not use the word recognition to specifically refer to fame or ambition, that he would reserve the term for the recognition achieved between the actor and judging consciousness. But Hegel never explicitly says this. Instead, I think it would make more sense to say that fame and ambition are types of recognition that need to be treated here because they are part and parcel of the striving that led to the struggle that instigated the master/slave dialectic. Hegel's point in discussing them here is in no way to delegitimate them. On the contrary, as in the earlier sections on the "Way of the World" and "Animal Kingdom of the Spirit," the pursuit of fame and ambition are validated. The "antithesis of singularity and universality" turns out, at least at this point, not to be much of an antithesis at all. Every action, according to Hegel, has a universal side and a particular side. It is here that he quotes the saying: "No man is a hero to his valet; not because he is not a hero, but because the valet is a valet." It is the judging consciousness that is in the wrong here, as it is the moral valet of the acting consciousness. The acting consciousness must be brought to see the disproportion between purposes and actions, and to acknowledge its hitherto unperceived "hypocrisy" through a confession to the judging consciousness. One should not be misled by the reference to the acting consciousness as "evil" into thinking that it is in the wrong. It is only mistaken to the extent that it fails to make the proper connection between its motivation and its action and to see itself as necessarily situated in a larger whole.[36] It is the judging consciousness that really takes a beating in this section. It claims to be judging on the basis of the universal, but it fails to connect with others—specifically, the actors. It judges on the basis of whether actions are based on conviction, but, as the "beautiful soul," it is unable to act. These deficiencies are its "hypocrisies," which are discerned by the acting consciousness.

Problems crop up every step of the way in this section. The claim that acting from conviction or "Conscience" does justice both to the singularity of the individual and society is obscure.[37] The claim that language is more determinate than actions is unpersuasive, and the argument that lying is not at issue in expressing one's conviction is impenetrable. Also, Hegel makes little attempt to say which parts of earlier stages are retained in this section, although some must be. However, I will focus on three problems with this section that are most relevant to the issue of universal, equal recognition.

The first of these is the question of universality. The question of the scope of the terms "Conscience" and "Geist" is unavoidable. Who has a conscience? According to Hegel, conscience is a historical product. Initially, only post-Kantian Germans have a conscience, although conscience presumably can and will spread much farther afield. Conscience arises as a late stage of *Geist*, so now we must consider the scope of *Geist*. Does *Geist* consist of all human beings? all language speakers? Europeans? Christians? German-language speakers? Post-Kantian Germans? European Christian German-language speakers? The question has been pursued by readers

36. Hegel says on two occasions that the acting consciousness is "taken to be evil" by the judging consciousness. It is not clear that the acting consciousness should be thought of as evil; the withdrawal of the judging consciousness fits most directly Hegel's definition of evil. The exact way in which evil in the conventional sense is forgiven through these two dialectical figures is not very clear, but the conclusion that it is indeed forgiven through them is inescapable.

37. Is this established solely by the idea of acting from conviction, or does it require all of the steps that occur in this section?

of Hegel without result, and I think there is no answer to this question. Similarly, we need to know who participates in the final reconciliation of the acting consciousness and judging consciousness, after they acknowledge their likeness to each other in their deficiencies ("hypocrisy") and forgive each other. Commentators tend to spend their time pointing out which Post-Kantian historical or literary figures were Hegel's models for the various positions in this section. But we need to know the scope of this recognition. Who can recognize? Who can be recognized? Must one live at the time (and after) these historical figures live out this dialectic? How explicit must one's understanding of the dialectic be? How explicit must one's confession be? Does it even need to be explicit at all? Again, I think that there are no answers to these questions in Hegel's text. I would opt for a broader interpretation in which all of the dialectical tricks that Hegel uses to broaden the scope of *Geist* would also be brought into play here.[38] Indeed, the "confession" is stated in terms so general (may one say "abstract"?) as to make it perfunctory, perhaps even dispensable. But it would also appear that all of the reasons that scholars have provided for thinking that various "others" are excluded from Hegel's conception of the spiritual community apply as well.

The second problem I wish to raise has to do with, to put it very mildly, unpleasant aspects of this scene of recognition as mutual confession and forgiveness. The final turn takes place after the acting consciousness has discerned the deficiency of the judging consciousness and admitted its own. The judging consciousness refuses to acknowledge its own deficiency, becoming the "hard heart" that refuses to soften its condemnation of the acting consciousness. Moltke Gram has argued that Hegel derived the figure of the "hard heart" from nattering nabobs of negativity (not Gram's phrase) like Hölderlin (or his characters), who judge the world only in terms of sweeping condemnations of political oppression and destructive mediocrity.[39] The reconciliation that takes place after the "hard heart" is broken and returns the confession it has received and forgives the acting consciousness has momentous implications that go far beyond the particular individual(s) on which Hegel modeled this figure. "The wounds

---

38. These dialectical tricks would also bring back the problem of gradation, since one of the terms in the various oppositions involved (e.g., implicit/explicit) is valued more highly than the other.

39. Moltke Gram, "Moral and Literary Ideals in Hegel's Critique of 'The Moral World-View'," in Jon Stewart, ed., *The Phenomenology of Spirit Reader: Critical and Interpretive Essays* (Albany: SUNY Press, 1998), pp. 327–29.

of spirit heal without leaving scars."[40] Here we have made the transition to absolute spirit. What has happened here?

I suggest that *Geist* is forgiving itself for all of the atrocities that its actors have committed over the course of its development. The "acting consciousness" and the "judging consciousness" are both parts of the social subject that is *Geist*, and the actors in the previous historical worlds making up the development of *Geist* have made the error attributed to the acting consciousness: they failed to discern the larger whole of which they were part. Slavery, the Terror, and all of the atrocities of the slaughterbench of history are wiped away: "spirit in the absolute certainty of itself, is master over every deed or actuality and can throw them away and make as if they never happened."[41] In sum, through the continuity provided by their *Geist*, contemporary members of the community of "equal recognition" forgive their forebears (and contemporaries[42]) for their atrocities. Only this sort of forgiveness explains how the proposed solution to an abstruse problem in the Kantian theory of moral action can enable the transition to absolute spirit.[43]

The third problem to be mentioned here has to do with the two types of recognition with which we are left at the end of this chapter of the *Phenomenology*, one of which is hierarchical (fame/ambition) and one of which is not (equal recognition of confession and forgiveness). Both are legitimate and necessary, according to Hegel. But I see no argument for the claim that the egalitarian version matters more than the hierarchical kind. As Pierre Bourdieu has pointed out, egalitarian ideals can always be interpreted as a matter of making a virtue of necessity by those in the subordinate levels of the hierarchy. I would suggest that if Kojève's discussion of what is at stake in the master/slave dialectic has had such appeal, it is because his definition of what is at stake (desire for the desire of the other) seems, rather obviously, to cover recognition. Mutual recognition in

---

40. Hegel, *Spirit*, p. 156.

41. Ibid., p. 155.

42. I do not see how this conclusion can be avoided, given that the various positions occupied in the *Phenomenology* (and argued therein to be historically refuted) still existed, and were known by Hegel to exist, in Hegel's time.

43. In his later System, Hegel makes the involvement of the reader in historical atrocity even tighter, since the achievement of the System is not merely a cognitive achievement but also an act of will. In completing the system, the reader must actually will it in its entirety, including world history. Thus, according to Hegel's later System, understanding the world requires that one be an accomplice in its atrocities!

terms of a very abstract deficiency has far less appeal, to the point of not seeming much like recognition at all. It should also be kept in mind that hierarchical recognition of fame brings with it its own privileged terms and practices of forgiveness.

Hegel, then, cannot solve Taylor's problem. So what can be learned from Hegel's treatment of recognition? Exactly what generations of readers of Hegel have learned: that recognition must be concrete.[44] And it must be concrete in two ways, one external to the one recognized, one internal. First, self-perception and self-evaluation are intersubjective—or, to use Taylor's word, "dialogical." There must be others who grant recognition in concrete ways. Second, recognition can only be granted because of a particular characteristic of the person recognized. This latter point derives from connecting the master/slave scenario to Hegel's critique of Kant's deontological ethic, which abstracts from all empirical characteristics, an abstraction that Hegel thinks is at the root of the tragedy of the Terror.

With regard to the external characteristic, I think we can extend Hegel's account and say that recognition manifests itself in one or more of three ways. Recognition is manifested through emulation, association, and/or gratification. Emulation and association are relatively straightforward; people try to be like and associate with those whom they admire. They also aim to give things of value to those whom they admire, and this is what I mean by "gratification." Recognition of a musician or a band involves copying their style (emulation), wearing their T-shirt (association), or paying the musician/band for the T-shirt (gratification). Of course, these are merely the first examples that leap to mind, and one could come up with innumerable others. Recognition may, but need not, involve all of these three. All of these ways of recognizing others are matters of degree.

There may be other ways of manifesting recognition. One candidate would be understanding. A scientist might think that his or her recognition is wanting if others know them as "a famous scientist" (say, as a Nobel Prize winner) but know nothing of their work, even if they wish to associate

---

44. We may actually want to credit Fichte with first claiming that recognition, to be genuine, must be concrete. He says that one must be recognized by a particular person, that one must "actually *act* in the sensible world" in order to recognize someone, recognition must involve people who reciprocally interact. J. G. Fichte, *Foundations of Natural Right*, ed. Frederick Neuhouser (Cambridge: Cambridge UP, 2000), pp. 42–43.

with and gratify the scientist.[45] This might be thought of as a deficiency of gratification. Others may wish to buy the scientist drinks but be unwilling to grant their time to study the scientist's work. (I am sure anyone reading this realizes how valuable giving time is, especially the time to study difficult work.) On the other hand, others do their best to hide the steps taken to achieve a result. For example, those having cosmetic surgery would prefer that others not understand how they achieved their beauty. The desire to understand the work that goes into producing beauty would seem to be a deficiency of recognition rather than a manifestation of it.

We can also extend Hegel's account of the internal characteristic of recognition. This latter establishes that there is a veristic aspect to recognition. Since one can only be recognized if there is a particular characteristic, activity, or achievement for which recognition is granted, the person must actually have the characteristic for which they are being recognized. So, if the Grammy awards are a means of recognizing musical ability or achievement, Milli Vanilli was not recognized when they won one. (If the Grammys are a means of recognizing contribution to the production of musical spectacle, then we will need a different example.) This is not a trivial implication. It establishes that recognition is not the same as symbolic power. Bourdieu's concept of symbolic power involves the ability to obtain one's desires from others, but it does not differentiate between cases where someone has a particular ability antecedent to the obtaining of their desire and cases where they do not. This distinction is otiose on Bourdieu's view, because through acts of consecration, awards create the abilities and achievements for which they supposedly are bestowed. Hence, misrecognition is the key concept for Bourdieu, not recognition. A discussion of these concepts is beyond the scope of this paper, but a few points can be made here. The Milli Vanilli example shows that Bourdieu's universalization of his concept of "acts of consecration" is an exaggeration. Second, to the extent that Bourdieu thinks that his theory of the struggle for symbolic power serves to capture the insights of Hegel's master/slave scenario, as suggested by his reference in *Distinction*, this would be an internal problem for Bourdieu's theory.[46]

45. Here there are two levels of understanding. One level is understanding the meaning of the theses or equations; the other, deeper level is understanding the accomplishment of discovering or proving those theses.

46. "Verbal virtuousities or the gratuitous expense of time or money that is presupposed by symbolic appropriations of works of art, or even, at the second power, the self-imposed constraints and restrictions which make up the 'asceticism of the privileged'

What else can we conclude from Hegel's account? Can we conclude from the master/slave scenario that recognition must be mutual and equal? The conclusion is drawn from Hegel's claim that the master is unsatisfied with recognition from the slave. Some of the problems with this conclusion have already been addressed. In addition we can note that the master has achieved recognition: the slave gratifies and emulates (to the extent possible, that is, the slave wanted to be a master before capitulating) the master. What more is there?[47] Hegel's answer is that there is recognition from an independent (*selbständig*) consciousness, not a dependent consciousness. We have already seen that the reduction to two positions is unjustified and merely finesses the problem of gradation. Once we add more people to the scenario, we can say that there would be recognition from a more talented slave or a less talented master. At best, we might conclude that there is something vaguely unsatisfying about being at the top of the hierarchy—especially if we consider understanding to be a manifestation of recognition and can establish that those who are lower in the hierarchy are incapable of understanding those above them. But there seems no reason to conclude that a failure to achieve complete satisfaction is somehow a "refutation" of a social situation that provides a reason to think that there could be a better one. Constant striving might be a bad infinity, but this is hardly a refutation. Since recognition must be earned for a specific characteristic (even if this characteristic is inherited), free bestowal to all could not satisfy the desire for recognition.

Can we conclude from Hegel's account, as Williams does, that recognition cannot be coerced?[48] This would only be true in some cases, depending on what people wanted to be recognized for. If one wanted to be recognized for having power, as the combatants in Hegel's scenario

(as Marx said of Seneca) and the refusal of the facile which is the basis of all 'pure' aesthetics, are so many repetitions of that variant of the master-slave dialectic through which the possessors affirm their possession of their possessions." Pierre Bourdieu, *Distinction: A Social Critique of the Judgement of Taste* (Cambridge, MA: Harvard UP, 1984), p. 256.

47. Sometimes it is claimed that the master is dependent on the slave for recognition, and that this dependence is what leaves the master unsatisfied, as it turns him into a slave. But there is an important asymmetry between the dependence of the master and the dependence of the slave. The master is dependent on having a slave, not on any particular slave. The slave is dependent on this particular master. The economic consequences of this asymmetry were drawn out by Marx. I see no reason to think that the recognition satisfaction would be more deficient than the economic satisfaction derived from this asymmetry.

48. Williams, *Hegel's Ethics of Recognition*, pp. 59, 63.

do, then recognition can be coerced. If one valued force, then losing a contest of force—being forced—is a legitimate (and perhaps the only) way to obtain one's recognition. If one were concerned with recognition for something other than force—say, one's achievement as a poet—then it would indeed appear to be the case that recognition could not be coerced. There are two cases that raise difficulties, because they suggest that even in this case force can lead to, or has an important role to play in, recognition. One involves the case of murdering one's competition. Suppose one is considered the fifth-best living poet. One way to become the best living poet is to improve one's poetry. But another would be to kill the four better poets. (And what about the case where the other four died of natural causes?)[49] A second, more serious difficulty concerns the way power is needed to attain success in life's endeavors. As Bourdieu points out, to be a successful artist requires a certain amount of privilege, since one needs to spend long hours of unpaid labor attaining mastery. One also needs to establish contacts with leading figures for one's apprenticeship. An aspiring artist who has to work at Starbucks will be at a competitive disadvantage with those who have more resources and the leisure that they bring. Whether people desire recognition for power or for other matters is an empirical matter.

IV.

One way of thinking of the issues at stake in this paper is to consider it as an episode in the dispute over the status of morality. For Kant, morality was internal to human life because it involved laws that reason sets itself. However, to Hegel, Kantian morality appears to be an external "ought." Hegel followed Fichte's introduction of the concept of recognition because he thought that it provided a way of grounding moral claims internally to human life, specifically through desire. If my analysis is correct, he failed to do so, and claims for universal, mutual, equal recognition remain external oughts, no different from the claims that we should value ability at tic-tac-toe more than ability in music, chess, or basketball.

In no way should this be taken as an argument in support of a Kantian approach. Some of the flaws in Kant's approach have been pointed out above, and there are many others. We can follow Taylor in seeing Kant and

---

49. Here again it seems that memory—specifically with regard to the way one has attained one's position—has a role to play in any analysis of recognition.

Hegel as trying to extend and work out problems in Rousseau's attempt to mediate between condemnations of honor and discourses of honor. But it would appear that the entire tradition is a failure.[50] The sheepishness with which Taylor raises the metaphysical presuppositions of this tradition is worth considering:

> The politics of equal dignity is based on the idea that all humans are equally worthy of respect. It is underpinned by a notion of what in human beings commands respect, however we may try to shy away from this "metaphysical" background.[51]

And yet ideas of essentialism, and especially attempts to base politics on some human nature, have been thoroughly discredited.

Taylor's account of the shift from aristocratic politics to democratic politics should be seen as part of an account of how a political system, based on a set of mistaken presuppositions, came to be replaced by another political system, more just, whose rhetoric invoked a different set of mistaken presuppositions. When one (or some) social hierarchies came to be correctly seen (most notably by those in power) as baseless, a discourse of equality arose. This discourse of equality initially attempted to justify itself by claims about natural rights, and then split into two separate traditions: one turned to recognition, the other (outside the scope of this essay) turned to utilitarianism. The discourse of equal recognition arose for two reasons, which can be designated as Marxian and Wittgensteinian, respectively. First, this discourse was (and is) useful rhetorically for gaining support from groups that think (wrongly) that they will share equally in the benefits. In addition to this ideological function, this discourse is the sort of overgeneralization from one or few examples that typically leads to metaphysical beliefs: the idea that recognition is equal sometimes is taken to be sufficient justification for thinking that it can be equal all of the time. The idea of a recognition that is equal and universal as relied upon by theorists is typically metaphysical in a second way, in that it is supposed to provide all of the benefits of recognition without any of the detriments.

It cannot be denied that this mistaken metaphysics has led to, and still leads to, positive consequences. In the eighteenth century, hierarchies of

---

50. It is curious that Mill is never mentioned in Taylor's genealogy of liberalism.
51. Taylor, "The Politics of Recognition," p. 41.

aristocracy and slavery were widely seen to be groundless; since then, others—such as racial, colonial, and sexual hierarchies—have followed. In addition, I understand that this sort of discourse provides solace for destitute, homeless people. And, in the last fifty years, Kantian discourse has possibly done more to spread ideas of human rights internationally than other sorts of discourse. For these reasons, theorists are rightfully worried about any critiques of ideals of equality.[52]

In addition to these pragmatic uses of egalitarian discourse, appeals to "equal recognition" have strong emotional resonance. Partly, this is a matter of mistake. I think much of what is called to mind by the phrase "equal recognition" is a matter of politeness, of not making a public display of one's successes, and this hardly falls within the concept of recognition. Partly, this is a matter of thoughtlessness. People think of the "equal recognition" they desire from those above them in various hierarchies, but they fail to think of the "equal recognition" that they disdain for those at lower places. And partly, this is a matter of the powerful experience of comfort and freedom that sometimes can be attained in equal recognition, when one interacts socially with those of equal social status. These experiences have this power, according to Bourdieu, because they form a sort of oasis, where one feels as if one has stepped out of social hierarchy.[53] But these "utopian moments" are thoroughly conditioned by broader social hierarchy and can in no way be extended universally.

But these positive consequences and powerful experiences in no way make this discourse of equal recognition any more tenable. To the extent that they require more grounding than the unmasking of specific claims of privilege, universal rights will need to find some other sort of intellectual grounding. I hope to have shown that appeals to the concept of recognition are not more successful in grounding democratic politics than appeals to natural rights.

52. I think these worries are valid but exaggerated. Prior to World War II, the rhetoric of utilitarianism had far more progressive influence than Kantian rhetoric. Even in the last sixty years, in which Kantian discourse about "human rights" has led the way in international law and constitutional change, at the local level I wonder if utilitarian considerations are not still often more influential.

53. Pierre Bourdieu, *Language and Symbolic Power* (Cambridge, MA: Harvard UP, 1991), p. 71. Additional qualifications are needed for this claim, as Bourdieu uncharacteristically exaggerates the extent and availability of this zone of freedom. The rules of the broader hierarchies traverse relations among equals through their relations to those broader hierarchies. A prime example relates to Bourdieu's own discussion of the "trajectory" of social actors.

Bourdieu's theory comes closest to modeling society as a zero-sum struggle for recognition, given the proximity of his concept of symbolic power to the concept of recognition.[54] But in establishing the distinction between the two concepts, we can raise the question: what motivates people more deeply, recognition or symbolic power? If the answer is recognition, then we have one small—perhaps very small, compared with the ambitions of theorists to ground all of democratic politics on the concept—internal moral check on the struggle for power.[55]

54. Although it may seem as if Bourdieu treats the maximization of symbolic power as the only goal in life, his theory does include another. People seek comfort, specifically the comfort to be found in living within a habitus within which one grew up. Of course, the convergence of these two goals can only be attained by those at the top of the hierarchy. This is part of the meaning of privilege.

55. Many thanks to Kevin Thompson, Dan Breazeale, and Jim Wilkinson for discussions about Hegel and Fichte which saved me from a number of errors.

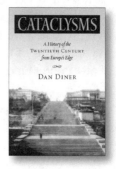
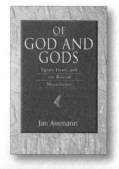

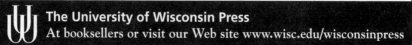

One Hundred Years of Orthodoxy

James V. Schall, S.J.

> I had always felt life first as a story; and if there is a story, there is a story-teller.
>
> G. K. Chesterton, *Orthodoxy*[1]

> This at least seems to me the main problem for philosophers, and is in a manner the main problem of this book. How can we contrive to be at once astonished at the world and yet at home in it? How can this queer cosmic town, with its many legged citizens, with its monstrous and ancient lamps, how can this world give us at once the fascination of a strange town and the comfort and honour of being our own town?
>
> G. K. Chesterton, *Orthodoxy*[2]

I.

Initially, let me say that no man can write anything about Chesterton's *Orthodoxy* that will be better than reading or re-reading *Orthodoxy* itself. But the glory of the sun ought not to prevent us from seeing *what is* in its light. Indeed, if we see only the sun, we will see nothing else, which not seeing is neither the point of the sun nor of Chesterton. The temptation to "explain" Chesterton better than Chesterton explained himself is the hazard that comes with loving Chesterton. Though under no illusions, I freely confess to having succumbed to this insidious enticement frequently as I

---

1. G. K. Chesterton, *Orthodoxy* (1908; San Francisco: Ignatius Press, 1985), in *Collected Works*, vol. 1, p. 264. This volume also includes the text of *Heretics*.

2. Ibid., p. 212. (Additional references to this edition will be cited parenthetically in the text.)

have written a monthly column, entitled *Schall on Chesterton,* for three decades now, plus numerous other essays that found inspiration in him one way or another.

Something uncanny surrounds the experience of selecting almost any paragraph in Chesterton, only to discover, on mulling it over, that it eventually leads to almost everything worth knowing and loving. On finishing one of his sentences, I often can barely wait to tell someone about what I just read in one of Chesterton's essays or books, which are fortunately plentiful. The man was prolific. How often do we say or write, "as Chesterton said somewhere"? Only we do not remember exactly where he said it, but we do recall what he said and how he said it. More often than not, we remember what he said because it is so amusingly true and aptly put.

Of course, I do not deny that very, very good essays and books are written about Chesterton. I own a number of them. Happily, hundreds upon hundreds of them exist. It is amazing how many authors try their hand at it, from Belloc and Maisie Ward to Hugh Kenner, Joseph Pearce, Garry Wills, Christopher Hollis, Stanley Jaki, Dale Ahlquist, Margaret Canovan, Ian Boyd, Michael Ffinch, Quentin Lauer, Alzina Stone Dale, David Fagerberg, and Dudley Baker, among others. There is even a *Schall on Chesterton* tome. And I have a tape of a lecture that Chesterton gave in the 1930s on the Canadian Broadcasting Company. Just hearing his rather high-pitched voice adds to his fascination. We know him mostly as a writing man, while those of his time knew him also as a speaking man, which is probably a better way to know a man. I think Plato thought it was the only way.

Indeed, Chesterton wrote his own *Autobiography,* still one of the most remarkable of his many memorable books. This book began with the ultimate challenge to modern scientific methodology, to wit: "Bowing to blind credulity, as is my custom, before mere authority and the tradition of the elders, superstitiously swallowing a story I could not test at the time by experiment or private judgment, I am firmly of the opinion that I was born on the 29th of May, 1874, on Campden Hill, Kensington...." One's own birth involves an act of utter trust, the doubt of which puts one on the high road to skepticism in all other things, including the fact of our being born.

Ignatius Press in San Francisco, moreover, continues to bring forth volumes of Chesterton's *Collected Works,* many of which are now published. Then there are the used-book stores that carry earlier Chesterton editions. *Orthodoxy* itself can be found on Amazon.com, in used and new, hardback as well as paperback. A Google search turns up several online versions of the text. *The Chesterton Review* and *Gilbert Magazine* are devoted to publishing essay after essay about him and his ambiance. Even in the daily press, Chesterton is still one of the most widely quoted authors in our language, and not just our language. I caught the present Pope referring to him, as did John Paul I, in a famous letter-essay in his *Illustrissimi*. The very nature of the good is that it inspires and draws forth something else that is likewise good. *Bonum est diffusivum sui.* I have often thought that Chesterton somehow exemplified what is meant by finality, rightly understood. That is, like the Greek divinity, it is a final, not an efficient, cause. It draws things to itself by being *what it is.*

In reading about Chesterton's public life and his many friends, it is striking how often the word "good" comes up in describing his heart. He is famous for the fact that those who may have disagreed with him still loved him. Once I gave a lecture about him that I entitled: "On the Enemies of the Man Who Had No Enemies" (*Vital Speeches*, July 15, 1998). A few of the duller sort of our kind profess annoyance over his paradoxes, his trademark for seeing the inner- and inter-relationships of things. Still, almost everyone loved and enjoyed him and his wit. The testimony on this latter point is strikingly universal. Chesterton was a man happy with the "abundance" of things. He would have laughed over an intended philosophical play on words, namely, words that simultaneously covered both his fully rounded girth and the scope of his mind, which widely ranged over all things large and small.

Chesterton's *Orthodoxy* was published in 1908, when he was thirty-four years old. He seems so young to have known so much. He died in fact on June 14, 1936, after having already sensed the upcoming dangers with Hitler, and, even later on in our days, with Islam. I have often, unabashedly, stated that *Orthodoxy* is the greatest book published in these hundred years, 1908–2008, that, in the meantime, have passed us by. No doubt, such a bold affirmation of the book's importance will be considered by many readers to be either nonsense or an exceedingly minority opinion, but so be it. It is a metaphysical statement. *Orthodoxy* is a sword drawn and plunged through the middle of our minds. No book came closer to describing just about what did happen in our minds in the intervening century. Nor did any one else but Chesterton do so more delightfully or, in his own way, more ominously.

Concerning truth, Chesterton was often chided for being too amusing to be serious about it. He was unmoved by this absurd accusation. The opposite of "funny," he explained in *Heretics*, is not "serious." The opposite of funny is "not-funny," nothing else. No real reason can be found for thinking that truth cannot be contained in what is otherwise full of laughter. Indeed, it is probably more likely to be found in humor than anywhere else. The connection between metaphysics and laughter, as well as that between joy and truth, is intimate. We do not laugh unless or until we see in our own active mind, where truth alone exists, the relation of this thing to that, this word to that, and thus, by implication, of all things to each other. And once we understand this astonishing inter-relatedness of the *things that are*, we are prepared to understand more profoundly the surprising word about the divinity that concludes *Orthodoxy*, the word that was concealed to us in the Incarnation. That word was "mirth." It is intended to tell us that, though we be in a vale of tears, we are created in joy and intended for joy.

This fullness of the experience of joy is also why we have the famous Chestertonian experience of being "homesick even at home," of loving one woman and, as a result, of finding all other things worth having, as he put it in his famous essay "In Defence of Rash Vows."[3] The true origin of joy is the greatest mystery of the universe. Why, in addition to the universe itself, does joy also exist within it? Ultimately, we are its recipients, not its cause, at least not without its first having been caused in us. In one sense, the whole of *Orthodoxy* depicted a man who looked for a source, a cause, a person to whom to be grateful for this surprising and unavoidable adventure in living a real life full of joy, once he experienced it even in the littlest of things. Such is the meaning of the sentence that I cited in the beginning: "*I had always felt life first as a story, and if there is a story, there is a story-teller.*"

II.

On this one hundredth anniversary of *Orthodoxy*, I do not intend to write a particularly "scholarly" article. How could I? Though scholars diligently study him, Chesterton, thank God, is beyond scholarship. Indeed, like the truths of scripture itself, I sometimes think that Chesterton disappears when he is subjected to what we innocently call "scholarship." He wrote for, as the title of one of his posthumously published books averred, "the

---

3. G. K. Chesterton, "In Defence of Rash Vows," *The Defendant* (London: Dent, 1914), pp. 18–26.

common man," the man who was something of a practitioner of common sense, for the man not overly impressed by the men of the academy. The line that divides the wise and the unwise does not necessarily pass through the academy. For this we can be grateful. It is not that Chesterton did not himself read widely. He did. He deliberately called himself, however, a "journalist," not a scholar, because the journalist was more likely than the scholar to be in touch with the ordinary, every day things, including the sins and foibles, of humanity.[4] But just at the point where we discover that scholars do not read him because he was not "scholarly," we realize that the common man does not trust the scholar for the same reasons. Chesterton saw and spelled out, in terms the common man could grasp, the contradictions and peculiarities found in the elaborate systems of the academic mind.

No one has ever read a "scholarly" work about Chesterton, no matter how heavily documented or steeped in philosophic lore, that is more interesting or insightful than Chesterton himself. Any time I read an essay or book on Chesterton that has myriads of footnotes, I shake my head. It is not that he cannot be misquoted or misunderstood. He often is. But the reason for misquoting him, I sometimes think, is to blunt the impact of the truth he sees. In this sense, Chesterton is very dangerous in a disordered intellectual culture. This awareness of his danger may be why he is seldom read even in universities presumably sponsored by the Church.

Chesterton is himself, again recalling Plato, a veritable "city in speech." That is, those who read him suddenly "wake up," suddenly "turn around," to gaze anew on *what is*. I have seen it happen again and again. Students exclaim, "Why have I never heard of all this before?" The real reason is not "because he was an obscure English journalist." The reason is that he undermines most of the philosophy that the students have ever heard thrown at them, but Chesterton puts it in order. Students who read Chesterton are likewise dangerous. An annoyed student once came to complain to me that he was not allowed to cite Chesterton's *St. Francis of Assisi* in a paper because it was "unscholarly." Bemused, I told the student to relax. "He now could understand more clearly on the basis of experience why 'scholarship' was not necessarily the same as 'truth.'"

Chesterton is wise, not scholarly; he sees the whole even in seeing what is part of the whole, as his book on *St. Thomas Aquinas* demonstrates. In this sense, the man drives us to despair, as Gilson happily said

---

4. See my essay "G. K. Chesterton: Journalist," *Schall on Chesterton* (Washington, DC: The Catholic Univ. of America Press, 2000,), pp. 1–20.

of Chesterton on reading this same book on St. Thomas. Similar to his detective, Father Brown, in his mystery stories, Chesterton was anything but naïve. Recalling the admonition of Plato in the *Republic*, he knew the mind of a criminal or a libertine without himself being a criminal or a libertine. We were, he thought, to commit murders every day but in our novels and detective stories.[5] It was not a perfection of the mind to "know no evil," however much it was an imperfection of the soul and will to do evil.

Chesterton was fond of telling the story of the Oxford undergraduates who thought that the original of Father Brown, a certain Father O'Connor, being a priest, was "innocent," whereas Chesterton had just taken a walk with him across the moors during which the priest explained to him the real depths of evil among us. The Catholic priest, though alas too often he is not, is to strive to be sinless. Nevertheless, he is not supposed to know nothing of what sin is. Rather, he should know exactly what it is in all its various forms. Even more profoundly, he should know those scholarly theories that deny sin's possibility, that deny free will or personal responsibility for our chosen actions. Such theories are largely what *Heretics* and *Orthodoxy* are about. Again, this insight into the disorder of soul is why they are dangerous books, largely forbidden in the academy.

I have never read even the shortest essay of Chesterton, of which there are literally hundreds and hundreds, without learning something, and in reading it again without learning something else. A good definition of a truly "liberal" or "freeing" education is simply: "reading Chesterton." We often do not see because no one points our gaze in the right direction. We always come away from Chesterton, however, seeing things that we did not see before because no one told us where to look. He guided us to look where the truth could be found. The truth is not found because it does not exist but because we often do not know where or how to look for it.

I have been reading Chesterton ever since I discovered him in my younger yeas as a Jesuit. I do not even remember now where I first consciously encountered him. But finding Chesterton was one of my life's blessings. With him, I knew there was light in the darkness. Indeed, with him, I also learned what intellectual darkness might mean. Chesterton was not unfamiliar with despair or doubt. He often said, however, that "gratitude" is our only proper response to *what is*. If the Communion of Saints means anything, it means that we can thank the dead for their gifts to us.

---

5. See G. K. Chesterton, "In Defence of Detective Stories," in ibid., pp. 118–23.

Indeed, in *Orthodoxy*, being grateful to the dead was one of the bases of democracy, of tradition, of what set our past apart from sheer blankness. Chesterton clearly understood that in the past we could find real human beings and what they actually did, whereas in the future, to which we now turn our minds, we find only abstractions.

If I search around for someone to thank for the gift of Chesterton, I start with Dodd Mead, Sheed & Ward, the *London Illustrated News*, Methuen, John Lane, Hodder and Stoughton, Cecil Palmer, and, as if born out of due time, Ignatius Press. These and many other publishers printed what he said for us still to read with delight and anticipation. Chesterton was so prolific. *The Chesterton Review*, *Gilbert Magazine*, and *The Defendant* in Western Australia still publish things we have only rarely, if ever, seen before.

Now that we have almost lost its public celebration, Chesterton is still there to tell us, in so many ways, what Christmas is, in case we have forgotten, which so many of us have. No one writes better about Christmas than Chesterton, often seen through the eyes of Dickens. Chesterton's biography of *Dickens*, published in 1906, between *Heretics* and *Orthodoxy*, is, indeed, still one of the most wonderful of books. Its last paragraph, something I often cite, I think changed my soul forever and I am grateful for it. Let me cite it here:

> The hour of absinthe is over. We shall not be much further troubled with the little artists who found Dickens too sane for their sorrow and too clean for their delights. But we have a long way to travel before we get back to what Dickens meant: and the passage is along a rambling English road, a twisting road such as Mr. Pickwick traveled. But this at least is part of what he meant; that comradeship and serious joy are not interludes in our travel; but that rather our travels are interludes in our comradeship and joy, which through God shall endure for ever. The inn does not point to the road; the road points to the inn. And all roads point at last to an ultimate inn, where we shall meet Dickens and all his characters: and when we drink again it shall be from the great flagons in the tavern at the end of the world.[6]

That life is a journey many writers and philosophers have told us, including Chesterton himself. But what is important about the road is its end, the place to where it leads. On this destination, with its "great flagons" at the

6. G. K. Chesterton, *Dickens* (San Francisco: Ignatius Press, 1989), in *Collected Works*, vol. 15, pp. 208–9.

"tavern at the end of the world," no one is better than Chesterton. His sane piety is something that common men understand, whatever the scholars might think about it.

I have just finished rereading *Heretics* and *Orthodoxy* with a class here at Georgetown. I always save the best thing on my class syllabi for last. It is not just a question of aesthetics, though it is that. It is closer to the theological virtue of hope, that if a thing can be so good, if we find so much delight in what this man sees, we need not doubt that the real world to which he points us through the world *that is* contains, as he says in *Orthodoxy*, the answers to the riddles of our existence. If Aristotle said that our end was happiness, Chesterton confirmed it by being a happy man who taught us to laugh while knowing the truth of things.

Chesterton finished *Orthodoxy*, as I have indicated, by telling us that the one thing that God hid from us while He was on earth, in His Incarnation, was His "mirth." Only a man of "mirth" could suspect, even after having examined, as he did in *Orthodoxy*, the aberrations of the optimists and the pessimists, after contemplating the Man of Sorrows, that we too are made for joy. He recalled in his *Autobiography* that his Scottish grandfather, after whom he received his middle name, had said that he would thank God for his existence even if he ended up (or down!) in hell. I have always loved that grandfather, who had no doubt about the possibility that we might, indeed, end in hell. He understood, in other words, what free will really meant. There really is a risk to our existence, the risk of losing, of choosing to lose, what we really want. Yet, he knew that without such a risk, the possibility of our kind of being could not exist at all.

III.

No doubt the most charming chapter of *Orthodoxy*, the one that students invariably comment on, as it explains something that they have wondered about all their short lives, is that chapter called "The Ethics of Elfland." Since the film versions of J. R. R. Tolkien's *The Lord of the Rings* and C. S. Lewis's *The Chronicles of Narnia* have graphically drawn our attention to the subject of what are thought to be "fairy tales," this famous chapter, admired by both Tolkien and Lewis, has a certain contemporary pertinence. We even have educators who warn us, as their predecessors did in Chesterton's time, not to read fairy tales, at least ones not expurgated of the wonder, the good and the bad characters, so that children would not be upset.

The notion that children should not be prepared by literature for the real world in which they are to live always amused Chesterton. Traditionally, it was through fairy stories that children became prepared for what would, in due time, occur in their lives. Fairy tales, Chesterton thought, were the defense of the normal boy and girl against the cosmos. Chesterton constantly reminded us of the astonishment at seeing the world for the first time and forgetting, on seeing it a second or fiftieth time, the wonder that anything could exist at all. The real surprise was that there was anything at all to see, yet there it was.

Here, I want rather to say some things about the chapter in *Orthodoxy* entitled "The Suicide of Thought." It is this chapter that I have always found to be particularly prophetic, intellectually prophetic. One can find examples of this peculiar "suicide" almost every day in the papers and certainly in most academic journals and halls. Actually, Nietzsche, whom Chesterton cites rather often in *Orthodoxy*, died just five years before *Heretics* was written. He had already seen what Chesterton in his own way saw, namely, that the modern mind is not coherent with itself. Nietzsche, in realizing that the modern mind contradicted itself, gave up on reason. Chesterton, with the same experience, rediscovered reason by following the logic of the contradictions. At the limits of reason was not "irrationality," but something closer to "superabundance." This contrast is why Nietzsche ended with "power" whereas Chesterton ended with "truth."

The Doubleday Image edition of *Orthodoxy* (1959) contains a brief half-page "Preface," which Chesterton evidently wrote sometime later than the original text. This "Preface" is not in the Ignatius Press *Collected Works* edition of *Orthodoxy*, nor in my 1924 reprint of the John Lane, The Bodley Head original.[7] In this reflective "Preface," Chesterton explains that *Orthodoxy* is meant to be a companion to *Heretics*. Critics had maintained that in *Heretics*, Chesterton "merely criticized" current philosophies without offering any "alternative philosophy." Thus, *Orthodoxy* is conceived as "an attempt to answer the challenge." And he is delighted to take up the challenge.

This rather polemical stance meant that *Orthodoxy* would be "unavoidably autobiographical." It would set down precisely Chesterton's "personal

---

7. This edition was originally printed in London and was given to me as a used book. It was previously owned by All Souls Priory, Old Headington, Oxford, and later by the Marian Centre, 1835 Halifax Street, Regina Saskatchewan, where it was classified under "Classics." Each book has its own history.

philosophy." Chesterton recalls that Newman was in much the same situation in writing his *Apologia pro Vita Sua*. That is, he was "forced to be egotistical in order to be sincere." No one can explain what he holds without talking about himself, since that is what the "challenge" was about in the first place: "Do you believe it and what is it that you believe?" There is no sense in telling someone what we think as if we were pretending to be someone else. For the first modern problem is whether anyone holds anything as true, and if so, why so?

The word "sincere" is ambiguous here. For sincerity does not refer to the truth of a position and its proofs but to whether someone actually holds interiorly what he says he holds. The greatest of idiots and tyrants, as well as many a professor, can be quite sincere and, simultaneously, quite wrong. All such can be "sincere." After we find out whether someone in fact really "holds" this or that opinion, we still need to decide whether what is held is rubbish or not. Sincerity is both attractive and dangerous. This double possibility is why it is not, by itself, the criterion of truth.

The motive of Chesterton in writing *Orthodoxy* is clearly stated: "to attempt to explain, not whether the Christian faith can be believed, but how he personally has come to believe it." Thus, we may think someone a fool for believing such absurd doctrines, but our judgment of such foolishness must itself include the reasoning of someone, like Chesterton, who thinks a case can be made in reason for his being sane. It is "credible" at least to one man. This book, he tells us, is thus arranged in the format "riddle and answer." One can already sense why Chesterton is a defender of fairy tales and detective stories. Unless someone has encountered the "riddles" of existence in his own soul, he will not know whether answers are addressed to it either from reason or transcendence. Chesterton has a way with "riddles" that expresses the perplexities of the average man before the mysteries of being. He first states what problem it is that he was dealing with, and then how his questions were solved by "Christian theology," as he calls it.

In considering the nature of mind, what particularly interests me are the last two sentences in this "Preface." They read: "The writer regards it (riddle and answer) as amounting to a convincing creed. But if it is not that it is at least a repeated and surprising occurrence." That is, one may answer one or two riddles by chance or luck, but when the same source provides more and more sane answers to recurring perplexities, the question must arise about the origin. It begins to seem less and less due to chance and more and more due to some background of *logos* or intelligence.

Chesterton was especially fascinated with those elements in Christianity, say, the peculiar doctrine of original sin, where we should expect it to be wrong, but where in fact it most corresponds to what does occur in our experience. We might expect the most intelligent men to be the most reasonable and virtuous, as Plato sometimes seems to imply. But if we understand about original sin, we see better that what more often happens is that the most intelligent, in pursuit of their own explications, are often the ones most likely to undermine the truths of the human soul. This result is not because they are not intelligent. It is because they choose what they shall be in spite of any objective truth about themselves. They know or suspect what they ought to be, but still, as Aristotle explained in the seventh book of the *Ethics*, knowingly rejecting it in the way they live.

Yet, Chesterton's position is delicately stated. What Chesterton attests throughout *Heretics* and *Orthodoxy* is that what he found most intriguing about Christianity was not the apologists who presented the case in its favor, people whom he never in fact read, but those philosophers and essayists who vigorously presented the case against it. He was bemused by the fact that one set of critics would say that what was wrong with Christianity was that it was too pessimistic, while the next set claimed that it was too optimistic. After innumerable instances of such curiosities recorded in *Orthodoxy*, he decided that the contradictory evidence of the heretics showed that Christianity, on most things, was just about what made most sense and was, in fact, most reasonable, if by "reasonable" we mean what most conforms to the reality that most people experience in their lives. Chesterton has great fun really with this approach, but, at the same time, he is quite taken with its force, which is, in the end, a force of reason.

Indeed, Chesterton even suggests at one point, not entirely playfully, that he would have himself devised Christianity but, much to his relief, found that it was already invented.[8] And it is just this offhand remark about his thinking that he might have "invented" Christianity by himself that brings me back to the last sentence in the "Preface." Obviously, if Christianity is what it says it is of itself, namely, precisely a "revelation," then to claim that one "could" have concocted it by himself is nothing less than a divine claim. Chesterton by this logic would be his own heretic! On the other hand, revelation does claim to address itself to philosophic reason precisely when such reason is being itself most explained to itself in

8. See James V. Schall, "Chesterton: The Real 'Heretic': The Outstanding Eccentricity of the Peculiar Sect Called Roman Catholicism," *Logos* 9 (Summer 2006): 72–86.

philosophic terms. This particular revelation thus does not conceive itself to be anti-philosophic. Its effect is the increase, not decrease, of philosophy itself. Thus, when Chesterton remarks that, when Christianity repeatedly and surprisingly has an answer to the "riddles" that he posed, it may not constitute a "proof," but it certainly does present an enigma that goes back to the problem of whether there is a storyteller.

In the last chapter of *Orthodoxy*, entitled "Authority and the Adventurer," Chesterton writes: "I am a rationalist. I like to have some intellectual justification for my intuitions. If I am treating man as a fallen being it is an intellectual convenience to me to believe that he fell; and I find, for some odd psychological reason, that I can deal better with a man's exercise of free will if I believe that he has got it" (347). Aside from being quite amusing, that passage has a particular profundity to it. It is not merely that he "sincerely" holds to such a thing as a "fall" and another thing called "free will," but that it is precisely these realities that explain why it is that we do not do what we would do and why it is that we are responsible for what we do "do" when we do it.

It is this thought that brings me back to Chesterton's chapter on "The Suicide of Thought." By almost all accounts of the century between ourselves and the initial writing of *Orthodoxy*, what has happened is not that Christianity has been proved "unreasonable" but that "reason" has proved itself, or better claimed itself, to be "unreasonable." This situation was pretty much what Nietzsche had also figured out, as Chesterton also understood. The difference is that Nietzsche went on to propose "the will to power" as a "non-reasonable" substitute for reason, while Chesterton took a second look at reason and saw that it did explain what it set out to explain, provided that one granted that the human being had the power of reason in the first place.

"The modern world is not evil," Chesterton observes in the beginning of the chapter; "in some ways the modern world is far too good" (233). The world is full of "wild and wasted virtues." It is the balance of the virtues that has been lost, the seeing things out of proportion. "The modern world is full of the old Christian virtues gone mad." We have justice without mercy, cleanliness without godliness, sex without consequences. Modern relativism is famous for telling us that we can be certain of nothing except our capacity to affirm nothing. Not only that, following Descartes and Kant, we do not even have, contrary to the famous notion that we are "rational animals," a power capable of knowing rationally, or at least capable of knowing *what is*. The only "reason" we acknowledge is our "practical reason," especially the *ratio factabilium*, the reason that "makes." But it apparently just sits out there with no relation to metaphysics, and hence it is free with no grounding.

The insistence that we do not have any "power" or "faculty" that can "know" the truth is our last protection against the question of why we do not accept and live the truth of a natural law addressed to our very being and the revelation addressed to it. If we maintain a theory of the fall and free will, we can pretty much suspect why we do not live virtuously, if we do not. Greek hubris and Augustine's "pride" remain central. But if we maintain that we are not fallen and if our epistemology claims that we are not free, if our mind cannot know any objective order, then we can really "do" nothing wrong in any moral sense. Whatever we do, simply is. Our whole moral order is left open for us to do what we please, even if we claim we are not free in doing it. And this reasoning about morals may, in fact, be the real reason for the epistemological problem. Without it, we would have to face the issue of our deliberately rejecting what we ought to be and how we ought to live, the classical moral questions. We thus use philosophical theory to escape ethical responsibility.

Chesterton already saw the core of the problem. "What we suffer from today is humility in the wrong place," he wrote. "Modesty has moved from the organ of ambition. Modesty has settled upon the organ of conviction; where it was never meant to be. A man was meant to be doubtful about himself, but undoubting about the truth; this has been exactly reversed. Nowadays the part of a man that a man does assert is exactly the part he ought not to assert—himself" (234). One could hardly find a more prophetic passage in a world of "self-fulfillment." Since there is no "truth" that is theoretically possible, the only world that anyone can live in is the one that man "asserts" or proposes for himself. The truth of *what is*, on the contrary, meant that everyone could live in the same world because we could, each of us, know what was not ourselves. We could check our minds by a reality that was there. The "truth" of modernity, by contrast, is that no one can live in the same world because there is no "same" world to live in, or, if there were, there is no way to discover it.

This "new humility" about our rational powers "makes a man doubtful about his aims, which will make him stop working altogether" (235). The final cause is always the first cause. This doubt about aims is as true of a civilization as it is of the men who compose it. Indeed, it is the doubt in the souls of men about their own powers to know the truth that causes the problem in the first place. "We are on the road to producing a race of men too modest to believe in the multiplication table." Yet, as Benedict XVI said in his Regensburg Lecture, it is precisely the multiplication table, with its abstraction from existing being, that is almost the sole clue we have to wondering about why the multiplication table, mathematics itself, works when we use it on things. "The whole modern world is at war with reason," Chesterton continues. It does not know what is reasonable unless its own reason defines reason in such a way that reason has no check outside of itself.

Thus, if we follow theories of progress, nationalism, fascism, communism, existentialism, historicism, positivism, liberalism, conservatism, to deconstructionism and nihilism in their intrinsic logic, we see that what they have in common is a denial that reason knows things, that it knows a reality that is actually there to be known by powers given to us whereby to know. To obviate this danger is the reason why the classical definition of truth was precisely "the conformity of mind to reality," wherein mind was to be open to a world in which intelligibility was already found and not simply imposed by the same mind.

IV.

What Chesterton is particularly concerned with in *Orthodoxy* is the positive relation of religious authority to reason, to philosophy. This relationship was exactly the issue that was the concern of John Paul II's 1998 encyclical, *Fides et Ratio*. It is what is behind Chesterton's memorable conclusion in *Heretics* that "we shall be left defending not only the incredible virtues and sanities of human life, but something more incredible still, this huge impossible universe which stares us in the face. We shall fight for visible prodigies as if they were invisible. We shall look on the impossible grass and the skies with a strange courage. We shall be of those who have seen and yet have believed" (207). Why are the "virtues and sanities of human life" called "incredible" even when "they stare us in the face"?

The paradox of these last words of *Heretics* is not to be missed. In the classic way of thinking, belief and reason were seen not as contradictories but as two different ways of knowing a real, objective truth found in things. One way was to see or to reason to them; the other way was by the testimony of a witness who saw the fact and attested it. Neither way was subjective. Once the very integrity of the faculty of knowing was questioned from Descartes, however, it took an act of faith to give any credence to what we saw or to the powers by which we saw them. Descartes famously needed to prove the existence of God before he could be sure that his senses told him that a bird was perched on the tree outside his window singing its song.

In the earlier logic, "seeing is believing," that is, since one saw, he did not need to "believe." Seeing the bird was clearer than the philosophic proof of its existence. What Chesterton recognized already in 1905, in *Heretics*, was that in modern philosophy the "visible" things no longer have any persuasive meaning of themselves. In the end, he thought, the only "realists" who trusted their senses would be the believers whose very "belief," however, is founded on the reality of *what is*, on the reality of the visible things and their assured existence. Without this initial grounding, belief in the transcendent had no passage between the visible and the supernatural world.

"The modern critics of religious authority," Chesterton continues, "are like men who should attack the police without ever having heard of burglars. For there is a great and possible peril to the human mind, a peril as practical as burglary. Against it religious authority was reared, rightly or wrongly, as a barrier. And against it something certainly must be reared as a barrier, if our race is to avoid ruin" (236). We live in a world in which, like the burglars, the opponents of arms and armies do not recognize that they have any enemies or what these enemies are against.

Chesterton says "somewhere" that we should never tear down a sign or fence until we know why it was put up in the first place. This advice contains his point about burglars and police. We may have problems with our police, but until we understand our problem with burglars, we will never understand why we have police at all. It is the order of mind that decides what is what, what is a policeman, what is a burglar. Notice how, in this passage, Chesterton again becomes almost prophetic—the "great peril" to the human mind, a human race that has to "avoid ruin." The very defense of civilization begins with and depends on a defense of the integrity of mind itself. A mind that cannot tell the difference between burglars and police is no mind.

But what, in the end, will defend this mind from itself? The peril is first to be named: "The peril is that the human intellect is free to destroy itself." Neither God nor nature will destroy it; rather, it can only destroy itself. Yet, without this intellect in the world functioning as it should, as intellect, the world is strictly speaking, from its inside, "mindless," "clueless." This condition was not originally intended to be the status of the world. And how, we wonder, would the intellect go about destroying itself? After all, it is not like a withered hand or diseased appendix, which we might simply cut away. The intellect is a spiritual power that is designed to know *what is*; it is what allows us to be what is not ourselves. The only way it could possibly destroy itself is for it to refuse, by an act of the will, to understand what it is or to refuse to function according to its own rules or order.

Thus, Chesterton continues, "one generation could prevent the very existence of the next generation, by all entering a monastery or by all jumping into the sea." Following this vivid analogy, Chesterton concludes, "so one set of thinkers can in some degree prevent further thinking by teaching the next generation that there is no validity in any human thought." Needless to say, such destructive thinking has long been in place among us. Chesterton saw it a hundred years ago. Notice that it is by "teaching" one generation that another generation influences it, even destroys it. It is possible to lose our tradition by not studying it or by not living it or by not passing it down. But that refusal is not nearly so disastrous a loss as affirming that our very faculties of reason function in a way that makes them incapable of knowing the truth.

"It is idle to talk always of the alternative of reason and faith. Reason is itself a matter of faith." This affirmation is rather what is meant by a "first principle" or "first thing." We cannot "prove" by some more clear argument than actually seeing it that the grass is green. Finally, we come to what we cannot doubt. And if we still insist on doubting it, we, in effect, deny our very power to know. If we did not know that the rose that is there before us is really there, why would we ever cut it and put it on the table? Let alone how would we know to plant it in the first place?

This first principle is what Chesterton means by the "act of faith" in the very power of reason. "It is an act of faith to assert that our thoughts have any relation to reality at all." Logically, if we deny that our thoughts have any relation to reality, we would not be able to say, as Chesterton again says somewhere, "thank you for passing the butter." In other words, our lives fortunately are often broader than our philosophical theories.

This great chapter in *Orthodoxy* is the ultimate defense of things. "If you are merely a skeptic, you must sooner or later ask yourself the question, 'Why should *anything* go right; even observation and deduction?' 'Why should not good logic be as misleading as bad logic?' They are both movements in the brain of a bewildered ape?"[9] If all that counts in the mind of the "bewildered ape" is the electronic brain movements, intelligibility about the difference between logic and illogic does not matter. The whole point is that it does make a difference if, in building a bridge or a computer, we make a mathematical mistake. If so, the thing will not function. Unless the mind as mind is connected with things, there is no sense in using our mind to deal with things or to learn from things how the things we did not make function.

Chesterton sums up this line of thought by observing that "[t]he young sceptic says, 'I have a right to think for myself.' But the old sceptic, the complete sceptic, says, 'I have no right to think for myself. I have no right to think at all.'" If everyone "thinks for himself" but no one thinks the same thing, then the very word "thinking" becomes meaningless. There is no way that "thinking for oneself" is not "thinking for oneself." Whatever we think is what we think, and that is the end of it. On such a hypothesis, there are no grounds for thinking anything outside of ourselves at all, as the old sceptic in Chesterton's memory understood.

What is clearly at issue, then, is the integrity of the thinking power to be what it is. If it can know nothing but itself, if it acquires no knowledge of anything but itself, there cannot be one world. Such thinking creates as many worlds as there are brains. Aristotle thought that all brains could know the same world, which was there to be known. Moderns think that no brains know anything but their own world. But none of the modern "brain worlds" is responsible to the others. This awkward result brings us back to the first proof of all classic philosophy, without which no philosophy is possible. This is the initial refutation of skepticism. That is, if it is "true" that there is no truth, there is either one affirmation itself that must be true or else the mind is useless. But if this one thing is true, this "first principle" that a thing cannot be and not be at the same time in the same way grounds all philosophy, all capacity to distinguish this thing from that, to know of *what is* that it is, and of *what is not* that it is not, as Plato said.

All of this argument brings us back to why *Orthodoxy* remains such an important book. It is the book that explains why the wars sometimes had to be fought, why *logos* itself needs a protected place in which to exist

9. See James V. Schall, "Why Should Anything Go Right?: On the Curious Relation of Revelation, Reason, and Reality," in *The Sum Total of Human Happiness* (South Bend, IN: St. Augustine's Press, 2006), pp. 94–110.

against its enemies.[10] "Dialogue" cannot deal with those who will not dialogue; with those who deny that dialogue is possible. "There is a thought that stops thought. That is the only thing that ought to be stopped. That is the ultimate evil against which all religious authority was aimed." That is to say, as Benedict XVI intimated, that revelation is directed to *logos*.[11]

The independent integrity of philosophy is the basis for understanding the intelligibility of what is revealed, of what it means to be revealed. Religious authority recognizes the importance of reason as reason; otherwise it could be neither authority nor religious. Religious authority does not substitute for reason, but it defends its integrity as reason. H. G. Wells "has written a delicate piece of scepticism called 'Doubts of the Instrument,'" Chesterton writes. "In this he questions the brain itself, and endeavours to remove all reality from all his own assertions, past, present, and to come" (236–37). The minute we doubt our knowing powers, the difference between what is "past, present, and to come" disappears.

What follows? Chesterton recognizes what many will not understand, that the institutions in which reason itself exists and flourishes must be protected from violence:

> But it was against this remote ruin that all the military systems in religion were originally ranked and ruled. The creeds and the crusades, the hierarchies and the horrible persecutions were not organized, as is ignorantly said, for the suppression of reason. They were organized for the difficult defence of reason. Man, by a blind instance, knew that if once things were wildly questioned, reason could be questioned first. (237)

This observation is not only an understanding of history that we seldom hear, but it is a prophecy of the present in which the same enemies of reason are again at war with it for the same philosophical reasons that, explicitly or implicitly, deny the very possibility of reason.

"The authority of priests to absolve, the authority of popes to define, the authority even of inquisitors to terrify: these were all only dark defences erected round one central authority, more indemonstrable, more supernatural than all—the authority of man to think." Two types of theory exist that deny this "thinking authority." The first denies the power of logic

10. See James V. Schall, "When Wars Must Be the Answer," *Policy Review* 128 (December 2004): 59–70.

11. See James V. Schall, *The Regensburg Lecture* (South Bend, IN: St. Augustine's Press, 2007).

and mind; the second identifies mind with will. The one denies that the mind itself can know what it is not itself; the other claims that God is not *logos*, that *Deus Voluntas Est*. The one finds no order in the universe; the other changes the order at will so that there is no "understanding" it, only "obeying" it.

V.

"Thinking," Chesterton writes, "means connecting things, and stops if they cannot be connected" (238). To "connect things," we must first distinguish them. We must say what they are and what they are not. We must look for their causes. If things are not what they are, we cannot connect them. And if there is not a principle that connects all things in being, there can be no philosophy that wonders about them and how they relate to one another. It is in this context that Chesterton sees to be the consequences of a theory of "progress" that, far from distinguishing things from one another, merges them into one another. It does not preserve them, but makes them disappear.

This constitutes Chesterton's take on modern historicism: "Akin to these is the false theory of progress, which maintains that we alter the test instead of trying to pass the test. We often hear it said, for instance, 'What is right in one age is wrong in another.' This is quite reasonable, if it means that there is a fixed aim, and that certain methods attain at certain times and not at other times" (238). The trouble with both modern liberalism and conservatism is found here in whether a fixed standard can be found that it not itself culturally variable. If in principle the standard changes, all things are possible. Ultimately, everything is everything else. "If the standard changes, how can there be improvement, which implies a standard?" We may make progress in building a better mousetrap so long as we know what mice and what traps are. Once we think the mousetrap is a bicycle or that a mouse is a shark, all progress ceases, because there is no longer any standard for either the mouse or the trap.

The second half of this chapter on "The Suicide of Thought" is much concerned with Nietzsche. "Nietzsche started a nonsensical idea that men had once sought as good what we now call evil; if it were so, we could not talk of surpassing or even falling short of them." Nietzsche's *Beyond Good and Evil* was always faced with the problem of whether what was "beyond" was itself good or evil. Chesterton was less forgiving than I would be. Nietzsche did see the illogic of the modern mind and insisted that it live with its own conclusions. Chesterton was more concerned with the coherence of Nietzsche's proposed substitute, the "will to power."

Nietzsche, perhaps reluctantly, accepted the fact that modern Christians did not believe in Christianity. He was certain that the modern mind could not function on the premises on which it had based itself, whereby the mind could only know itself and not reality. "The main point here, however, is that this idea of a fundamental alteration in the standard is one of the things that make thought about the past or future simply impossible. The theory of a complete change in standards in human history does not merely deprive us of the pleasure of honouring our fathers; it deprives us even of the more modern and aristocratic pleasure of despising them" (239). We cannot honor or despise our ancestors if we do not have the same standards that they did. In other words, if we keep changing the standards, we keep changing our ancestors and even our descendents.

"I agree with the pragmatists that apparent objective truth is not the whole matter; that there is an authoritative need to believe the things that are necessary to the human mind," Chesterton remarked. "But I say that one of those necessities precisely is the belief in objective truth. The pragmatist tells a man to think what he must think and never mind the Absolute. But precisely one of the things that he must think is the Absolute" (239–40). If we are to judge things by their "results," we must acknowledge that results do result from our actions, which originate in the human mind. If things really exist and we can know them, we cannot "practically" avoid the question of their origin, the question of the Absolute.

As Nietzsche saw, we do not live in a world in which doubt, skepticism, and atheism "may" come about. We live in a world in which they are already here. The consequences of modern thought are not merely things that "might" or "will" happen. They are things that have happened.

> What we are looking at is not the boyhood of free thought; it is the old age and ultimate dissolution of free thought. It is vain for bishops and pious bigwigs to discuss what dreadful things will happen if wild skepticism runs its course. It has run its course. It is vain for eloquent atheists to talk of the great truths that will be revealed if once we see free thought begin. We have seen it end. It has no more questions to ask; it has questioned itself. You cannot call up any wilder vision than a city in which men ask themselves if they have any selves. You cannot fancy a more sceptical world than that in which men doubt if there is a world. (240)[12]

12. See James V. Schall, *The Order of Things* (San Francisco: Ignatius Press, 2007).

The doubt of whether there even is a "world," an ordered cosmos, is one of the direct consequences of the primacy of the will in metaphysics and morals. If everyone lives in his own world, the one he "chooses," there can be no common "world."

The classical and medieval philosophical controversies over the relation of intellect and will were not politically neutral. Overemphasis on either faculty had its consequences. The voluntarists, be them classical, medieval, Muslim, or modern, perhaps in despair over reason, replaced reason with will, even in the Godhead. What does this mean?

> They see that reason destroys; but Will, they say, creates. The ultimate authority, they say, is in will, not in reason. The supreme point is not why a man demands a thing, but the fact that he does demand it. I have no space to trace or expound this philosophy of Will. It came, I suppose, through Nietzsche, who preached something that is called egoism. (241)

The relation of will and reason is central to all philosophy. As Aristotle said, reason by itself does not move or act. Will by itself if blind.

"They say that choice itself is the divine thing." Modern political culture has been premised on the primacy of "choice," with no attention to the object of choice. In this sense, "will" destroys since it need not ask what it is about. Will "wills" no matter what it wills. Its blindness is said to be a "freedom," whereas it is the most lethal power of modern times. Choice is only a "divine" thing if it remains within the divine being and *logos*. Political wars for this reason often have theological overtones. If the Divine can will whatever it chooses, subject to no *logos*, there can be no order in being but what was last willed. Will, by itself, is not "creative." "He [Shaw] says that a man does not act for his happiness, but from his will. He does not say, 'Jam will make me happy,' but 'I want jam'" (241). His wanting of jam obviously presupposes his knowing what jam is. He would not "want" it if it were a poison.

Thus, *Orthodoxy* is not only an examination of thought but, perhaps more fundamentally, an examination of what it is to "will." "The worship of will is the negation of will. To admire mere choice is to refuse to choose" (242). The worship of the will for its own sake denies the kind of power it is, the power to choose *what is* when the mind knows what this *is* "is." Chesterton is quite right: "to admire mere choice is to refuse to choose." Why? Because opposite things can be chosen with no concern about what they are. The choice of the murderer to murder and the choice of the doctor to cure are both choices. They do not differ as choices, only in what is chosen.

The will as will is the power to reach particular reality, the different things that exist. "You cannot admire will in general, because the essence of will is that it is particular." Once we set out to act, we must decide what sort of act we will put forth. "Every act of the will is an act of self-limitation. To desire action is to desire limitation. In that sense every act is an act of self-sacrifice. When you choose anything, you reject everything else" (243). If, on going on a journey, we have made no choice about where to go, we will go precisely nowhere.

Chesterton restores the proper relation of will and intellect. Will is indeed the basis of our freedom, the power of the particular. But will in turn depends on what it is we use this freedom for. The will is open only to what the intellect presents to it. We always must use it for this and not for that. Every "yes" is a "no." We do not just "choose" to choose. We always choose something, a this, not that. This power is both our freedom and our responsibility. "The moment you step into the world of facts, you step into a world of limits." The glory of the human mind and will is that it does live amid the myriads of finite things. Among these it must, as part of its actually seeking *what is*, seek the Absolute. Modern relativism is indeed premised on the supposition that there is no Absolute.

One of the striking characteristics of Chesterton's mind was its ability to carry through to its logical conclusion what is implied in a seemingly innocent philosophical position. For instance, one takes the modern "rebel" to be a rather romantic figure. He is someone who makes his name by protesting against something, whatever it is. He is the man who stands for nothing so that he can be against everything. "The new rebel is a sceptic, and will not entirely trust anything. He has no loyalty; therefore he can never be really a revolutionist. And the fact that he doubts everything really gets in his way when he wants to denounce anything. For all denunciation implies a moral doctrine of some kind…" (244).

No one can be against something if there is no standard upon which to take one's position. This affirmation is why, when Chesterton was challenged to state what he was for, what was his philosophic position, he did so. On the other hand, "the modern man in revolt has become practically useless for all purposes of revolt. By rebelling against everything he has lost his right to rebel against anything" (245). If nothing is wrong, what replaces whatever is rebelled against cannot be right.

Orthodoxy, as I have said, has always struck me as a prophetic book. Chesterton often spoke as a prophet. He understood that political and cultural disorder first occurred as disorders in the mind. Indeed, he understood that the greatest disorder of all was that which undermined the very capacity of mind to be mind.

> I can see the inevitable smash of the philosophies of Schopenhauer and Tolstoy, Nietzsche and Shaw, as clearly as an inevitable railway smash could be seen from a balloon. They are all on the road to the emptiness of the asylum. For madness may be defined as using mental activity so as to reach mental helplessness; and they have nearly reached it.... He who wills to reject nothing, wills the destruction of will; for will is not only the choice of something, but the rejection of almost everything. (246)

It would not have surprised Chesterton, at the end of the twentieth century, to hear that most universities are now defined as inheritors of Nietzsche and of a liberalism that sees positivism and historicism as their only justification, that sees, in other words, that the mind cannot know anything other than itself. There is no order in things, including human things, to know.

The doubt that the mind is mind goes hand in hand with the claim of the will to replace mind with its own "power." "*He who wills to reject nothing, wills the destruction of the mind.*" As I have said, Chesterton is something of a prophet. He even says so himself in the last chapter of *Orthodoxy*:

> Every man is womanized merely by being born. They talk of the masculine woman; but every man is a feminised man. And if ever men walk to Westminster in protest against this female privilege, I shall not join their procession. For I remember with certainty this fixed psychological fact; that the very time when I was most under a woman's authority, I was most full of flame and adventure. Exactly because when my mother said that ants bit they did bite, and because snow did come in winter (as she said); therefore, the whole world was to me a fairyland of wonderful fulfillment, and it was like living in some Hebraic age, when prophecy after prophecy came true. (360)

The central meaning of the mother in the family in this past century has grounded the validity of Chesterton's thought, especially those found in his books *What's Wrong with the World* (1910) and *Eugenics and Other*

Evils (1922). Chesterton was aware that this question of the family and its survival would be at stake in the century to come. And ironically, the whole issue of the family turns on the centrality of the will and whether it has any object, on whether the "choice itself is a divine thing" or whether it is only divine in the context of what in particular it chooses.

The final thing about *Orthodoxy* remains its defense of the gift and goodness of things. "The mass of men have been forced to be *gay* about the little things, but sad about the big ones. Nevertheless (I offer my last dogma defiantly) it is not native to man to be so. Man is more himself, man is more manlike, when joy is the fundamental thing in him, and grief the superficial one" (364). It is in this context of joy that Chesterton wondered in 1908, "How can we at once contrive to be astonished at the world and at home in it?" That we can eventually accomplish is the burden of *Orthodoxy*. If the intellect knows and the will chooses from the particular things that are, we eventually must wonder where both intellect and will find their origins, for we know we did not give them to ourselves but found them already in our being. "*I had always felt life first as a story, and if there is a story, there must be a story-teller.*" One hundred years of *Orthodoxy* have left us with the urgency of this "feeling" ever more present in our souls whenever we grant that the intellect is a power given to us to know *what is.*

The Dialectic of Monotheism: St. Paul's "Letter to the Romans"

Aryeh Botwinick

There is a way of looking at Christian doctrine as classically formulated by St. Paul in "Letter to the Romans" that enables us to see it as proceeding in a quite rigorous sense to introduce variations on monotheism (excavating and defining new dialectical pathways) that had been inaugurated by Judaism. The structure of Jewish belief that confronted St. Paul and his contemporaries had given rise to certain jarring paradoxes that St. Paul, with his Rabbinically trained mind[1] that is amply in evidence in the text of Romans, sought to resolve. I would like to map the emergence of these paradoxes in a deliberately anachronistic way (although many of its key elements already suffuse the cultural and religious climate that nurtured St. Paul[2]) in order to highlight the audaciousness and imaginativeness of St. Paul's Christian reconfiguration of monotheistic teaching:

1. The search for reasons and causes of events and phenomena would proceed without letup—without any prospect of satisfaction—unless we postulate God as Prime Mover, First Existent, or First Cause.

---

1. In his defense before the Jerusalem Jews, Paul says: "I am a Jew, born in Tarsus in Cilicia, but brought up in this city. At the feet of Gamaliel I was educated strictly in our ancestral law and was zealous of God, just as all of you are today" (Acts 22:3).

2. In what follows in the text, I am schematizing Maimonides' distillation of his Rabbinic predecessors as recorded in the first section of his *Code* (*Mishneh Torah*) called, "Laws Concerning the Foundations of the Torah." Some of his precursors whose teachings Maimonides is condensing and paraphrasing were contemporaries of St. Paul. A very good English translation of the first four chapters of these Laws is to be found in Ralph Lerner, *Maimonides' Empire of Light: Popular Enlightenment in an Age of Belief* (Chicago: Univ. of Chicago Press, 2000), pp. 141–53.

2. The concept of God can only satisfy the search for ultimacy in explanation if He is posited as subsisting in an infinite dimension beyond the reach of finite man and his finite methods and outcomes of probing.

3. The infinite regress that drives the search for reasons and causes to come up with the concept of God resurfaces after the idea of God is pronounced. The guise that the regress takes is that the propounder of the idea of God must now be able to elucidate how the Infinite intersects with the finite so that the idea of God can indeed bring the explanatory quest to a halt. But if this connection could be explicated, then the regress would continue and the idea of God would not have solved anything.

4. Reverting to one horn of the dilemma (let us call it the ultimacy horn, in contrast to the unintelligibility horn), we must affirm that our whole vocabulary of Divinity is irredeemably metaphoric. A whole range of mighty descriptions are invoked to describe an entity—namely, God—whose status as God would be diminished if any of these descriptions applied literally to Him.

5. There is a dilemma within the dilemma—or a paradox within the paradox. If the denuding of God of literal attributes were our last word about God, then we would have penetrated the Infinite sufficiently to know that our human vocabularies do not apply to God. In the course of ostensibly following through on our project of situating God as the ultimate explanatory factor, we would have betrayed it (Him). We would know something that the very protocols of our exploration—the ground rules delimiting our quest—debar us from knowing.

6. Having gone full circle in our exploration of God under the aegis of a negative theological construal of the premises of monotheism (that we can only say what God isn't, but not what God is), we are left with two alternatives. Being stalked by contradiction every step of the way in our inquiry into the monotheistic God, we might adopt a generalized agnosticism that leaves the door open to the normalization of contradiction encoded in any one of the modern logics devoted to elaborating this possibility. A generalized agnosticism suggests that the question of God is undecidable by us—and

that God is beyond the ken of human understanding, which is the original premise of monotheism. We will have gone through all of these labors to disclose a possibility monotheism wants to seal as a matter of faith. Faith wants to institutionalize in the present what human reason shows to be open with regard to the future.

7. Or, given how the negative theological critique of monotheistic doctrine neutralizes itself so that even its delimitation of what God isn't cannot be literally applied to God, we might elect to chart a mystical route toward the engagement of God. God is unspeakable and unformulable in humanly tractable terms. It is only by withdrawing from speech and the rational plotting of the elasticities of speech that we create space for God. Elijah's *Kol Demama Daka* ("the sound of thin silence"[3]) is the name that we retrospectively apply to our configuration of silence.

It is at this juncture that we can conceptualize St. Paul as intervening and determining that since the finite doesn't immediately connect with the infinite in the way that the Jewish rational and theological quest would like to project, it becomes compelling to make a move in the contrary direction of connecting the finite with the finite—and identifying the human partner to the human connection as God. By translating God (or one portion of the Godhead) into man, the theological paradoxes associated with Divine transcendence—including the one that points to how acts of conceptual divestiture of literal attributes integral to articulating that transcendence cannot be coherently formulated because there is no substratum of Divinity that can be literally grasped and therefore "peeled away"—appears to be overcome in one fell swoop. It was the sustaining of that transcendence in its pristine Jewish form that gave rise to the Pauline critique that lies at the theological core of Christianity. In accordance with the Jewish theological dispensation, mechanisms of law regulating the life of the religious community need to supervene between God and man, and, as a result, the dualism of "commander" and "commanded"[4] remains inextirpable within the heartland of monotheistic religion. If God is unrelieved, unmitigated transcendence, then the promise of radical oneness augured by the very

3. 1 Kings 19:12. See my discussion of this phrase in "Post-Shoah Political Theology," *Telos* 121 (Fall 2001): 56.
4. This imagery is echoed by St. Augustine in *City of God*, bk. 19, chap. 27.

name of monotheistic religion is being willy-nilly withheld from the community of monotheistic believers. "Oneness" (from a Jewish perspective) subsists only as an abstract theological premise that is logically impervious to any kind of verbal paraphrase and cataloguing of attributes—let alone into a set of religious institutions and practices that would offer emotional solace to the believer. The Pauline innovation—the move and the moment that heralds the birth of Christianity—is to posit an exceptional human being who is now stipulated as being part of the Godhead (God the Son). By engaging in this move, it would appear that the logical paradoxes surrounding God's transcendence become superseded or suspended—and the believer is able to reap the emotional benefits offered by a humanly embodied ideal of oneness. The menacing dualism paradoxically represented by uncompromising Judaic monism appears to have been overcome.

Christianity might even claim from one perspective that it is more faithful to monotheistic (i.e., negative theological) premises than Judaism. By refusing to invest a human being with divine powers, it looks like Judaism reifies negative theological distance and makes it a function of the impossibility of transforming physical entities into supra-physical entities. Christianity, by contrast, by investing one human being with a Divine component—if it were to be coupled with the negative theological imperative to immediately discount that investiture and acknowledge that we do not know what it signifies—dramatizes the idea that Divine distance and its correlative of human limitation are purely a function of language and of the paradoxes attendant to piercing its limits by literalizing the notion of God, and do not disclose to us anything about God.

To have an impact upon molding and restructuring human lives and institutions in the world, Christianity, of course, has to resurrect on a historical plane of existence the very dualism of which, on a sheerly theological level, it is such a bitter enemy. Christianity can only navigate and leave its imprint on the world between Redemptive Moment One and Redemptive Moment Two (the Second Coming) through mechanisms of law—with their explicit and implicit dualisms of commander and commanded.

Moreover, the Christian swerve concerning the locatability of God is also logically and theologically vulnerable. If the fundamental theological impulse identified with monotheism is one of transcendence, then making Jesus divine does not really heal the residual dualism of monotheism but only provides it with a new arena in which to rear its head. In terms of monotheistic principle, God the Son is as theologically inscrutable as God the Father. If all of the terms attached to the latter turn out to be "uncashable" metaphors, the same is true concerning all of the terms attached to the former designation. The theological vocabulary in both instances is situated in a relationship of ever-receding distance to the theological entities it is purporting to represent. Despite St. Paul's most determined efforts, we need to come on to the hierarchical, regulatory mechanisms of law that, as a matter of theological necessity, take root in communities of monotheistic believers in order to theologically access, relate to, and worship God the Son. This is to say that suppressed dualisms of law inevitably resurface within a Christian theological setting.

Christianity to some extent grows out of that strand of Jewish thought reflected in *Pirkei Avot* (loosely translated as the *Ethics of the Fathers*) and elsewhere which emphasizes that doing good deeds—performing *Mitzvot* (Divine commandments)—is entirely independent of mechanisms and apparatuses that correlate our actions with rewards and punishments. The reward for a Mitzvah is the engagement in the Mitzvah itself.[5] Christianity merely extends suspicion of the mechanism of rewards and punishments into a deflation of the role of Mitzvah altogether in defining man's relationship to God.[6] However, the initial impulses of suspicion directed toward theological frameworks emphasizing rewards and punishments stems from profound negative theological affirmation. It is because God is utterly metaphysically transcendent that rewards and punishments loom as theologically absurd and counterproductive.

Running parallel to the dialectic surrounding the concept of law in monotheistic religion—with Christianity's rejection of the dualism of commander and commanded setting the stage, during the course of the historical development of Christianity, for the reintegration of law as intimately governing the rhythms of the lives of the community of believers—is a dialectic surrounding the notion of love. Are the means of love—the approaches to and expressions of love—as passionate and

5. This is one way of making sense of *Ethics of the Fathers*, Chap. 4, Mishnah 2.

6. I have found the following works especially helpful in explicating St. Paul's relationship to Rabbinic Judaism: E. P. Sanders, *Paul: A Very Short Introduction* (Oxford: Oxford UP, 1991); E. P. Sanders, *Paul, the Law, and the Jewish People* (Philadelphia: Fortress Press, 1983); E. P. Sanders, *Jesus and Judaism* (London: SCM Press, 1985); James D. G. Dunn, ed., *The Cambridge Companion to St. Paul* (Cambridge: Cambridge UP, 2003); James D. G. Dunn, ed., *Paul and the Mosaic Law* (Grand Rapids, MI: Eerdmans, 2001); A. Andrew Das, *Paul and the Jews* (Peabody, MA: Hendrickson, 2003).

ecstatic as the ends of love? Here, too, the exchange of roles and the merg-
ing of opposites become characteristic of monotheistic religion.

In the *Phaedrus*, for example, Plato suggests that the supreme lover is
the non-lover.[7] The lover, paradoxically, is prone to smother and to over-
whelm his love object—and therefore to destroy the possibility of love.
The philosophical lover, on the other hand—imbued with an appreciation
of the unimaginable distances that separate philosophical reflections from
their targets, and the persistently non-logically rigorous overlap between
words and things—has cultivated a sensibility that is readily able to assimilate the notion that the objects of human desire are beyond human grasp.
The philosopher has reared himself to be the consummately skilled and
practiced non-lover—which is to say, the optimal lover.

From a Platonic perspective, therefore, the Divine love expressed by
the Crucifixion has to be negatively theologically glossed. The inconceiv-
able One delineated in the *Parmenides* (which some scholars have traced
as a source for the negative theological construal of the tenets of monotheism[8]) cannot be regarded as loving in a straightforwardly passionate
human sense. Divine love as configured in Christian doctrine has to be
negatively theologically discounted as a metaphor whose cognitive and
emotional content cannot be literally grasped and applied.

A textual analysis of Romans yields a vision both of the thrust toward
the reallocation of monotheistic priorities constitutive of Christianity, and
of traces of the causes and factors leading to the extreme set of tensions
imposed by the reallocation. In stating his theme concerning salvation by
faith at the outset of Romans, St. Paul's ostensible prooftext comes from
a verse in Habakkuk: "For I am not ashamed of the gospel. It is the power
of God for the salvation of everyone who believes: for Jew first, and then
Greek. For in it is revealed the righteousness of God from faith to faith; as
it is written, 'The one who is righteous by faith will live.'"[9] A more literal
translation of the Hebrew of the prophet Habakkuk would read: "The Tzad-
dik [the righteous man] will live with his faith." The Babylonian Talmudic
Tractate of Makkoth states: "It is Habakkuk who came and based them all

7. See the discussion of the *Phaedrus* in my book, *Skepticism and Political Participation* (Philadelphia: Temple UP, 1990), pp. 81–84.

8. See the discussion in my book, *Skepticism, Belief, and the Modern: Maimonides to
Nietzsche* (Ithaca, NY: Cornell UP, 1997), pp. 24–25.

9. Rom. 1:16–17, citing Habakkuk 2:4. The translation comes from *The New American Bible* (World Publishing, 1987), p. 1211. Further references to Romans will be to this
edition and will be cited parenthetically within the text.

[the 613 commandments of the Torah catalogued by the Rabbis] on one [principle], as it is said, 'But the righteous shall live by his faith.'"[10]

In order to be able to appreciate the contrasting ways in which Judaism and Christianity relate to this verse, it is important to note that the key word in this verse—*Emunah*, in Hebrew—is systematically ambiguous, connoting both faith and faithfulness. The two sets of emotions and attitudes that are conjured up by these two words are in tension with each other. The person who has committed himself to faith has in some ways given up on faithfulness. To have faith (as the expression goes) means that one suspends one's own efforts—reposing confidence in a Higher Power (or Higher Powers) that it (or they) will engineer an outcome that is hospitable to one's needs and aspirations.

To be faithful (in contrast to having faith) suggests that one recognizes that there is a subtle means-end relationship attendant to the nurturance of faith itself. On has to cultivate (exercise) faith faithfully—by not succumbing to the illusion that one already has it or that it will "deliver" those ends of action that one originally hoped for in adopting it. If one merely has faith, then one is treating faith as a durable entity—a source of certainty, a guarantee of eventual triumph over the vicissitudes of human existence. To have faith is to be unfaithful to the project of cultivating faith. To ensure that the means of faith do not vitiate or undermine the ends of faith, one can only strive to be faithful—investing each act in which one engages with the hope that it will have the desired efficacy. To be faithful means to mobilize the energies of will to triumph over the twin, antithetically alluring dangers of demoralization and overconfidence. To be faithful means to remain endlessly a doer. To act at all in the world (and certainly to engage in action on an ongoing basis, as the Jewish conception of Maasei Mitzvah [the doing of religiously-ordained deeds] envisions) is the keenest expression of faith.

There are two verses in the Psalms that apply the word *Emunah* to God in a way which reinforces this reading of faithfulness. In Psalms 33:4, we find the verse: "For the word of God is upright and all His deeds are done with faithfulness." This idea is spelled out a little bit more fully at Psalms 92:3: "To declare Your lovingkindness in the morning, and Your faithfulness in the night." What both verses appear to be referring to is God's faithfulness in sustaining a natural order in which night follows

10. *The Hebrew-English Edition of the Babylonian Talmud: Makkoth*, trans. H. M. Lazarus. (London: Soncino Press, 1987), 24a.

day and day follows night with obsessive, unbroken regularity. Given the organizing principle of monotheism that God's transcendent Oneness militates against a literal translation of any of the attributes and actions ascribed to Him in the Biblical text, we need to make sense of these two verses in the Psalms in the general mold of how the Rabbis interpret the Biblical imperative of "V'Halachta B'Drachav"—"And you should walk in the ways of God."[11] The Rabbis ask how is it possible for human beings to walk in the ways of God, who is described as an all-consuming fire? So the verse must refer to human imitation of Divine attributes: Just as God is merciful, so you, too, must be merciful; just as He is compassionate, so you, too, must be compassionate. Extending this hermeneutical principle to the verses in question from the Psalms, we might say that just as God practices faithfulness in upholding the natural order, so must we, too, practice faithfulness in our mode of relating to Him.

In Romans 1:20, St. Paul invokes an Argument from Design: "Ever since the creation of the world, his invisible attributes of eternal power and divinity have been able to be understood and perceived in what he has made" (Rom. 1:20; p. 1211). St. Paul's invocation of this Argument already presupposes the truth of negative theology. This Argument locates its proof for the existence of God squarely within the human world—not by way of a direct reading of nature that culminates in God, but by way of analogy with the work of human artificers. Its insistence on proceeding analogically—and therefore staying in the human world in developing its proof of God instead of attempting to straightforwardly trace a direct relationship between the world and God—highlights both the negative theological background postulate to the Argument and its inability to be coherently stated. The Argument must resort to analogy in making its case for God, because God is utterly aloof and transcendent in relation to things in this world. At the same time, however, that aloofness and transcendence prevent the Argument from having any import for the nature and existence of God. The ground rules and presuppositions of the Argument sever its tie with the conclusion that it seeks to serve.

At Romans 2:6, St. Paul invokes the verse from Psalms 62:13, which says that God "will repay everyone according to his works" (p. 1212).

---

11. The relevant Talmudic and Midrashic sources for the discussion in the text are the following: Babylonian Talmud, Sotah 14a; Ketuboth 111b; Shabbath 133b; Vayikrah Rabbah 25:3.

The verse in Hebrew is arresting for two reasons that are elided by this English translation. In Hebrew, the word for "works" appears in the singular—"K'Maaseihu"—and not in the plural—"K'Maasav." The verse clearly has in mind all of the actions that a person performs, and yet it refers to them in the singular rather than the plural. This suggests that the verse might be alluding to how a person's actions add up to fashion (i.e., to delineate) a human being. A person's actions ultimately yield and define him. This is their most significant reward or punishment. We become limited—and delimited—for ourselves and for others—by our actions. The verse in the Psalms begins with the phrase: "Unto Thee, O Lord, belongeth mercy [lovingkindness]." God's kindness to us is manifested in His letting our actions become their own reward and punishment. God's unbridgeable distance from us itself becomes a source of great kindness in that willy-nilly our own actions become decisive in defining who we are and what our trajectory of being is.

Paul pounces upon the intense paradox attendant to the whole idea of Divine punishment: "But if God's truth redounds to his glory through my falsehood, why am I still being condemned as a sinner? And why not say—as we are accused and as some claim we say—that we should do evil that good may come of it?" (Rom. 3:7–8; p. 1213). The very efficacy of Divine punishment undermines the idea of Divine punishment. If God's Glory is enhanced by His imposition of punishments upon sinful human beings, then through our sinning we have contributed to the greater glory of God and are therefore not appropriate recipients of punishment. Punishment undercuts itself—and, in the course of being applied, delegitimates the right to its own exercise.

The three factors that I have cited—Paul's theological rationalism that undergirds his citation of an Argument from Design, the Argument from Design itself, and his impugning the coherence of the theological apparatus of rewards and punishments as traditionally conceived—point to Paul's affirmation of the principles of negative theology. If this reading is at all on the right track, then it sets the stage for a reading of Romans as Paul's series of strategies for grappling with the dilemmas and paradoxes that negative theology engenders.

So, when Paul announces, not far from the beginning of Romans, "One is a Jew inwardly, and circumcision is of the heart, in the spirit, not the letter" (Rom. 2:29; p. 1213), the best reading of this withdrawal is probably Jacob Taubes's: "Interiorization is not a dividing line between "Judaism" and "Christianity"; it signifies a crisis within Jewish eschatology itself—in Pauline Christianity as well as in the Sabbatian movement of the 17th century. How else can redemption be defined after the Messiah has failed to redeem the external world except by turning inward?"[12] In response to a struggling—and overtly failing—messianic movement, in a context in which God does not literally speak, inwardness for St. Paul becomes the rallying cry for the expression of religiosity.

St. Paul emphasizes again and again that law, sin, and punishment are circular constructs. There are only human beings worthy of being punished by the law because of the categories of sin defined by the very law that punishes transgressors: "Since no human being will be justified in his sight by observing the law; for through the law comes consciousness of sin" (Rom. 3:20; p. 1213); "Though sin is not accounted when there is no law" (Rom. 5:13; p. 1215); "The law entered in so that transgression might increase" (Rom. 5:20; p. 1216); "For sin is not to have any power over you, since you are not under the law but under grace" (Rom. 6:14; p. 1216).

The category of "sin" is correlative with the category of "law." Once the notion of law is dislodged from the human pantheon of highest values, the category of sin is distanced—or even abolished—along with it. St. Paul implicitly subscribes to the idea of the underdetermination of theory by fact. Sin is not a fact in the world but is a function of a legal set of categories and conceptualizations. The ultimate theological paradigm lending support to the concept of underdetermination is the concept of the monotheistic God Himself, who is theorized as being so utterly and uniquely transcendent that all human strings of words and descriptions—no matter how diverse and contradictory they might be in relation to each other—fail to describe Him. Our theological vocabularies remain underdetermined by the utterly conceptually aloof and remote monotheistic God. Since the premises of monotheism affirming God's total transcendence cannot be breached even in this negative, indirect way, which invests literal credence in His complete transcendence, then we must transfer the analytical apparatus of "underdetermination" away from Divine matters to human things. What results is the Pauline emphasis on the categorial dependence of human sinfulness upon the notion of law. In a universe saturated with

12. Jacob Taubes, "The Price of Messianism," *Journal of Jewish Studies* 33, nos. 1–2 (Spring–Autumn, 1982): 596. I am grateful to Joshua Gold for calling this article to my attention.

monotheistic categories of understanding, our ontologies remain in a state of suspended animation, dependent upon our categorial ingenuity and inventiveness.

The transition to a mode of existence unburdened by the category of law and its correlative of sin is accomplished through the Crucifixion of Jesus: "We know that our old self was crucified with him, so that our sinful body might be done away with, that we might no longer be in slavery to sin. For a dead person has been absolved of sin" (Rom. 6:6–7; p. 1216). There is something highly secular—and even radical—in this formulation. Human beings are envisioned by St. Paul as owning their own deaths. Death is an event in a human life that is on a par with all of the other events that compose that life. Projecting our own death as harboring a certain signification enables us to restructure our lives in order to enhance our sense of mastery in the present. Very paradoxically, St. Paul, by investing death with supernatural meaning—that we have all been purified by the Crucifixion of Jesus, that we have all vicariously participated in his death and have therefore been liberated to partake of a life of grace without sin—has naturalized death, made it thoroughly available for human uses to regenerate human life in the present. Hobbes's theorizing of the role of death in *Leviathan*, as facilitating the nurturance of a life devoted to the pursuit of endless felicity, represents to some extent a secularization of this vision.

In the faith-governed universe to which St. Paul catapults us, the negative theological strains are still paramount. St. Paul says: "You have become obedient from the heart to the pattern of teaching to which you were entrusted" (Rom. 6:17; p. 1216). In an utterly transcendent mono-theistic universe, God does not directly impart to us or communicate to us anything. The metaphor that captures the tenuousness and obliqueness of the lines of interaction between us and God is that of "trust." The idea of trust brackets off the possibility of secure knowledge. God "entrusts" us because He cannot speak to us in any literally defined and explicable way. By the same token, we can only be "entrusted" with the Divine teach-ing because our allegiance to it is not predicated upon the attainment of certainty—or even complete assurance that it is emanating from God. The mobilization of our volition, of our will to believe, constitutes a prerequi-site for our trusting—and our being entrusted.

Pursuing the logic of his argument, St. Paul subsumes compliance with *Mitzvot* (Divine laws and commandments), which either insinuate or define the categories of sin that they are geared to curb and restrain, under the rubric of "flesh"—and identifies Jesus' redemptive love which circumvents both law and sin as "spirit": "For if you live according to the flesh, you will die, but if by the spirit you put to death the deeds of the body, you will live" (Rom. 8:13; p. 1218). At this juncture, one can point to an internal contradiction in Paul, invoking Paul against Paul. If Paul is committed to the view of the underdetermination of words by things so that "sin" becomes a function of the category called "law," then what "flesh" and "spirit" as metaphysical categories refer to are not immediately given and intuitively self-evident, but are a function of contingent couplings and de-couplings, groupings and de-groupings. Spirituality can be "substantialized" and "fetishized," and love of the material and concrete and momentary and fleeting can be transformed into a spiritual principle. We can then appropriately respond to St. Paul by saying that it is neither "flesh" nor "spirit" that will sustain us in life or kill us, but the skill and subtlety with which we learn to cathect and associate and de-cathect and disassociate a mass of experiences and things with an unfolding repertoire of words and categories, including "flesh" and "spirit" and their cognates.

In the chapter from which I am quoting, Paul goes on to say: "No, in all these things we conquer overwhelmingly through him who loved us. For I am convinced that neither death, nor life, nor angels, nor principalities, nor present things, nor future things, nor powers, nor height, nor depth, nor any other creature will be able to separate us from the love of God in Christ Jesus our Lord" (Rom. 8:37–39; p. 1219). It is arresting to juxtapose these sentences to Plato's theorizing of the superiority of the non-lover to the lover in the *Phaedrus*, and the implicit metaphysical connection between this and Plato's theorizing of the One in the *Parmenides* discussed earlier. The category of "love," too, is underdetermined by the intensity of the emotion that one feels. The strength of one's yearning and longing—the depth of one's craving for embeddedness—can mask and feed into a powerful urge to domination. I am so emotionally and existentially dependent upon you, my beloved—whether God or another human being—that, out of sheer reciprocity and acknowledgement of need, you must restrict your range of options to make your nurturance and solicitousness of me become the major way in which you express your love. Through the sheer frenzy of my dependence, I surge toward total domination. If my beloved is the Pauline God, with Jesus as the mediating Divine element, then I have foreclosed overwhelming monotheistic metaphysical distance by the fashioning of an idolatrous emotional artifact that is beholden to me.

The anti-monotheistic corruption that develops from the way that St. Paul portrays and projects the love of Jesus for a humankind hankering after redemption sets the stage for our invoking against St. Paul a parallel criticism to the one he levels against Judaism. He argues that sin does not have an independent, ontologically autonomous existence but is categorially dependent upon the notion of law for its emergence and salience. Sin—transgression—is correlated with legal normativity. Once you abstract the primacy being assigned to law, then sin becomes a theological non sequitur—a conceptual hangover from a theologically more "primitive" age. The Pauline substitution of love for law is vulnerable to an analogous critique. "Love" and "faith"—like "sin"—in order to be properly meaningful need to be subsumed under a more overarching category (or categories) that specifies their function in the inner life of human beings. The category that St. Paul selects to play this role, influenced by · his cultural climate, is that of "redemption." However, the formal, analytical level upon which St. Paul seeks to discredit the Jewish preoccupation with law can also be mobilized to discredit the Pauline preoccupation with love and faith in the context of redemption. Love and faith work to define a distinctive mode of being for the *homo religiosus* only in an antecedent setting that identifies redemption with these emotions and attitudes. If one conceives of redemption in more partial, ameliorative, and provisional terms, then "love" and "faith" represent too holistic a lurch toward transcendence, which can have the counterproductive effects of destroying love (we do too many hateful things in its name) and undermining faith (by creating too large a gap between our otherworldly loyalties and our this-worldly translations and arrangements). If St. Paul's critique of the centrality of law in Judaism is at least to some extent a formal, analytical critique, then it becomes a double-edged sword that can be mobilized against St. Paul's official transvaluation of the values emphasized in Judaism.

There is a crucial hedging in the teaching of St. Paul. While, on the one hand, in his image of the loving, saving Jesus, he makes God answerable to a human craving for redemption, on the other hand, in his resolution of the conundrum surrounding the coexistence of Divine omnipotence with human free will, he reconfirms the austerity of monotheistic distance in all of its starkness. At Romans 9:18–19 (p. 1220), St. Paul says: "Consequently, he has mercy upon whom he wills, and he hardens whom he wills. You will say to me then, 'Why [then] does he still find fault? For who can oppose his will?'" In this passage, St. Paul affirms an unbridgeable metaphysical distance between Divine omnipotence and the exercise of human freedom. God can exercise His judgment and power as He wills (He bears ultimate responsibility for everything that occurs in the world), and we are still culpable for faulty exercises of our freedom: "He still find[s] fault." Divine omnipotence and human freedom run on independent tracks that never meet. Apparently, then, from St. Paul's perspective, faith in Jesus is not able to alleviate or redeem this distance.

This suggests that the Divine love expressed by the Crucifixion of Jesus does not completely overcome monotheistic distance, but just gives it another arena in which to operate. The relationship between Divine love and human action in the presence of God in Christian thought remains as dense and impenetrable by human reason as the relationship between preoccupation with compliance to law and action undertaken in the presence of God within Judaism. Replacing law with love, St. Paul ends up with the same theological predicament and the same literally indecipherable pattern of resolution that is definitive of Judaism.

At Romans 9:30–33 (pp. 1220–21), St. Paul formulates the credo of the new monotheistic religion that he is working to found: "What then shall we say? That Gentiles, who did not pursue righteousness have achieved it, that is, righteousness that comes from faith; but that Israel, who pursued the law of righteousness, did not attain to that law? Why not? Because they did it not by faith, but as if it could be done by works. They stumbled over the stone that causes stumbling, as it is written: Behold, I am laying a stone in Zion, that will make people stumble and a rock that will make them fall, and whoever believes in him shall not be put to shame."[13] St. Paul in this passage (as well as in several others that one could cite) becomes the great architect and advocate of Christianity as the monotheistic religion that substitutes justification by faith for justification by works. Judaism, in its preoccupation with elaborating upon and fulfilling the precepts of the law, makes it look as if the individual believer can satisfactorily justify

---

13. A literal translation of the last part of the sentence from the Hebrew of Isaiah 28:16 would read as follows: "He that believeth shall not make haste." The words "in him" are nowhere to be found in the Hebrew original, but are an interpolation either by St. Paul or by some redactor of his work.

himself both in his own eyes and in the eyes of God by conforming to the requirements of the law. The innovation of Christianity consists in substituting justification by faith for justification by works.

It is important to note, however, that this substitution accomplishes nothing—and leaves Christianity exposed to the same sort of critique that St. Paul levels against Judaism. Stated tersely, the theological problem attendant to justification by works is not "works." It is "justification." Because I have complied with Divine commandments—done a sufficient number of "works"—I am entitled to Divine favor and acceptance. However, by substituting "faith" for "works" very little has changed in the structure and dynamics of the argument. The only factor that has altered is the entity that I rely on in order to secure Divine favor and affirmation. From St. Paul's newly innovated Christian perspective, that factor becomes "faith" rather than "works." But as long as I can come up with a humanly intelligible and coherent argument why "faith" should net for me Divine favor, I feel that I have appropriately rationally justified myself in the eyes of God—and that He now owes me the goods (rewards) promised by the religion. The argument supporting justification by faith is not hard to come by. It resides close to the surface of St. Paul's text. If I do not repose confidence in the theological efficacy of my own actions (even if those actions consist in attempts to comply with Divine edicts and pronouncements) but acknowledge in advance the numerous ways, from ambiguity and self-interestedness of motives to incomplete grasp of the Divine ends to be attained through compliance with Divine law, in which my actions might boomerang and fail, and therefore shift the basis of my overall allegiance and daily devotion to God from works to faith, then I am justified. I achieve a greater level of coherence in my own eyes and become a more coherently worshipping member of a Divine faith community by designing and theorizing my religious approaches from the perspective of "faith" rather than "works." On the basis of St. Paul's premises, however, one could say that as long as I remain engaged in a justificatory project, shifting the basis of justification from "works" to "faith" does not accomplish anything. Either way, I am attempting to breach the overwhelming distance that separates man from God by conceiving of my pattern of religious behavior (whether predicated on the primacy of the principle of "faith" or of "works") as being uniquely appropriate for serving and relating to Him.

The point that we need to become aware of is that if Christianity can be let off the hook at this juncture, so can Judaism. To validate "justification by faith" from a monotheistic perspective, one would have to say that the point of "justification by faith" is not to transparently clarify for us that we are fully acceptable in God's eyes but to help convince us that within a human frame of understanding we are organizing our religious lives in a maximally coherent way. "Justification by faith" merely assures us that we are measuring up in our own eyes—and tells us nothing about how we shape up on the Divine horizon. The gap between us and God can still be affirmed as conceptually unbridgeable.

The same kind of analysis is directly relevant for the idea of "justification by works." Our compliance with and fidelity to Divine commandments is a function of our wanting to improve the caliber of our own lives—our earthly existences—which we believe are exalted to a higher, more purified plane by our efforts to conform to (what we take to be) Divine requirements. Our structuring of our lives to meet what we take to be Divine demands is entirely compatible with our acknowledging that our actions have no impact upon and are not needed by God, and that His way of registering them remains entirely inscrutable to us, so that the terms Reward and Punishment in relation to God have no sustainable sense and no discernible reference in a human setting. "Justification by works," just like the concept of "justification by faith," can only be enunciated, defined, and defended with the human parameters of self and communal structuring in mind and an unconditional relinquishing of any claims to Divine connection and acceptance.

It is very interesting to note that in Romans 10:5 (p. 1221), St. Paul cites a text that would be used by the Rabbis of the First Century to invalidate the sacrificial death of one human being for another, of precisely the sort that is manifested on the grandest possible scale by Jesus. St. Paul says that "Moses writes about the righteousness that comes from [the] law, 'The one who does these things will live by them [Lev. 18:5].'" In the Babylonian Talmudic tractate of Yoma 85a, the following question was raised: "Whence do we know that in the case of danger to human life the laws of the Sabbath are suspended [i.e., that one can violate those laws in order to save a human life]?" At 85b, the Talmud reports that "Rab Judah said in the name of Samuel [quoting the verse cited by St. Paul]: 'He shall live by them,' but he shall not die because of them."[14] In the Babylonian

---

14. *Hebrew-English Edition of the Babylonian Talmud: Yoma*, trans. Leo Jung (London: Soncino Press, 1986).

Talmudic tractate of Baba Mezia 62a, we find the following braita:[15] "If two are traveling on a journey [far from civilization], and one has a pitcher of water, if both drink, they will [both] die, but if one only drinks, he can reach civilization.—The Son of Patura taught: It is better that both should drink and die, rather than that one should behold his companion's death. Until Rabbi Akiva came and taught: 'That thy brother may live with thee' [Lev. 25:36]: Thy life takes precedence over his life. ['With thee' implies that thy life takes priority, but that he, too, has a right to life after thine is assured.]"[16]

The Rabbis thus block—delegitimate—any kind of vicarious atonement within Judaism by emphasizing the primacy of each individual life. To atone through one's self-consciously assumed death for the sins of others presupposes that one is certain of one's spiritual superiority—one's moral elevation—over other human beings. Given God's total and utter transcendence in relation to things human, this is knowledge that no human being can be presumed to have. From a monotheistic perspective, deepened knowledge of God consists in a greater appreciation of the metaphysical distance separating us from Him. Rabbi Akiva's famous gloss on "Thy brother shall live with thee"—that in a moral crunch, in a moment of potential triage, or in a moment of supreme spiritual ecstasy when you feel driven to sacrifice your life for the benefit of humanity, your life has priority over your fellow human beings—seeks to neutralize and to classify as a large-scale monotheistic transgression the temptation to martyrdom. In his project of fashioning a monotheistic religion in which faith, love, and grace predominate over works and law, so that a monumental act of sacrifice becomes necessary to serve as the object of the faith and the conduit of the love, the internal logic of monotheism as Paul comes to understand it in the light of his earlier discipleship of the Rabbis dictates that the human being who sacrifices be conceived as divine—have at least one component of his being that is totally other than human. In order that Jesus's death be seen as supreme sacrifice rather than sacrilege, he must already be God at the moment of the Crucifixion. Otherwise, he is a hapless Jew who simply misunderstands his own creed.

15. Statements by the early generations of Rabbis that were not codified in the Mishnah were collected in braitot and are very often cited in the Talmudic text to support particular points of argument.

16. *Hebrew-English Edition of the Babylonian Talmud: Baba Mezia*, trans. H. Freedman (London: Soncino Press: 1986).

Aside from the larger logico-metaphysico factors leading to the invest-ment of Divinity in a human being that I discussed earlier, there is a more local, internal factor constraining the divinization of Jesus. Given how the postulates of monotheistic distance enshrined in Judaism work to assign overriding importance to each individual human life—life is supreme given the metaphoric character of all of the theological, metaphysical, and moral pegs that one can point to beyond the range of the human—we can say that internal to the logic of Judaism it is only someone who subsists beyond the level of the human who can justify the sacrifice of a human life (in this case, his own). Jesus has to already be God—he has to be outside of the framework of the human—in order to sanction the sacrifice of his life for the sake of humanity. What makes Christianity look so adversarial to Judaism (the claim to divinity advanced in behalf of Jesus) is actu-ally a function of how closely it is conceptually and theologically tied to Judaism.

St. Paul's genius consists in universalizing monotheism by making love—rather than law—the organizing principle of monotheistic religion. Law particularizes and establishes boundaries and barriers. Love univer-salizes and erodes boundaries and barriers (between people, nations, and cultures). In this context, it is important to recognize that in his political quietism and passivity, St. Paul simply displaces law out of a religious domain and onto a secular one—endorsing the civil status quo. He does not get rid of law on the human scene. He merely rezones it to another locale within the traditional mapping of the human: "Therefore; whoever resists authority opposes what God has appointed, and those who oppose it will bring judgment upon themselves. For rulers are not a cause of fear to good conduct, but to evil. Do you wish to have no fear of authority? Then do what is good and you will receive approval from it, for it is a servant of God for your good. But if you do evil, be afraid, for it does not bear the sword without purpose; it is the servant of God to inflict wrath on the evildoer. Therefore, it is necessary to be subject not only because of the wrath but also because of conscience" (Rom. 13:2–5; p. 1224).

Judaism, by contrast to this programmatic formulation by St. Paul, in focusing upon law and making the elaboration of law and compliance with it central to its monotheistic project, has the opportunity to place in circulation values and standards that can serve as a critique of existing political, economic, and social arrangements. For example, the laws of the sabbatical and the jubilee years within Judaism (Leviticus, Chapter 25), which require the land to lie fallow for three years after six years of regular

cultivation, enshrine values such as respect for the environment and equal-
ization and redistribution of property that can serve as the basis for critique
of existing civil and positive law. St. Paul's passionate universalism leads
to a dismantling and discrediting of this invaluable critical resource.

A very subtle and trenchant critique of Pauline theology is implicit
in Jacques Derrida's theorizing of the gift.[17] This theorizing constitutes a
gloss on Christian theology and can be read as being deeply subversive of
it. According to Derrida, in order for there to be a gift, there cannot be a
giver or a recipient or indeed even a gift. Even the conceptual registering
of these three entities militates against their this-worldly translation and
realization. If something is denominated as a gift, it opens up a whole
range of multifarious possibilities, only some of which converge with our
commonsensical understanding of what a gift is. If you contrast gift with
sale, then a gift is something that you give and get for free. If you contrast
"gift" with other modes of ingratiating yourself to other people, such as
an overt personal display of affection, then a gift is an instrumentality for
trading certain goods with other people. In order to dissociate itself from
these other possibilities, a gift would have to be pre-verbal, pre-concep-
tual. In order to qualify as a gift, a gift couldn't be a gift.

This suggests that perhaps the only way a gift can be a gift is if it is
insinuated from within the interstices of other social and linguistic practices. For example, Judaism with its mechanisms of law for regulating all
levels of human relationship, from the intra-psychic to the inter-personal
to the public and governmental, conjures up a contrasting image of more
spontaneous and less organized modes of human relationship. Instead of
God being viewed as the Supreme Lawgiver, He is seen as the Supreme
Dispenser of love and good feeling. Given that words only signify in
relation to contrasting sets of words that they feed off, "Divine Love" is
already being communicated to us in the texts that focus on "Divine Law."
The love that issues forth in Divine Grace and God's other inestimable
gifts showered on human beings is thus being placed before us in the only
manner where conceptualization does not sully it—obliquely, indirectly.

The underdetermination of meaning by text that makes the gift vocabulary so unstable and potentially self-contradictory also proliferates the
number of options available to us in construing the relationship between

---

17. Jacques Derrida, *Donner le temps. I. La fausse monnaie.* (Paris: Galilee, 1991).
The English translation of this work is: *Given Time. I. Counterfeit Money*, trans. Peggy
Kamuf (Chicago: Univ. of Chicago Press, 1991).

"law" and its contrasting meaning-conferring terms, "love" and "spontaneity." "Love," on one level, is the conceptual foil that enables the notion of "law" to click into place. But law—the ordaining and legitimating of regularized procedures for the structuring of human relationships—can also be theorized as a supreme manifestation of love in the Platonic sense discussed earlier. The establishment of a series of systematic boundaries for the actualization of human energies represents, as it were, God's supreme gesture of love. Jews who strive to abide by the norms of Jewish law are being nurtured in accordance with the ethos of the non-lover—the supreme manifestation of love in a Platonic and Biblical sense.

Anglicans in the Postcolony: On Sex and the Limits of Communion

Mary-Jane Rubenstein

At this point, it would be a considerable accomplishment *not* to be aware that there is something very strange going on in the Anglican Communion. Nearly every day brings fresh stories of increasingly complicated ecclesiastical warfare: Nigerian bishops in Virginia, Ugandan churches in California, same-sex blessings in Canada, threats of schism, charges of heresy—and perhaps you've heard about the gay bishop in New Hampshire?[1]

The current difficulties in the American Episcopal Church and the wider Anglican Communion can be traced back to a number of different events in the life of the church, depending on how deep the storyteller would like to go. The flashiest and most recent of these is the consecration of the Right Reverend Gene V. Robinson, a partnered gay man, as Bishop of the Diocese of New Hampshire in 2003. But the tension within the world's third-largest Christian family had already grown unbearable by its 1998 meeting at Lambeth Palace, when questions about gay clergy and same-sex blessings polarized the Communion to such an extent that none of the other matters (war, debt, poverty, HIV/AIDS, water) received

1. See Michelle Boorstein, "Conservative N. Va. Priest Installed as Anglican Bishop: Head of Episcopal Split to Lead Nigerian Offshoot," *Washington Post*, May 6, 2007; Jan Nunley, "Two California Parishes Vote Alignment with Uganda Diocese," *Episcopal News Service*, August 17, 2004; Diocese of New Westminster, "Information on Same-Sex Blessings," available at the diocesan website, http://www.samesexblessing.info; Peter Akinola, "A Most Agonizing Journey," available at the Church of Nigeria website, http://www.anglican-nig.org/main.php?k_j=12&d=88&p_t=index.php; and James Solheim, "Amid Cheers and Protests, Robinson Consecrated in Diocese of New Hampshire," *Episcopal News Service*, November 2, 2003.

nearly the attention it deserved.[2] This millennial conflict at Lambeth had been brewing at least since the Episcopal Church's "irregular" ordination of women to the priesthood in 1974, which threatened to split the Communion between proponents and opponents of women in Holy Orders.[3] There have been few decades, in fact, in which some faction of this global church has not accused another of an unacceptable departure from tradition. Such a dispute can even be said to have formed the Anglican Communion itself: the first Lambeth Conference was called in 1867 in response to the excommunication of J. W. Colenso, Bishop of Natal, South Africa, whose biblical scholarship the Bishop of Cape Town found to be heretical.[4] And, of course, the efficient cause of the English Reformation in the first place was Henry VIII's refusal of papal authority on matters of sexual conduct. The contemporary crisis among Anglicans worldwide is therefore not qualitatively different from skirmishes they have encountered before. That having been said, the current *quantity* of internecine rancor might ultimately prove too much for the Communion to bear.

The vast media coverage of recent events tends to explain the conflict as an ideological battle between "liberal" and "conservative" members of the Communion, who simply cannot agree on the status of homosexual people within the church. Most Anglican leaders believe, at least in principle, that lesbian and gay people should not be the objects of ridicule or abuse.[5]

2. The Lambeth Conference convenes roughly every 10 years at the invitation of the Archbishop of Canterbury; see the official website, http://www.lambethconference.org, for the history of the Conference as well as archives of its resolutions. In relation to Lambeth 1998, see Stephen Bates, *A Church at War: Anglicans and Homosexuality* (New York: I. B. Tauris, 2004), pp. 125–41; and Mary-Jane Rubenstein, "An Anglican Crisis of Comparison: Race, Gender, and Religious Authority, with Particular Reference to the Church of Nigeria," *Journal of the American Academy of Religion* 72:2 (2004): 341–65.

3. The first woman to be ordained in Anglican Communion was actually Florence Li Tim-Oi, ordained in 1944 in occupied Hong Kong. The controversy that ensued prevented her serving as a priest until she emigrated to Canada. On the history of women's ordination within the Communion, see Norene Carter, "The Episcopalian [*sic*] Story," in *Women of Spirit: Female Leadership in the Jewish and Christian Traditions*, ed. Rosemary Ruether and Eleanor McLaughlin (Eugene, OR: Wipf and Stock, 1998), pp. 356–72; and Henry R. McAdoo, *Anglicans and Tradition and the Ordination of Women* (Norwich: Canterbury Press, 1997).

4. See Peter Hinchliff, "Colonial Church Establishment in the Aftermath of the Colenso Affair," in *Religious Change in Europe 1650–1914: Essays for John McManners*, ed. Nigel Aston (Oxford: Clarendon Press, 1997), pp. 345–63.

5. Lambeth Resolution 1.10 declares that while homosexuality is "incompatible with scripture," the members of the conference commend gay and lesbian people to the pastoral

But does the principle of Christian love demand that they be healed, or celebrated? Should same-sex partnerships be blessed, or condemned? And can a gay man be a model of Christian living to a parish? To a diocese? The yea-sayers seem to include the majority of the American Episcopal Church and the Anglican Church of Canada, who see the "full inclusion" of lesbian and gay people as an urgent matter of justice.[6] The nay-sayers are said to include the disaffected members of the Episcopal Church, along with the churches of the "Global South." The self-appointed spokesperson of this body is the Most Reverend Peter J. Akinola, Archbishop, Metropolitan and Primate of All Nigeria, who believes the rise of gay advocacy amounts to a "satanic attack" on the church.[7] As for the Church of England and the Archbishop of Canterbury, they have done their best to remain on the theological fence, allowing clergy (but not bishops) to live in same-sex relationships so long as both partners remain celibate.[8] While this global schematic can perhaps be helpful for the purposes of a news brief, the problem is that it ultimately fails to account for the vast range of opinions within specific Anglican provinces, dioceses, parishes, and even families—not to mention entire continents and hemispheres. This is particularly true of "the Global South," and of "Africa" in particular, which is almost always represented as univocally ultra-conservative. It should be said from the outset that this is hardly the case.

In a recent speech to the Ecclesiastical Law Society in Liverpool, England, Bishop Musonda Trevor Selwyn Mwamba of Botswana ventured that there were at least three major strands within Africa; "conservative," "liberal," and "moderate." Mwamba explained that the conservative voice is represented by Archbishop Akinola of Nigeria, who views homosexuality

care of their priests and bishops and "condemn irrational fear of homosexuals" (Lambeth Conference website, http://www.lambethconference.org/resolutions/1998/1998-1-10.cfm).

6. On the position of the Episcopal Church, see The Episcopal Church (USA), *To Set Our Hope on Christ: A Response to the Invitation of Windsor Report* (New York: The Episcopal Church Center, 2005), par. 135. On the position of the Anglican Church of Canada, see "Same-Sex Blessings not in Conflict with Core Doctrine," available at the Anglican Church of Canada website, http://www.anglican.ca/news/news. php?newsItem=2007-06-24_m.news.

7. See Jane Little, "Schism Looming for Anglican Communion," *BBC News*, December 18, 2006.

8. Celibacy was officially recommended to gay clergy in *Some Issues in Human Sexuality* (London: Church House Publishing, 1991). The 2003 controversy over Jeffrey John's candidacy for the episcopate in Reading demonstrated that this leniency does not, however, extend to bishops: see Bates, *A Church at War*, pp. 155–79.

as "a cancerous growth which needs to be removed in order to save the Communion from collapsing."[9] To that end, the Primates of Nigeria and Rwanda have each established missionary groups that consecrate American priests as bishops in Africa and then send them back to re-convert the New World.[10] This faction emphasizes a "plain" reading of Scripture over all other sources of authority and includes the leaders of the churches in Nigeria, Rwanda, Uganda, Kenya, and Tanzania. While there are certainly clergy and laity within these provinces who think otherwise, their bishops and archbishops usually claim to speak for the entirety of the continent when they call homosexuality "un-African, inhuman, unscriptural."[11]

The "liberal voice" to which Mwamba refers issues primarily from the Anglican Church of Southern Africa, its Primate the Most Reverend Njongonkulu Winston Ndungane of Cape Town. Much like his predecessor Desmond Tutu, Archbishop Ndungane approaches the issue of homosexuality from the perspective of South Africa's struggle against apartheid. As Tutu has recently said of the status of gay and lesbian people in the Communion: "It is a matter of ordinary justice. We struggled against apartheid in South Africa because we were blamed and made to suffer for something we could do nothing about. It is the same with homosexuality. The orientation is a given, not a matter of choice."[12] In addition to affirming Tutu's assertion of sexual equality as a human right, Archbishop Ndungane has challenged the hermeneutic inclinations of his more conservative brothers.

9. Musonda Trevor Selwyn Mwamba, "The Anglican Communion: Crisis and Opportunity," March 26, 2007, available at the Anglican Church of Canada website, http://www.anglican.ca/news/news.php?newsItem=2007-03-26_africa.news.

10. Rwanda, along with South East Asia, works through the Anglican Mission in America (AMiA), and Nigeria's group is called the Convocation of Anglicans in North America (CANA).

11. Dickinson Adeyanju, "Homosexual Priests: Nigerian Anglicans Will Not Succumb to Pressure From the West, Says Akinola," *The Guardian* (Nigeria), July 30, 2007.

12. Desmond Tutu in Bates, *A Church at War*, pp.129–30. The idea that homosexuality is inborn is a common position among liberals in the church, who are usually caught in the position of countering claims that God "did not make people gay." The most obvious retort to such an accusation seems to be, "yes, he did!"; but this leaves defendants vulnerable to the doctrine of original sin. (See Paul Zahl, "Last Signal to the *Carpathia*," *Anglican Theological Review* 86 (Fall 2004): 647–52.) This essentialist stalemate has been partially circumvented by *To Set Our Hope on Christ*, which reports that "contemporary studies indicate that same-sex affection has a genetic-biological basis which is shaped in interaction with psycho-social and cultural-historical factors" (*To Set Our Hope on Christ*, 2.22). Granted, this falls short of Judith Butler, but it manages to avoid collapsing same-sex behavior into either a biological defect or a whimsical "lifestyle choice."

Scripture, Ndungane argues, can only be approached in conversation with "reason, faith, culture, experience, and tradition."[13] Inasmuch as the Communion has experienced the dedication of its lesbian and gay members, Ndungane considers them to be gifts rather than cancers and has called upon the churches in Africa to recognize the episcopacy of Gene Robinson.[14] Other representatives of this "liberal" voice include members of African Anglican gay rights organizations, including Integrity Uganda and Changing Attitudes Nigeria.[15]

Finally, there is the "moderate" voice, which is embodied for Mwamba in the Anglican Church in Burundi. While Burundi's official position is critical of the consecration of Gene Robinson in New Hampshire and the development of a rite for same-sex blessings in New Westminster, Canada, it does not seek to expel the participants of either from the Communion. Rather, Burundi, along with other "moderate" Anglican churches, is calling both poles to reconciliation. The missiologist Titus Presler has suggested that this position comes out of Burundi's own context of genocide, which he distinguishes from the Rwandan context. In Rwanda, Presler explains, the recent genocide taught the church that the nation needs a strong, unified Christianity, which the "disease" of homosexuality can only destroy: "[W]e cannot afford," Presler paraphrases, "for our church to be contaminated in this crucial time of national reconstruction." In Burundi, by contrast, genocide taught the church to be suspicious of rigid theo-political positions: "What we have learned is that we must keep talking. Breaking relations is not a solution."[16]

Other parties within this "moderate" group include the churches in Latin America and the Caribbean who have declared themselves "The Global Center,"[17] and perhaps most significantly, the entirety of the Anglican

13. Njongonkulu Ndungane, "Scripture: What Is at Stake in Anglicanism Today?" in *Beyond Colonial Anglicanism: The Anglican Communion in the Twenty-First Century*, ed. Ian T. Douglas and Kwok Pui-Lan (New York: Church Publishing Inc., 2001), p. 253.

14. See Mwamba, "Anglican Communion," and Stephen Bates, "African Cleric Breaks Ranks on Gay Issue," *The Guardian*, September 8, 2003.

15. These groups are chapters of groups based in the Episcopal Church and Church of England, respectively, but their leaders maintain that, despite these affiliations, they remain locally organized.

16. Titus Presler, "Listening toward Reconciliation: A Conversation Initiative in Today's Anglican Alienations," *Anglican Theological Review* 89 (Spring 2007): 262–63.

17. These include the churches of Brazil, Colombia, El Salvador, Guatemala, Haiti, Honduras, Mexico, Nicaragua, Panama, Venezuela, and the Virgin Islands. See "Declaration of the Anglican Bishops of Latin America and the Caribbean (Global Center),"

Women's Network, which comprises two delegates from every province in the Communion—including Nigeria. The Network meets every two years at the meeting of the United Nations Commission on the Status of Women, and each time has unanimously affirmed its desire to remain in communion, regardless of who holds the crosier in New Hampshire. The statement from their 2007 meeting reads in part, "Given the global tensions so evident in our Church today, we do not accept that there is any one issue of difference or contention which can, or indeed would ever cause us to break our unity as represented by our common baptism. Neither would we ever consider severing the deep abiding bonds of affection which characterize our relationships as Anglican women."[18]

And so the notion that the Global South holds a unanimous opinion on human (that is, homo-) sexuality is simply false. This misconception is partly the work of a group of Primates who have appointed themselves the spokesmen for the whole of the southern hemisphere, partly the work of their North American allies, and partly the work of scholars and journalists who love a good postcolonial culture-clash. Indeed, among all parties concerned, the thesis Philip Jenkins sets forth in *The Next Christendom* has become common parlance: while church membership in the European and American mainline churches has been steadily declining for half a century, Christians have multiplied exponentially in Africa, South and East Asia, and Central and South America.[19] This means, Jenkins concludes, that the agenda of the global churches will now be determined by the people to whom Europe brought the gospel in the first place: as Archbishop Henry Orombi of Uganda has recently written, "the younger churches of Anglican Christianity will shape what it means to be Anglican. The long season of British hegemony is over."[20] This is undoubtedly the case. But what neither Jenkins nor Orombi nor the often sensationalist news analysts makes clear

available at the Anglican Communion website, http://www.anglicancommunion.org/acns/articles/40/50/acns4054.cfm. Vocal opponents of this centrism include the archbishops of the Central Cone and West Indies.

18. Anglican Women's Network, "Statement From the Anglican Women gathered at the 51st of the United Nations Commission on the Status of Women," March 3, 2007, available at the International Anglican Women's Network website, http://www.iawn.org/2007From_the_Anglican_Women_gathered_at_the_51st_UNCSW.htm.

19. See Philip Jenkins, *The Next Christendom: The Coming of Global Christianity* (Oxford: Oxford UP, 2002).

20. Archbishop Henry Luke Orombi, "What Is Anglicanism," *First Things* 175 (2007): 23–28.

is that the "younger churches" do not all speak with one voice. The problem, Bishop Mwamba explains, is that progressive Anglican voices from
the southern hemisphere are usually ignored and often silenced, so that the
Global South can be presented as univocal and uncompromising.[21]

And when "the Global South" is so presented—whether by journalists,
American Episcopalians, or African bishops—the choice for Europeans
and North Americans seems to be to side or not to side with the postcolonial
monolith. This means that the great divide within the northern churches
seems to fall between those who care about their sisters and brothers in
the developing world and those who do not; between Americans who take
global relationships seriously and American cowboys who do whatever
they please; in short, between proponents of relation within the Communion and proponents of autonomy. If the Global South speaks with one
voice and that voice condemns homosexuality, then northern supporters
of gay lives, rights, and practices are "choosing to walk apart"[22]—in other
words, abandoning their African, South American, and Asian siblings.

I would like to suggest, however, that a more useful picture—both ana-
lytically and ecclesiastically—emerges when one considers the full range
of commitment and opinion within the Communion. In conversation with
the work of French philosopher Jean-Luc Nancy, I will propose that the
Anglican Communion's crucial distinction falls, not between proponents
of ecclesiastical relation and proponents of ecclesiastical autonomy, but
rather between proponents of two different *kinds* of relation: one that aims
to bring all difference into identity, and another that seeks its identity in
and through difference. Both of these models can arguably find scriptural
and traditional justification, and yet they are proving to be fundamentally
incompatible as they vie for the souls—and the soul—of the Anglican
Communion.

Unworking Communion

In an essay titled "La communauté désoeuvrée," Jean-Luc Nancy reflects
on the nature of living in relation to others. He comes to distinguish
what he calls "communion," which replicates the logic of identity, from

21. See Mwamba, "Anglican Communion," and Pat Ashworth, "Listen to the Majority African Voice of Grace," *Church Times*, February 2, 2007.

22. See Akinola's accusation in Jordan Hylden, "The Episcopal Declaration of Independence," March 26, 2007, *On the Square* blog at the *First Things* website, http://www.
firstthings.com/onthesquare/?p=676.

"community," which names the interrelation of differences.[23] Like the roundly critiqued figure of the (Cartesian) individual, Nancy's "communion" understands itself to be self-identical and a soundly unified work, or *oeuvre*. A group of people "in communion" work at making themselves a work by retelling their communal myth, which assures them they all come from a common origin—that they are *essentially* all the same. Nancy calls this mode of relation "immanentism": once each existent is reduced to one common substance, or one "common-being," each of them is totally present to each of the others. It is perhaps obvious that "communion" thus understood becomes the focus of incisive criticism in Nancy's work, but the motivation behind this critique is no ordinary poststructuralist allergy to the "metaphysics of presence." Rather, Nancy's exposure of the immanentist logic of communion functions as a political critique of the kinds of violence that "communions" exercise in trying to assert their identity, reappropriate some mythic past of perfect unity, and purify their single essence.[24]

In distinction to communion's "common-being," which gathers all difference into identity, Nancy offers the "being-in-common" of community. Whereas a communion asserts itself as one massive individual, a community is composed of singularities that are only themselves in relation to *other*—essentially different—singularities. Refusing the self-identical appearance of communion, singularities can only "com-pear." "One cannot make a world with simple atoms," Nancy explains, "There has to be a *clinamen*. There has to be an inclination or an inclining from one to the other."[25] When being is understood not as common but as in-common, nothing properly *is* at all, except insofar as it is with others, toward others, touching others, and seeping into others. Far from being shared in common, a community's essence is shared out—communicated, fragmented, shattered—to such an extent that all community "is" is this inclining, this communication, this "with-ness" itself. "It is a groundless 'ground,'" Nancy writes, "made up only of the network, the interweaving, and the sharing of singularities."[26] Community's work, then, is to un-work

23. See Jean-Luc Nancy, "The Inoperative Community," in *The Inoperative Community*, trans. Peter Connor (Minneapolis: Univ. of Minnesota Press, 2001), pp. 1–42.

24. See Jean-Luc Nancy, "The Nazi Myth," trans. Brian Holmes, *Critical Inquiry* 16:2 (Winter 1990): 291–312.

25. Nancy, "The Inoperative Community," p. 3.

26. Ibid., p. 27.

itself; to become *dés-oeuvrée*; that is, to interrupt the formation of any single essence into which all its different singularities might be forcibly gathered. In other words, while "communion" must assimilate or destroy everything in its path, community's persistent interruption resists "the delirium of an incarnated communion. . . . Community is, in a sense, resistance itself: namely, resistance to immanence. Consequently, community is transcendence."[27]

After naming community "transcendence," however, Nancy goes on to note that such transcendence "no longer has any 'sacred' meaning." This is perhaps no surprise; one of the primary targets of Nancy's critique seems quite clearly to be ecclesiastical organizational structures. Christian communities can be said to function as Nancean "communions" *par excellence* insofar as they claim a common foundational myth (the life and death of one man in Judea), a common function (to "make disciples of all nations"[28]), and most importantly, a common essence: every Christian on earth is said to be a "living member" of the one body of Christ, himself "of one substance" with God the Father.[29] This substantial unity seems to be affirmed nowhere more clearly than in the words of St. Paul, often echoed in the Eucharistic liturgy: "We who are many are one body, for we all share in the one bread."[30] Along one reading, then, the Eucharist is the paradigmatic source of common being: it begins each time with a re-telling of the foundational myth ("on the night he was handed over to suffering and death, our Savior Jesus Christ took bread. . ."[31]); distributes the one body for internalization by the many; and proceeds to knit the multitudes into one, holy *communion*.

It would therefore seem that the churches are simply doomed to the "fascist" annihilation of difference that Nancy ascribes to communion,[32] and that historical and contemporary assertions of Anglicanism only confirm as much. When powerful men travel and replicate themselves overseas in order to purify their ranks and enforce sexual "order and

---

27. Ibid., p. 35.

28. This injunction is known as "the Great Commission." See Matt. 28:6–20.

29. This phrase can be found in the traditional English version of the Nicene Creed. Both this and the contemporary version can be found at http://www.cofe.anglican.org/worship/liturgy/commonworship/texts/word/creeds.html.

30. 1 Cor. 10:17.

31. *The Book of Common Prayer* (Episcopal Church) (New York: Church Hymnal Corporation, 1979), p. 362. Cf. p. 334.

32. Nancy, "The Inoperative Community," p. 35.

discipline"—whether in nineteenth-century Nigeria or twenty-first-century New Hampshire[33]—it stands to reason that they re-confirm the irreducibly totalizing nature of Christian "relation" itself. The question I would like to explore is whether there is there a way of configuring Anglicanism as a "community" in the Nancean sense, that is, as a network of interrelated, mutually constitutive, mutually *contaminating* singularities that resist the violence of enforced identity. In a more concrete idiom, the question is whether a church built on a colonial infrastructure can resist its own impulse toward colonialism. Rather than imposing order and discipline upon its recalcitrant subjects, can this—or any—Christian fellowship understand its identity as both constituted *and unworked* by difference?

Relation and the Windsor Report

After Gene Robinson's consecration in November 2003, the much-besieged office of the Archbishop of Canterbury appointed a group of bishops, clergy, and laypeople to a body called the Lambeth Commission. This group was charged with the task of writing a document that would examine the sources of and remedies for the church's seemingly irreconcilable differences concerning same-sex relationships and openly gay clergy and bishops.[34] The resulting Windsor Report, released in 2004, begins by addressing the unique structure of authority in the Anglican Communion. Unlike the Roman Catholic Church, it explains, the Anglican Communion has no curia—no centralized structure of control.[35] Rather, the Communion has been defined since its official formation in the 1860s as a set of autonomous churches, held in relation to one another through reciprocal "bonds of affection."[36] While Windsor affirms this "autonomy of individual provinces," it warns that "'autonomy' is a much-misunderstood concept."[37]

---

33. On the imposition of sexual order and discipline in early colonial Nigeria, see Ifi Amadiume, *Male Daughters, Female Husbands: Gender and Sex in an African Society* (London: Zed Books, 1987); Oyèrónké Oyěwùmí, "The Translation of Cultures: Engendering Yorùbá Language, Orature, and World-Sense," in *Women, Gender, Religion: A Reader*, ed. Elizabeth A. Castelli (New York: Palgrave, 2001), pp. 76–97; and Rubenstein, "An Anglican Crisis of Comparison."

34. The Lambeth Commission on Communion, *The Windsor Report* (London: Anglican Communion Office, 2004), par. 23.

35. Ibid., par. 42.

36. Robin Eames, foreword to *The Windsor Report*, p. 5.

37. *Windsor Report*, par. 72.

The Report explains that within Anglicanism at least, the concept of autonomy grew out of a colonial context, initially signifying "'independence from the control of the British crown.'"[38] Gradually, such independence gave way to liturgical and ecclesiastical expressions that varied from continent to continent, nation to nation, and town to town, so that with respect to strictly "local issues," provinces and dioceses were understood to be free from any sort of centralized control.[39] This freedom notwithstanding, autonomy in local affairs did not and does not extend to autonomy in *all* affairs; after all, the churches within the Anglican Communion can only be said to be autonomous insofar as they have been granted autonomy by those to whom they are responsible:

> A body is thus, in this sense, "autonomous" *only in relation to others*; autonomy exists in a relation with a wider community or system of which the autonomous entity forms part. The word "autonomous" in this sense actually implies not an isolated individualism, but the idea of being free to determine one's own life within a wider obligation to others. The key idea is autonomy-in-communion, that is, freedom held within interdependence.[40]

So far, this sounds strikingly like Nancy's account of singularities in relation: no body within in the Communion exists, except insofar as it relates to the other bodies composing the Communion. What, then, was the error of the Episcopal Church when it consecrated Gene Robinson, or of the Diocese of New Westminster when it developed a rite for same-sex blessings? Their fault lay in exercising autonomy as though autonomous decisions did not affect and rely upon others—or, to put it more simply, in doing what the rest of the Communion believed to be wrong. This is not the way that churches in communion are meant to behave: "[I]n communion," the Report explains, "each church acknowledges and respects the interdependence and autonomy of the other, putting the needs of the global fellowship before its own."[41] In short, the Episcopal Church and Diocese of New Westminster ought to have waited for—and obeyed—a communion-wide consensus on matters that their sisters and brothers tend to find "scandalous and offensive": "The relational nature of communion

38. Ibid., par. 3.
39. Ibid., par. 74.
40. Ibid., pars. 75–76.
41. Ibid., par. 49.

requires each church to learn more fully what it means to be part of that communion...seeking a *common mind* in essential matters of common concern: in short, to act interdependently, not independently."[42] As Windsor understands it, then, the crisis in the Communion comes down to a refusal of relation itself on the part of the offending dioceses.

What is troubling about this account is that it ends up equating relation with being of a "common mind," that is, with unanimity, or at least the opinion of the majority. If autonomy, like Nancean singularity, is only ever exercised in relation to others, then one would presume that autonomy and relation depend on *otherness* itself. Yet, such otherness is swiftly eclipsed as Windsor's analysis of interdependence reaches its practical, frankly utilitarian conclusion: "if a sufficient number of other Christians" oppose a particular practice, Windsor admonishes, then it ought not to be done.[43] For example, any "acceptable" candidate for the episcopate must be viewed as acceptable across national and hemispheric lines: "The question of acceptability could be posed in a number of ways. Is there any reason to expect that the appointment or election of a particular candidate might prejudice our relations with other provinces? Would the ministry of the individual be recognized and received if he or she were to visit another province? Would the individual be 'translatable'?"[44] The Report does note briefly that, since the Right Reverend Barbara Harris's consecration as Bishop of Massachusetts in 1989, many provinces have refused to recognize the episcopacy of any person who happens to be a woman. Women, in other words, are not quite "translatable" across the Anglican globe. Gender, however, is a degree of disagreement the Communion can bear.[45] Sexual expression, by comparison, is not.

"Not all 'differences' can be tolerated," Windsor explains. "(We know this well enough in the cases of, say, racism or child abuse; we would not say, 'some of us are racists, some of us are not, so let's celebrate our diversity.')"[46] These parenthetical parallels to the "difference" of homosexuality are hardly coincidental. They reflect, first, a persistent equation of (especially male) homosexuality with violence against children and, second, a simplistic and dangerous conviction that those who offend the

42. Ibid., pars. 93, 51 (emphasis added).
43. Ibid., par. 93.
44. Ibid., par. 131.
45. Ibid., pars. 12–21, 126.
46. Ibid., par. 89.

sexual sensibilities of "the Global South" are effectively racists. This highly complicated bind was summarized by the Reverend Martin Smith of Massachusetts, who explained to local Episcopalians that at Lambeth '98, "the few bishops who spoke up for gay and lesbian reality were literally hissed, and denounced in angry whispers as racists and imperialists, for if you supported gays you were opposing the witness of the third world bishops defending purity and scriptural authority."[47] As Bishop Barbara Harris told this same diocese, however, the bishops' "belief in the inerrancy and primacy of Scripture" mirrors the very colonial hermeneutic "that not only had been handed to their forebears, but had been used to suppress them."[48] So it is hard to determine who is colonizing whom.

To recapitulate before moving on, the Communion's official explanation of its own difficulty is that some of the "autonomous" churches have taken autonomy too far and ought to be mindful of their constitutive relation to others. But Windsor's account of "relation," far from designating identity in and through difference, eventually comes down to like-mindedness. Insofar as a province takes interdependence seriously, it will put others ahead of itself, which effectively amounts to submitting to the dominant—or loudest—position on any given matter. Relation thus construed is ultimately a matter of unifying different people by enforcing unanimity. In other words, the Windsor Report considers the Communion to be a "communion" in the Nancean sense: a unified body that, while speaking of autonomy in relation, seeks in the end to assert itself as one, whole, individual. Furthermore, because the most vocal critics of the American and Canadian churches' sexual politics are bishops in Africa, understanding the Communion as "communion" solidifies "the Global South" and its allies, on the one hand, against their alleged opponents, on the other. Given the number of Christians in the southern hemisphere, the former is taken to be the majority. If relation simply means submitting to the majority's opinion, then, heeding it means submitting to this ostensibly singular voice of the southern hemisphere. Resisting such submission is seen not only as a denial of responsibility to others, but also, and more gravely, as a refusal to take the "younger churches" seriously. In short, the northern churches' unwillingness to alter their stance on homosexuality amounts to a "refusal

47. James Solheim, "Sexuality Issues Test Bonds of Affection among Bishops at Lambeth Conference," *Episcopal News Service*, September 3, 1998.

48. James Solheim, "Bishops Interpret Meaning of Lambeth Conference for their Dioceses," *Episcopal News Service*, September 28, 1998.

of relation," which in this global context constitutes an act of neo-colonialism. And yet, again, the gospel defended by the developing Anglican world was a colonial imposition in the first place. Considering the history of the Anglican Church, it is hard not to think it may have brought this crisis on itself.

Axes of Colonialism

In his address to the third International Conference on Afro-Anglicanism in 2005, the Rev. Dr. Michael A. Clarke of Virgin Gorda reminded his sisters and brothers that "the Afro-Anglican Church had its origins, for the most part, either in the cauldron of colonialism or the branding-iron of slavery."[49] Whatever their political and theological inclinations, leaders of all the African churches find themselves in the difficult position of defending and spreading the tradition that helped to enslave and subject them in the first place. In the case of nations colonized by Great Britain, people who choose to remain Anglican do so because they see a crucial distinction between the church and the "cultural vessels" that brought it to Africa.[50] Contemporary Afro-Anglican thought and practice is therefore a matter of teasing out the Book of Common Prayer's distinction between "doctrine" and "discipline"; that is, of distilling the core teachings of the church from the socio-political tincture in which they were administered during the colonial period. As South Africa's Archbishop Ndungane has explained it, "Colonialism brought both pains and joys. It brought the gospel, and for that we shall be eternally grateful....Yet we have even had to work at understanding what the gospel message was and is for us. It came clad in the culture of those who brought it to our continent."[51] Since independence, it has been the task of African Christians to throw off this culture.

Different Afro-Anglican theologians and bishops tend to disagree about the extent to which the churches have overcome this cultural legacy. For example, Archbishop Ndungane believes the scriptural literalism of

49. Michael A. Clarke, "Claiming Elijah's Mantle: Young Adults and the Life of the Church," *Anglican Theological Review* 89:1 (Winter 2007): 64.

50. Conference on Afro-Anglicanism, "The Codrington Consensus: Agreed Statement from the Conference on Afro-Anglicanism," June 17–22, 1985, available at http://www.afroanglican.com/CodringtonConsensus/The%20Codrington%20Consensus.pdf.

51. Njongonkulu Ndungane, "Sermon: Grasping the Past, Taking Hold of the Future: The Challenge of Afro-Anglicanism," *Anglican Theological Review* 89:1 (Winter 2007): 22.

his ultra-conservative colleagues to be a western imposition.[52] Moreover, he argues alongside many of his northern colleagues that as distinct from Calvinists, Anglicans have never understood the Bible to be self-evident. Rather, they have appealed to the "three-legged stool" upon which Richard Hooker said the sixteenth-century Church of England rested: scripture, tradition, and reason. Ndungane therefore maintains that a more authentically African *and* more authentically Anglican theology would be one in which "African culture and tradition were treated as the primary source alongside the Bible."[53] As a place to start, he often suggests the South African teaching of *ubuntu*: "I am because we are."[54]

By contrast, the African bishops who uphold Scripture as "the central authority in our communion"[55] consider the three-legged stool itself to be an Enlightenment accretion to the core message of the gospel. The key to Anglican liberation from British culture, they argue, is the Bible, whose simplicity and trans-culturalism transcend social particularities. As Archbishop Henry Orombi of Uganda has recently written, it is scripture alone that has "ended the assumption that Anglican belief and practice must be clothed in historic British culture."[56] Because of their adherence to "biblical" standards, especially concerning sexuality, both Orombi and his colleague Archbishop Akinola understand their churches literally to be more Anglican than the Church of England itself. For while the Church of England has not committed the egregious offenses of its North American counterparts, it has also not condemned them nearly so roundly as either Orombi or Akinola would like. In fact, it seems to be hovering somewhere between these two poles. And so, upon hearing the news that Rowan Williams had authorized Church of England clergy to live in celibate, same-sex partnerships,[57] Akinola changed the name of his church from "The Anglican Church of Nigeria" to "The Church of Nigeria (Anglican Communion)." The church's constitution now claims to be in communion not "with the Archbishop of Canterbury," as the classic formulation would have it, but rather "with all Anglican Churches, Dioceses, and Provinces

52. Ndungane, "Scripture," p. 240.

53. Ibid., p. 241. Cf. L. William Countryman, "Reading Scripture—and Rereading It," *Anglican Theological Review* 86:4 (Fall 2004): 573–83.

54. Ndungane, "Sermon," p. 22.

55. Orombi, "What Is Anglicanism?"

56. Ibid.

57. Church of England, "House of Bishops Issues Pastoral Statement on Civil Partnerships," July 25, 2005, available at http://www.cofe.anglican.org/news/pr5605.html.

that hold and maintain the 'Historic Faith, Doctrine, Sacrament and Discipline of the one holy, Catholic, and apostolic Church.'"[58] In the light of this redefinition, Canterbury's half-acceptance of same-sex partnerships, along with its inability to call the renegade churches to repentance, has led Akinola publicly to inquire, "Is the Church of England an Anglican Church?"[59]

Since the North American churches have failed to adhere to scriptural discipline and Canterbury has failed to make them do so, "Africa" is taking matters into its own hands. "God has always looked to Africa to save his church," Akinola said in a recent interview. "When Christ sought safety from Herod, he found it in Egypt, in Africa, and when he was completely worn out, an African carried his cross."[60] Now as then, God is "us[ing] Africa to build his church, to save his church from error." The visible sign of this is the network Akinola has established overseas: the Conference of Anglicans in North America (CANA). American parishes that reject the authority of their own bishops and affiliate with CANA come under the diocesan oversight of the Church of Nigeria, which ultimately hopes to declare the Episcopal Church a schism and realign its faithful former members with the majority of the Anglican Communion. To this end, Akinola consecrated a disaffected Episcopal priest in 2006 as a bishop in the Church of Nigeria, and then a year later, traveled to Virginia to install him as chief pastor to Americans who have broken with the Episcopal Church. The Windsor Report, along with Primates' Communiqués, numerous resolutions of the Communion's consultative bodies, and the Archbishop of Canterbury himself, has urged Nigeria, Rwanda, Uganda, and now Kenya to stop interfering with provincial and diocesan structures of authority. But as Akinola understands it, he is "simply doing what Western churches have done for centuries, sending a bishop to serve Anglicans where there is no church to provide one."[61] When faced with charges of reverse colonialism, Akinola tends to lose his patience: "For God's sake let us be. When America invades Afghanistan it is in the name of world peace.

58. Constitution of the Church of Nigeria (Anglican Communion), available at the Church of Nigeria website, http://www.anglican-nig.org/main.php?k_j=1, 3.1. See also Mwamba, "The Anglican Communion."

59. Stephen Bates, "The Real Mr. Big?" *The Guardian*, February 14, 2007.

60. Sarah Simpson, "An African Archbishop Finds Common Ground in Virginia," *The Christian Science Monitor*, January 8, 2007.

61. Lydia Polgreen and Laurie Goodstein, "At Axis of Episcopal Split, an Anti-Gay Nigerian," *New York Times*, December 25, 2006.

When Nigeria moves to Biafra it is an invasion. When England takes the Gospel to another country, it is mission. When Nigeria takes it to America, it is an intrusion. All this imperialistic mentality, it is not fair."[62] Of course, Akinola is not criticizing imperialism so much as he is defending his own right to exercise it alongside everyone else. Which, all things considered, is understandable.

For as he sees it, planting Nigerian churches in North America is merely an act of self-defense. The true colonialists are those members of the northern churches who have imposed their schismatic beliefs, their gay bishop, and homosexuality itself upon the inhabitants of the southern hemisphere. As one Nigerian Anglican put it, "homosexuality is a western thing. In Nigeria we don't condone it, we don't tolerate it."[63] This perception is hardly limited to Anglicans; President Robert Mugabe of Zimbabwe has repeatedly called homosexuality a "'Western' phenomenon imported to Africa by the European colonists," and this view is shared by many in sub-Saharan Africa, including, most dangerously, health workers.[64] For the sake of their political as well as their physical well-being, African gay-rights groups have sought to offer evidence to the contrary. Nigerian activist Dorothy Aken'Ova has published a "Preliminary Survey of Homosexuality in Nigeria," which argues that "the fact that there is a name for [homosexuality] in various languages in Nigeria indicates that the practice existed well before colonialism."[65] Davis MacIyalla, a Nigerian Anglican and founder of the lesbian and gay-rights group Changing Attitudes Nigeria, argues that far from bringing homosexuality to Nigeria, the West brought sodomy laws and the British penal code. Not only does MacIyalla note that each of the local languages have terms for same-sex practices ("we call it *supe* in the south, *gwobo* in Yoruba, and *dandaudu* in the North"), but, as he explained to a group of New York Episcopalians in the spring of 2007, the priestesses of pre-colonial goddess traditions were

62. Ruth Gledhill, "For God's Sake," *The Times* (London), July 5, 2007.
63. Lydia Polgreen, "Nigerian Anglicans Seeing Gay Challenge to Orthodoxy," *New York Times*, December 18, 2005.
64. Kendall, "'When a Woman Loves a Woman' in Lesotho: Love, Sex, and the (Western) Construction of Homophobia," in *Boy Wives, Female Husbands*, ed. Stephen O. Murray and Will Roscoe (New York: Palgrave, 1998), pp. 223, 250.
65. Cesnabmihilo Dorothy Aken'Ova, "Preliminary Survey of Homosexuality in Nigeria," presented to the Commission of Status of Women, March 7, 2000, available at the International Women's Health Coalition website, http://www.iwhc.org/resources/homosexualitysurvey.cfm.

renowned for sleeping with women.[66] In other words, "the West didn't bring us homosexuality; it brought us homophobia."[67]

The most likely answer to this disagreement between opponents and proponents of gay rights in Africa is that they are both right. As Foucault demonstrates, the category of "homosexuality" was produced through the modern psychiatric cataloguing of sexual practices. While Foucault knows full well that there were men who slept with men and women who slept with women before the nineteenth century, he argues that it was only with the intensification of the *scientia sexualis* that homosexual practice was forged into an identity.[68] In this light, Ugandan priest and theolgian Kevin Ward argues that the West brought homosexuality *and* homophobia to Africa: "same-sex relations have always been present and, to a limited extent, acknowledged in African societies.... but without the essentializing of sexuality which has been characteristic of western constructions of homosexuality in the last hundred years."[69] Either way, to return to Archbishop Akinola's perspective, condoning homosexuality in the church would amount to a betrayal of Scripture and Africa all at once. The continent was converted one time, he seems to say, and will not simply accept theological revisions that the northern churches decide to hand down a hundred years later: "The missionaries brought the word of God here and showed us the way of life," he said in an interview with the London *Times*, "We have seen the way of life, and we rejoice in it. Now you are telling me this way of life is not right. I have to do something else. Keep it for yourself. I do not want it."[70]

Of course, from the perspective of the North American Anglicans who support the "full inclusion" of lesbian and gay people in the church, Nigeria is not being forced to revise its own position at all. It is being asked to live with difference, rather than uniformity, within the communion. As

66. Davis MacIyalla, address delivered at the Church of the Holy Apostles, New York, NY, July 19, 2007. Amadiume argues that relationships between women priestesses and their wives were strictly non-sexual; see Amadiume, *Male Daughters, Female Husbands*, p. 7. For a critique of Amadiume's disavowal of lesbianism, see Kendall, "'When a Woman Loves a Woman,'" pp. 238–39.

67. Davis, address to the Church of the Holy Apostles.

68. "The sodomite had been a temporary aberration; the homosexual was now a species" (Michel Foucault, *The History of Sexuality: An Introduction, Volume I*, trans. Robert Hurley [New York: Vintage Books, 1990], p. 43).

69. Kevin Ward, "Same-Sex Relations in Africa and the Debate on Homosexuality in East African Anglicanism," *Anglican Theological Review* 84:1 (Winter 2002): 87.

70. Gledhill, "For God's Sake."

Bishop Robinson has explained, "The Episcopal Church is not looking for agreement, only for permission to live out its life and ministry in the context in which we live. It is not asking the Church in Nigeria to raise up gay and lesbian priests and bishops. We are only asking to be allowed to do so because it seems to be where God is leading us in our context."[71] As is hopefully becoming clear, then, Akinola and Robinson are operating with two different notions of the nature of community. As far as Akinola is concerned, being in communion means being in agreement, while Robinson understands it to mean interdependency in and through dissonance. What Robinson does not quite acknowledge, however, is that community thus configured does not permit the easy separation of one "context" from another. As Nancy argues, being-in-common necessarily entails a mutual contamination between and among parties, and it is precisely this contamination that Robinson's opponents are most resolved to stave off.

The fear among conservative African leaders, sacred and secular alike, seems indeed to be a fear of contamination, as though laxity toward same-sex behavior will cause it to spread everywhere. Robert Mugabe has in this vein called homosexuality a "sickness" threatening to consume his nation.[72] Similarly, Akinola typically characterizes homosexuality either as a "cancerous lump" on the body of Christ,[73] or as an infection threatening to spread anarchy throughout Nigeria: "[I]f care is not taken, our country will be one where you can do whatever you want to do."[74] There is, of course, a scriptural remedy for infection, which is to cut ties to the infected. In a recent communiqué entitled "The Road to Lambeth," the primates of the Council of Anglican Provinces in Africa (CAPA) therefore remind the Communion of Paul's "requirement that believers not associate with openly immoral church members (1 Corinthians 5:9–13, 2 Thessalonians 3–14)."[75] In this Pauline spirit, they insist that, in order to remain in

71. Andrew Collier and Ruth Gledhill, "Church of England 'Would Shut Down' without Its Gay Clergy," *The Times* (London), July 27, 2007.

72. Andrew Meldrum, *Where We Have Hope: A Memoir of Zimbabwe* (New York: Atlantic Monthly Press, 2004), p. 103.

73. "Nigeria Bishops Scorn US 'Cancer,'" *BBC News*, July 4, 2006.

74. Gledhill, "For God's Sake."

75. Primates of the Council of Anglican Provinces in Africa (CAPA), "The Road to Lambeth," September 19, 2006, available at the Global South Anglican website, http://www.globalsouthanglican.org/index.php/comments/the_road_to_lambeth_presented_at_capa. Days after the communiqué was issued, Archbishop Ndungane of the Province of Southern Africa announced that not all the members of CAPA had been consulted before the communiqué had been released, and that a significant number of them disagreed with

the Communion, the North American churches must "reverse their policies and prune their personnel."[76] And while they are waiting for the bad leaves to be cut off the Anglican family tree, the leaders within CAPA will continue to plant bishops and churches in North America to minister to dissenting parishes. CAPA thus sees its missions to North America as a way of saving souls and stopping the spread of sinfulness at the same time. Archbishop Bernard Malango of Central Africa illustrates this dual-function with a parable about a neighbor's house that catches on fire: "[A]nd if [my neighbor] says to me 'I like my house to be on fire,' what do I do? Well, I go and rescue the children first of all, and then I put out the fire before it spreads to my house as well."[77]

The bishops of CAPA therefore understand what Robinson does not want to admit: that when bodies exist in community with one another, the integrity of each is constantly undermined and contaminated by otherness. It is for this reason that they are insisting upon the uniformity that characterizes a communion, rather than the mutual interruption of community. To be sure, the leaders of the Global South across the board have good reason to be suspicious of foreign interruptions. As Akinola knows all too well, African modernity has more or less consisted of a string of them:

In our human existence in this world, there was a time Africans were slaves, but we came out of it. But what again followed? Political slavery, under colonial administration. Somehow, we came out of it. Then economic slavery: World Bank, IMF would tell you what to do with your money and your own resources. Now it is spiritual slavery, and we have to resist this. They had us as human slaves, political slaves, and economic slaves. They want to come for spiritual slaves. Now we won't accept it.[78]

And so the Communion's original sin refuses to leave it alone: founded upon a strategy of socio-political imposition, every move it makes seems to one party or another a colonizing gesture. This being the case, the only available strategy seems to be reciprocation: England colonized Nigeria,

many of its arguments. See "Ndungane Disavows Global South Communique," *Episcopal News Service*, September 25, 2006, available at the Episcopal Church website, http://www.episcopalchurch.org/3577_78023_ENG_HTM.htm.

76. CAPA, "The Road to Lambeth."
77. Bates, *A Church at War*, p. 29.
78. Adeyanju, "Homosexual Priests."

which is looking to counter-colonize the very communities now threatening to re-colonize *it*.

The story grows even more complicated when one considers that the African resistance to North American sexual imperialism has been partially orchestrated by North Americans themselves. During the year leading up to the Lambeth Conference of 1998, members of the conservative American Anglican Council (AAC) organized preparatory meetings with potential allies from Africa, Asia, and South America. Such meetings took place in Dallas and the Great Lakes, and were intended as a means of solidifying a global majority opinion against the ordination of gay clergy and the authorization of blessings for same-sex couples.[79] At the Lambeth Conference itself, the AAC set up headquarters in a Franciscan center on campus. There, volunteers stood ready to provide the bishops of the southern hemisphere with food, tea, coffee, mobile phones to communicate quickly with their American colleagues, and "crib sheets" that reiterated the collective consensus against homosexuality. All told, this operation cost over £40,000 ($66,484 at the July 1998 rate of conversion) and was all financed by the AAC.[80]

Sources of funding for the AAC itself have become increasingly obscured over the last ten years, as public financial documents have become less and less detailed. What *have* been demonstrated are the organization's close financial and geographical ties (the two offices are next door to one another in Washington, DC) to the Institute for Religion and Democracy (IRD).[81] Founded by Michael Novak and Richard Neuhouse in 1981, the IRD works to inhibit the growth of "liberalism" within the mainline American churches. According to Jim Naughton's "Following the Money Trail," the IRD helped the AAC to target Howard F. Ahmonson, who has shouldered a rising percentage of the AAC's annual budget since he financed the Dallas meeting in 1997.[82] Most recently, the IRD has launched a "Reforming America's Churches Project," which seeks

79. See Christopher T. Cantrell, "The Dallas Statement: from the Anglican Life and Witness Conference," September 24, 1997, available at the Road to Emmaus website, http://theroadtoemmaus.org/RdLb/32Ang/Epis/DallasStmt.htm.

80. Bates, *A Church at War*, p. 131.

81. See Jim Naughton, "Following the Money," *The Washington Window* of the Episcopal Diocese of Washington, April 2006, http://www.edow.org/follow; Alan Cooperman, "Gay Bishop-Elect: Foes Have Agenda," *Washington Post*, October 24, 2003; and Bates, *A Church at War*, p. 186.

82. Naughton, "Following the Money," p. 3.

to "restructure the permanent governing structure" of the Presbyterian, Methodist, and Episcopal churches in order to "discredit and diminish the Religious Left's influence."[83] The "Episcopal Action" wing of this initiative looks to replace "theologically flawed" bishops, however duly elected, with men whose agenda matches their own. Therefore, whenever the AAC supports the consecration of a North American as bishop in the Church of Rwanda, Uganda, Nigeria, or Kenya, it is safe to assume IRD money is behind it.

As for Archbishop Akinola, when confronted with the suggestion that his crusade against homosexuality might be the product of vast financial and spiritual blackmail (or "whitemale," as one African Primate suggested to me), he charges that this is yet another instance of the West's unmitigated narcissism. "Like a joke," Akinola told a Nigerian reporter in response to accusations of having accepted American bribes, "they thought that as Africans, we don't know what we are doing; particularly the Americans and you know they always have their ways politically and economically."[84] In the same interview, however, Akinola proudly tells his interlocutor that his Conference of Anglicans in North America is growing by leaps and bounds, and that these defectors from the Episcopal Church "are not just ordinary Americans; they are leaders and well-recognized people—who is who in Washington, DC."[85] Clearly, then, Akinola is aware of these ties to powerful right-wing lobbyists, and yet he insists that the commitment to stamping out homosexuality above all else is his own: "[T]here is no price tag on Akinola's forehead."[86]

Accusations to the contrary are common, however—not only among liberal North Americans, but also among moderate African Anglicans themselves. In an address to the most recent Afro-Anglican conference, the former Provincial Secretary and Personal Assistant to the Archbishop of Central Africa asked his audience to consider "in reality who or what is driving the current debate: is it events in the West, politics in the West,

83. Cited in ibid., p. 1. Naughton's footnote references a document entitled, "Reforming America's Churches Project 2001–2004," by the Institute on Religion and Democracy, 200, Washington, DC, which I have been unable to find. Calls to the IRD have been met with an acknowledgment that they "worked on" such a document, but they do not know where it might be. The IRD directs all inquiries regarding the project to the Institute on Religion and Democracy website, http://www.ird-renew.org.

84. Adeyanju, "Homosexual Priests."

85. Ibid.

86. Ibid.

or money from the West? I only ask the question."[87] Similarly, the *New York Times* cites Archbishop Ndungane as asking, "'Whose agenda is this? Definitely in my view, this is not God's agenda.' Nor is it the average Anglican's agenda, he said. 'I interact with people on the ground. They don't care about the lifestyles of people in America.'"[88] More importantly, these "people on the ground" are being neglected by their leaders, who cannot seem to get their minds out of Gene Robinson's bedroom long enough to ensure that their people are fed and their schools and hospitals funded. Esther Mombo, Kenyan delegate to the Anglican Women's Network, has noted the irony of certain bishops' calling homosexuality un-African when "they seem to spend most of their time on it. Who is paying for these voices to be heard?... Who is using whom in this debate? For whose benefit is it taking place?... These and many more questions are being asked by those in the pews. Who will give them answers?"[89]

Of the many questions from the pews that call for answers, Mombo notes in particular her constituents' disbelief that their own bishops are dedicating themselves to what they see as a western debate, "at the expense of the far more pressing and urgent issues of mission and ministry... [such as] poverty, feeding the hungry, and dealing with the sick, especially those infected with and affected by HIV/AIDS."[90] The same point has been raised in public addresses by Archbishop Tutu[91] and by Archbishop Ndungane,[92] who adds to this list of errors Akinola's silence on the matter of stoning a woman to death in Nigeria.[93] British and American columnists have listed even more of the Archbishop's alleged failures, including his refusal to condemn either the rigged elections in Nigeria, or Robert Mugabe in Tanzania, or genocide in Sudan.[94] To all of this, Akinola responds, quite

87. George W. Brandt, Jr., "Celebrating the Gifts of Afro-Anglicanism," *Anglican Theological Review* 89:1 (Winter 2007): 33.

88. Sharon LaFraniere, "Inviting Africa's Anglicans to Gather under a Bigger Tent," *New York Times*, February 10, 2007.

89. Esther Mombo, "The Windsor Report: A Paradigm Shift," *Anglican Theological Review* 89:1 (Winter 2007): 77.

90. Ibid., p. 77.

91. See Derrick Z. Jackson, "The Antigay Obsession," *Boston Globe*, November 18, 2006.

92. See Njongonkulu Ndungane, "Sermon," and LaFraniere, "Inviting Africa's Anglicans."

93. Bates, *A Church at War*, p. 191.

94. See Bates, "The Real Mr. Big?" and Wayne Besen, "Anything But Straight: Nigeria's Frequent Flyer," *Falls Church News-Press*, May 3, 2007.

simply, that homosexuality is more important. "They are urging us to think more of our poverty, HIV/AIDS and other problems and forget this matter [of homosexuality]," Akinola told a Nigerian reporter. "But Jesus told his disciples that 'you will always have the poor with you.' We are talking souls, eternity and kingdom of God, and you cannot equate it with anything. HIV/AIDS will come and go; poverty will come and go. But the matter of faith is eternity. They are not the same level."[95] So that is that: homosexuality is worth more time and energy than poverty and disease, because the former kills the soul, while the latter simply kill the body. It is at this point that dialogue begins to look genuinely impossible.

Communication and Communicability

Since the Most Reverend Katharine Jefferts Schori was elected Presiding Bishop of the Episcopal Church in the spring of 2006, she has been asked how she plans to build bridges across the profound rifts in the Communion. After all, very few Anglican provinces consecrate women to the episcopate, and some dioceses as close as Fort Worth and San Joaquin still refuse to ordain women to the priesthood. Bishop Jefforts Schori's consistent response has been that she intends to go forward with the work of the church: to feed the hungry, heal the sick, and make peace in a world ravaged by war.[96] To focus this work, Jefferts Schori has appealed to the Millennium Development Goals[97] as a site of mutual concern across political and hemispheric lines. Two days before her installation in November, the Presiding Bishop-elect tried to initiate reconciliation in a letter addressed to four primates of the Global South, who intended to fly to Falls Church, Virginia, later that month to meet with Episcopal Church leaders who opposed Jefferts Schori's consecration. "In the spirit of Lambeth 1998," she wrote,

> the Episcopal Church has identified the Millennium Development Goals as the framework for our missional work in the coming years. I would hope we might see the common interest we all have for seeing these

95. Adeyanju, "Homosexual Priests."

96. Katharine Jefferts Schori, "Investiture Sermon," November 4, 2006, available at the Episcopal Church website, http://www.episcopalchurch.org/3577_79214_ENG_HTM. htm, and Schori, "Sermon for Seating Ceremony," November 5, 2006, http://www.episcopalchurch.org/3577_79270_ENG_HTM.htm.

97. See the UN Millennium Development Goals website, http://www.un.org/ millenniumgoals.

Goals met, as they provide a concrete image of the Reign of God in our own day, where the hungry are fed, the thirsty watered, and the prisoners of disease and oppression set free.... I hope that during your visit you might be willing to pay a call on me, so that we might begin to build toward such a missional relationship. If that is a possibility, I hope you will contact this office as soon as possible. I would be more than happy to alter my schedule to accommodate you.[98]

Archbishops Akinola (Nigeria), Gomez (West Indies), Nzimbi (Kenya), and Akrofi (West Africa) not only declined this invitation, but they also refused to sit or share the Eucharist with the Presiding Bishop at the 2007 Primates' Meeting in Dar es Salaam.[99] In "The Road to Lambeth," these and three other primates explained their refusal thus: "We recognize the strategy employed by Episcopal Church and certain Communion bodies to substitute talk of Millennium Development Goals for the truth of Scripture. These choices are false alternatives: it is Christ of Scripture who compels us to care for the poor and afflicted."[100] In other words, questions of poverty, hunger, and disease cannot even be addressed until all parties submit to the authority of Scripture;[101] and Jefferts Schori, who as Bishop of Nevada approved Gene Robinson's episcopacy, has not submitted.

The central message of "The Road to Lambeth" is that "the time has come for the North American churches to repent or depart." The bishops of the Global South Steering Committee have had enough of conversation with their recalcitrant siblings: "Due to this breakdown of discipline, we are not sure that we can in good conscience continue to spend our money and our prayers on behalf of a body that proclaims two Gospels,

98. Katharine Jefferts Schori, Letter to The Most Reverends Peter Akinola, Drexel Gomez, Benjamin Nzimbi, and Justice Akrofi, November 2, 2006, available at the Episcopal Church website, http://www.episcopalchurch.org/78703_79163_ENG_HTM.htm.

99. See Rachel Harden, "Primates Head into a Storm in Dar es Salaam," *Church Times*, February 9, 2007.

100. CAPA, "The Road to Lambeth."

101. This argument is strikingly similar to that which Cardinal Joseph Ratzinger made to Latin American bishops and scholars in 1984, chastising liberation theology for privileging politics and things earthly over true doctrine and things eternal: "[L]iberation is first and foremost liberation from the radical slavery of sin" (Congregation for the Doctrine of the Faith, "Instruction on Certain Aspects of the 'Theology of Liberation,'" August 6, 1984). The parallel may or may not have something to do with Ratzinger's public support for the conservative Anglican alliance, which he voiced in a letter to a 2003 meeting in Dallas, Texas (see Bates, *A Church at War*, p. 198).

the Gospel of Christ and the Gospel of Sexuality."[102] The primates add that they will not attend the Lambeth Conference of 2008 unless the North American churches are either absent or penitent. Either way, submission is the prerequisite of conversation: "Let the Western churches first affirm God's plan for the sexes, then let us dialogue."[103]

By imposing such a condition upon dialogue, however, "The Road to Lambeth" forecloses dialogue itself; for what kind of conversation could possibly take place only after all parties agree to say the same thing? What seems clear is that the "Road to Lambeth" signatories are seeking not conversation, but rather unanimity. Just as Christ is of one substance with the Father, so must his body on earth be perfectly, essentially *one*. Anyone who vitiates this unity is free to leave the Communion. We will recall that this is more or less the position of the Windsor Report, which gradually equates communion with "common-mindedness." "The Road to Lambeth" primates simply take this equation to its logical conclusion: since relation means respecting the majority opinion, the minority must either give way or forfeit relation itself. The question, then, is whether or not this is the only theologically justifiable way to construe Christian life together. I would submit that it is not.

In fact, a different understanding of the nature of communion can be found in the Episcopal Church's response to the Windsor Report, *To Set Our Hope on Christ*. Far from demanding uniformity, the "communion" sketched in this document names a nexus of differences akin to Nancy's concept of community:

> The unity maintained by Anglicanism, in contrast to other churches, has always been a unity in difference (*Windsor Report* 66), a rich and diverse unity (*Windsor Report* 62). A unity with this degree of internal diversity requires a communion that is exhibited and maintained, not by simple agreement among all parties, but by respectful listening to those with whom one disagrees (*Windsor Report* 65), by a willingness to render account to one another in love, and a readiness to learn from one another (*Windsor Report* 67).[104]

Despite the frequent indications of consonance with the Windsor Report, *To Set Our Hope on Christ* is actually offering a profoundly different vision of life in communion. First, rather than subsuming all difference

---

102. CAPA, "The Road to Lambeth."
103. Ibid.
104. ECUSA, *To Set Our Hope on Christ*, 4.17.

à la Windsor, this understanding of unity depends structurally upon the persistence of differences. Second, these differences are not papered over but rather drawn into relation, by means of constant communication. As we have seen, communication—or communicability—is precisely what Akinola and his colleagues are resisting, looking to remove cancers and cut out infections, lest their people fall prey to the same diseases of scriptural laxity that plague their sisters and brothers overseas. What *To Set Our Hope on Christ* suggests, however, is that there is no community without such a risk of contamination. Community's communicability means that it will never be at one with itself; nevertheless, this fragmentation constitutes the inessential essence of unity: "We are not a Communion in agreement on all matters, yet may God grant us to be a Communion that bears the wounds of Christ, a communion of differences yet reconciled in the Cross, a Communion broken yet united in love for the crucified and risen Savior."[105] The body of Christ, one might say, becomes itself precisely inasmuch as it unworks itself.

Contrary to the Windsor Report's assessment, then, finding a way forward for the Anglican Communion will not be a matter of waking parts of the church to relation, but rather of determining what sort of relation it ought to pursue. There are those for whom communion requires unanimity and those for whom unity only genuinely takes place across disagreement.[106] There are those who seek to impose "order and discipline" upon difference, and there are those, like the members of the Anglican Women's Network, who humbly propose that "perhaps church order and ecclesiastical discipline may not be the ultimate need for the Anglican Communion."[107] There are those who separate out "acceptable and unacceptable forms of diversity,"[108] and those who ask, *not that all difference be uncritically accepted*, but that all differences speak, communicate, and share themselves.[109]

Instances of the "communal" model of relation are in no short supply: nations, race, genders, and socio-economic classes all operate on the principle of subsuming distinctions under one essence. Instances of

105. Ibid., 1.6.

106. See ibid., 1.5.

107. Mary Sudman Donovan, "Anglican Women: Empowering Each Other to Further God's Kingdom," *Journal of Anglican Studies* 5:1 (2007): 67.

108. The Lambeth Commission on Communion, *Windsor Report*, par. 71.

109. The Episcopal Church draws a parallel between its current position and that of Peter, called to account for his irregular baptism of Gentiles (ECUSA, *To Set Our Hope*, 2.10).

community are harder to find, but an appeal to Archbishop Ndungane's theological apparatus of "scripture, reason, faith, culture, experience, and tradition" produces at least three. There is, first of all, the Eucharist. To be sure, one interpretation of this rite construes it as instituting and confirming perfect unity among its members. This is the reason some Primates have declared themselves "unable" to commune with the Primate of the Episcopal Church. Whether because of her gender or her stance on human sexuality, she is *essentially* different and therefore can only vitiate Eucharistic purity. Consequently, a different interpretation must animate those members who communicate despite profound differences and a very painful history. Along this interpretation, the Eucharistic rite creates communion not by enforcing uniformity, but by being *broken*, shared out, and taken up into different bodies *that remain different*. Even "essential" disagreements, then, are not inimical to the Eucharist; to the contrary, they allow it to take place in the first place. A second model for Christian being-in-common is the Trinity itself—the "'difference-in-relation' of the divine persons"[110]—whose essence is nothing but the loving movement between and among them. And finally, in searching for a way to open the communal monolith out to conversation, "interweaving, and the sharing of singularities,"[111] one could call with Archbishop Ndungane upon the South African concept of *ubuntu*. As Ndungane reminds his Anglican brothers and sisters, *ubuntu* "can only be experienced in rich, varied community" and names the relationship between vastly different people who nonetheless are committed "to live and care for others; to act kindly to one another."[112] Those bound and held apart by *ubuntu*, rather than separating themselves from potential contamination, affirm the admittedly frightening truth that, when being is in-common, this contamination is all there is; that "I am because we are."[113] In spite of all that "we" have failed to be.

110. ECUSA, *To Set Our Hope*, 4.19.
111. Nancy, "The Inoperative Community," p. 27.
112. Ndungane, "Sermon," p. 24.
113. Ibid., p. 22.

1968: The Birth of Secular Eternity

Zoltán Balázs

One of the most idiosyncratic features of human communities is the way they think of time, even though there has been little reflection on that in political theory. To mention just one example that indicates how different the collective experience of time may be, I allude to the South American Aymara people, who associate the past with the spatial front, and the future with the spatial back. That is, past is ahead of us, and future is behind us. In this framework *progress in time* makes perhaps less sense, since the very concept of progress is, at its root, advance in space, and we can hardly *move* back to the past. (In science fiction, time travel to the past is a problem just because we presuppose that in the past we would be as free to act as we are in the present, and shall be in the future—that is, we take our present back with us to the past!)

The dominant Western vision of time is, obviously, the opposite. We look forward and constantly move to the future, whereas the past becomes more and more distant. Of course, our tradition is not as simple or unanimous as this. There are different strands of conceptualizing and perceiving time in it. The modern age, for instance, has been marked by the epochal conflict between two profoundly different political attitudes: that of glorifying the distant past, and that of awaiting the fulfillment of all political prophecies. What is common in these different strands of time-perception is, as Hannah Arendt discovered, the significance that both progressivists and reactionaries attribute to birth, to the beginning. Not only individuals but also political communities are born, miraculously or planned. The present is interesting only either because we need it to nurture what was born long ago, to amend and augment the past, as Arendt says, or because it is pregnant with the future. The obsession with the beginning is, thus, central to both the conservative and the liberal mind, and makes them share the same conception of time, in which past and future, represented by the corresponding political forces, fight the ultimate war of Western political history.

In my view, this great and, in some ways, apocalyptic struggle has come to an end, at least in Europe. In Western Europe, the Second World War ushered in liberal democracies run by parties that essentially gave up not only the political contest between the forces of past and future, but also the pursuit of moral ideals. And they made a compromise to deal only with welfare affairs. Old Europe died, was buried, and no new Europe was born. Nor was there any reason to wait for a new one.

In Eastern Europe, the final victory of the Communist ideology, with Lenin's prediction that in Communism the state would no longer exist, or would require only the most primitive administrative skills to manage, led to a similar result. The "last fight" was faced and won, so what? The newborn had to be protected, of course, but conservatism just does not fit professional progressivists and revolutionaries. Yuri Gagarin's 1961 journey was not a first, but a last one. It was the last beginning. And, in some ways symbolically, he died in 1968.

This is, I think, what the 1968 revolutionaries failed to see at first. Contrary to their presuppositions, the forces of the past did not exist any more. Contrary to their perceptions, the present was not pregnant any more. Hence—and this is my thesis, put inevitably in rough terms—1968, at least in Europe, essentially changed the conception of time and introduced the present as the ultimate category of political thinking. However, this is not a present related to the past or to the future, that is, a present favored against past or future, yet still understood in their terms. This is an eternal present, characterized by a consciousness cleansed from any reference either to the past or to the future.

The eternal present is basically a timeless, atemporal time. It is a theological notion, of course, and may be interpreted in two ways. God does not need time, for He created it and exists ontologically independently of it. But theologians tend to think that both the saved and the damned will still experience something like time, for, as Kant put it in "The End of All Things," a state in which there is no time is a dreadful state, since no change, no reflection, no emotion, no pleasure, and no pain is conceivable there. But, as he himself stresses, we cannot help yearning for eternity, which must, therefore, contain something humane as well. For him it is our eternal, unchanging moral maxims that give us a pre-taste of an eternity that is not inhumane. For theologians, the saved live in the state of the *visio beatifica*, enjoying the sight of God, yet they are still *waiting* not only for a new Heaven but also for a new Earth.

How can such a relativized (that is, not entirely atemporal) conception of the eternal present make sense in our world? Only analogically, of course. But analogies must be grounded in aspects of real identity.

One of them was already mentioned. Contemporary Europe is not a result of the epic wars of modernity. She is after the Apocalypse. But she is not related to it. *She was not born.* And this was finally revealed to her in 1968. One great and enduring act of that year was the ultimate condemnation and rejection of politics, of anything related to power, to political ideals, to institutions, to collective forms and norms. Communism died that year, too. It just took twenty more years to bury it, but the guiding principle of 1989 was still Václav Havel's and György Konrád's antipolitics. But politics is made within time, it presupposes time, being a joint business of past, present, and future. In the eternal present, however, time is unreal, and there is no room for politics, for collective action. European governments look more and more like ghosts on the stage of world politics, and whereas they have agreed upon a constitution that proclaims its independence from past and future, they simply lacked the political power to tie it up with the present. The new French president wanted to overcome the ghosts of 1968. But isn't he himself one of them?

Second, does the eternal present entail a sort of hedonism? Hedonism, the enjoyment of the present, favoring it over future and past, is no doubt related to eternity. But it is still a heroic attitude, so to speak, a fight within time, fought on two fronts, against ancestors and descendants. It is still part of the old framework. It is only when severed from any time-reference that enjoyment becomes an aspect of eternity. But this is no more a kind of hedonistic, orgiastic pleasure. Remember: *visio beatifica* is seeing and getting saturated by the sight of God. We, the heirs of 1968, are fully accustomed to the comforts of modern life, and rarely think we enjoy them. What we are more often called to enjoy are things to see and watch.

Third, in eternity there cannot be suffering. The dominant, that is, essentially 1968-type of liberalism tends to think that cruelty and coercion are the greatest vices for they cause suffering that is absolutely intolerable and unacceptable.[1] The main purpose of society is to minimize or avoid suffering. The classical liberal maxim, the harm principle, which permits everything for everybody provided that no harm to others is caused, is now generally thought to be inefficient. The political community has a primary duty to alleviate or terminate suffering, without regard to its causes and circumstances, and without regard to the scope and depth of intervention. The ground for it is that suffering and pain dehumanizes and thus makes us unfit for eternity. They are not simply bad; they are outrageous. The right for euthanasia is most firmly grounded in the emotions that the sight of suffering elicits in us.

Fourth, it is hard to find anybody in mainstream European politics who does not subscribe to the idea that human rights, and especially human dignity, overrides any other moral and political value. The aspect of the eternal present is unmistakable here. Human rights do not change, neither in collective nor in personal histories. Like Pallas Athene, modern children are born with a complete armory— composed not of weapons, but of human rights. Rights cannot be defended or attacked; they cannot be debated or speculated about, like justice, order, freedom, loyalty, and other moral concepts. Perhaps, in Edmund Burke's time, metaphysical rights really were like "rays of light which pierce into a dense medium," but in eternity we see them as and what they are: transparent and unchanging.

1. For a penetrating criticism of this view, advanced most notably by Judith Shklar and Richard Rorty, see John Kekes, *Against Liberalism* (Ithaca, NY: Cornell UP, 1997).

Fifth, we tend to favor the present in everyday practices, too. Again, this is not a hedonistic and individualistic feeling of *carpe diem*. This is a collective, rather than an individual, obsession with time, or with being up-to-date. Unlike Faust, we do not want to stop time because our goals have been achieved. We are already lords of time, hence we must make it pass. Our communication means, mobile phones, Internet access, reality shows, news channels, digital and web cameras, our passion for watching sporting events, especially those where new records can be expected, serve this collective purpose: to make time pass together, and to prove ourselves to be masters of time.

Kant thought that divine eternity would be dreadful for us. We saw that the eternal life is probably different for us human beings. It is dynamic rather than static. But dynamism does not necessarily imply the old conception of time, consisting of past, present, and future. We know what Kant did not, for we experience it, that the eternal present thrives on change. First of all, note the endless *talk* about change. Talking about change has not changed a bit in the past two decades. It is as if we were never allowed to stop to think about talking. And since social discourses deal mainly with change, we are almost never allowed to think otherwise than in terms of change. In the perfect present, as in Communism, change was ultimately prohibited. In the eternal present, change is practically prescribed.

But are we really masters of time? Everything that is being done now, will be forgotten in the next moment, for there is only one present: the eternal one. Anything that once existed but does not exist anymore, never did exist. Anything that does not exist yet, will never exist. It seems we have no power over time, after all. And therefore we do not know where we are. This is why anguish and sadness fills the earthly eternal present, lurking behind the joy of the saved. The inhabitants of the earthly eternal present are nowhere. They are not anxious and agitated by fear. Rather, they are sad and anguished by their powerlessness. For those living in the eternal present lack the basic human political, i.e., community-creating, capacities recorded by Hannah Arendt: the power to forgive and the power to make promises. By forgiving, we have power over the past. By promises, we have power over the future. But in order to forgive, we need the past; and to make promises, we need the future. Without them, we lose our power. And since we have no past, we cannot remember, we cannot enliven it, we cannot forgive—we cannot act. Since we have no future, we cannot make plans and anticipations, we cannot justify our actions, we cannot make promises—again, we cannot act. Only God, who alone is Lord of Eternity, knows where the way back to time lies.[2]

---

2. The comparisons drawn between the last four types owe much in spirit to Aurel Kolnai's seminal paper "Three Riders of the Apocalypse," in *Privilege and Liberty and Other Essays in Political Philosophy*, ed. Daniel J. Mahoney (Lanham, MA: Lexington Books, 1999).

Baseball Stadiums
and American Audiences

Kenneth H. Marcus

What is happening to America's favorite national pastime? There seems to be something new afoot with baseball stadiums and the audiences who frequent them. A sense of nostalgia characterizes the creation of many new stadiums in the United States, and it accompanies a change in class among the audiences who fill those stadiums. Together, these two aspects are altering a sport that, in the words of cultural historian David Nasaw, traditionally represented a form of social democracy.[1] In contrast, baseball today is transforming itself into a middle- and upper-class pastime for audiences, especially families, willing to spend enormous sums to enjoy a nostalgic experience at the ballpark.

Consider the new AT&T Park in San Francisco. Opened in 2000 to herald the new millennium as the new home of the Giants, it is a combination of both old and contemporary that recalls the classical ball fields of Fenway Park in Boston, Ebbets Field in Brooklyn, and Wrigley Field in Chicago. The seats are relatively close to the players, with some seats "within 48 feet of the playing field."[2] Riveted steel girders underpinning the stadium are plainly visible, which recalls early twentieth-century designs. The asymmetrical outfield configuration also reminds the viewer of those earlier ballparks. Even the location is telling: it lies adjacent to an old section of the city rather than apart from it in the suburbs. But don't let the nostalgia fool you. There is an explosive sound system with widescreen video, and attached to your seats are containers for drinks, as if you were watching the game in a movie theater or in front of your entertainment center at home.

Who are the audiences at the AT&T Park? Despite the incessant rock music that pounds out between changes at bat, the target is clearly families: middle-class folks who want a safe, controlled environment, complete with a playground (such as a slide and a giant glove provided by the Coca-Cola Company) and plenty of concessions for the kids. The men's bathrooms even have places to change diapers. In terms of class, the prices alone are telling; paying between $42 and

---

1. David Nasaw, *Going Out: The Rise and Fall of Public Amusements* (Cambridge, MA: Harvard UP, 1993), p. 102.
2. HOK Sport website, "AT&T Park," http://www.hoksport.com/projects/att.html.

$98 for regular, weekend seats (somewhat less on weekdays) suggests that the working class—the traditional base of fans of the sport since its earliest days—is scarcely able to afford the price of admission, let alone the high prices at the food stands.

Nor is AT&T Park alone. Across the country, similar ballparks are quietly rising up, imbibing nostalgic touches that had been almost nonexistent a generation earlier, while targeting middle- and upper-class audiences. Jacobs Field in Cleveland, Ohio, which opened in 1994, shares AT&T Park's asymmetrical outfield configuration, with some seats only 58 feet from the batter. The PNC Park in Pittsburgh, Pennsylvania, which opened in 2001, also has distinct similarities with AT&T Park, with its "ample sidewalks, and strategically located urban plaza [that] encourage community interaction."[3] Another company-named ballpark that opened in 2004, Petco Park, is even more out front about audiences' proximity to the action; one section, the Terrace Level, is "only 34 feet above the field, creating a sense of intimacy reminiscent of the great old ballparks."[4] Moreover, these parks are not in the suburbs; they were built within or adjacent to the city, much as earlier ballparks had been. In several ways, it would appear, baseball fans want to be closer to a sport that is becoming more distant from the class base that had long supported it and from which most players traditionally sprang.

One aspect that enforces this architectural uniformity among Jacobs Field, PNC Park, Petco Park, and AT&T Park is that they were all built by the same company, HOK. This international powerhouse specializes in building ballparks and sports stadiums around the world, and its American projects retain similar qualities in the design of its baseball stadiums: the nostalgic architecture, the often asymmetrical seating layout that enables a closeness to the players, and the geographic proximity to a city. Proud of its record, HKO claims to be "the only sports architecture firm to have been bestowed with our industry's most prestigious design awards," which include American Institute of Architects National Honor Awards for Jacobs Field, Oriole Park at Camden Yards, and others.[5] AT&T Park alone received several awards, such as the New Park of the Year in 2000, the San Francisco Architectural Landmark Award, and the San Francisco Chamber of Commerce Award in 2005. Clearly, nostalgia pays.

3. HOK Sport website, "PNC Park," http://www.hoksport.com/projects/pnc.html.

4. Designers of the park even integrated an original building on the site, the "Western Metal Supply Company," as a restaurant/café with a direct view of the ballpark. See the Official Site of the San Diego Padres, "PETCO Park," http://sandiego.padres.mlb.com/sd/ballpark/index.jsp.

5. HOK Sport website, http://www.hoksport.com. The website further claims that HOK's "global client list is diverse and comprehensive, and it includes 24 Major League Baseball franchises, 30 NFL franchises, 80 professional and civic arena clients, 40 soccer and rugby teams and 120 colleges and universities."

The contrast in the size of ballparks built in the decades after World War II is immediately evident. When Dodger Stadium opened in April 1962 in what was once a suburb of Los Angeles, Chavez Ravine, it offered parking for over 16,000 cars and seating for 56,000 people, with the stadium able to be adapted to seat 85,000 for special events. Angel Stadium in nearby Anaheim, California, also a suburb of Greater Los Angeles, increased from 43,000 in 1966 to a peak of 64,593 in 1979. Candlestick Park in San Francisco, which opened in 1960 and which AT&T Park replaced as the home of the Giants, had a seating capacity for 43,765, which increased to 59,080 in 1975.[6] While several of these stadiums were built for multiple use, they served to remind residents of the enormous popularity that baseball enjoyed throughout the nation during much of the postwar era.

Compare with more recent parks. AT&T Park seats 41,000, while Jacobs Field seats 42,000, as does the Great American Ballpark in Cincinnati, Ohio, which opened in 2003. Petco Park has 42,445 seats, while PNC Park in Pittsburgh seats only 37,992. Oriole Park in Camden Yards, which won architectural honors for HKO, has a relatively magisterial seating capacity of 48,876—or 10,000 to 25,000 fewer seats than most ballparks a generation earlier.[7] Some of the stadiums built in the 1950s and 1960s, in turn, are scaling back. Angel Stadium in Anaheim has recently reduced its capacity to about 45,000 seats, and as of this writing Dodger Stadium is preparing to do the same. As baseball franchises are targeting middle- and upper-class families, they are also seeing their audiences shrinking, and stadiums are built to match a decline in those audiences. Little wonder, then, that as fewer people attend, prices escalate to accommodate the enormous sums that baseball franchises pay their players and the management of the franchises. In other words, in baseball today, the fairly wealthy are supporting the very wealthy.

What a difference from earlier times.

When baseball grew in popularity among Americans during the second half of the nineteenth century, ballparks tended to attract almost solely men and boys. This aspect made baseball unique among most urban entertainment for the era; as David Nasaw asserts, "The availability of alcohol and gambling at the ballpark preserved the type of old-fashioned, male-only ambience that was disappearing from other commercial amusement sites." According to Nasaw's estimate, women in Gilded Age America made up only ten percent of baseball audiences.[8] Family

6. Ballparks by Munsey & Suppes website, "Dodger Stadium," http://www.ballparks. com/baseball/national/dodger.htm.

7. See the HOK Sport website; the San Diego Padres official website.

8. Nasaw, *Going Out*, p. 96. The first enclosed ballpark in the nation was Union Grounds, which opened in 1862 in the Williamsburg section of Brooklyn, New York. It included "one section for women and another for gamblers." Steve Springer, "50 Years Ago: Brooklyn to Los Angeles, Out at Home," *Los Angeles Times*, October 8, 2007, p. D13.

entertainment this was decidedly not. Baseball's then-reputation for "rowdy-ism"—that working-class audiences would spark riots spurred on by beer-soaked enthusiasm—assured the presence of private police forces or hefty "ushers" who sought to prevent any contact between the upper- and lower-classes. In short, ballparks were hardly for the meek or faint of heart. With the freedom to curse, spit, or engage in other familiar male rituals, the early ballpark represented what we could call a "location of release" for male fans. Baseball was thus much more than mere entertainment; it was at the heart of how urban American men defined their masculinity and, even more importantly, allowed them to exhibit it in all its loud bravado.

Nor did this makeup of the audiences change much in the ensuing decades prior to World War II, although those audiences did change in size. Admission to big-league baseball doubled during the first decade of the twentieth century; Forbes Field in New York, for example, built in 1909, could seat only 25,000, while Braves' Field in Boston, built in 1915, represented a decided improvement in seating up to 40,000.[9] The sport's audiences remained both overwhelmingly male and segregated, not only among race but also among class: wealthy customers enjoyed special, enclosed seats behind home plate or along the baseline, while the hoi polloi had the opportunity of sitting in the open seats most exposed to the sun, hence "bleachers."[10] Nonetheless, the sport retained its democratic spirit, which prompted the early twentieth-century social reformer Jane Addams to ask rhetorically, did not baseball belong to "the undoubted power of public recreation to bring together all classes of a community in the modern city unhappily so full of devices for keeping men apart?"[11]

Building on this democratic tradition, the post–World War II era demanded stadiums that responded to changes in policies concerning racial segregation. As any baseball historian or enthusiast will readily relate, baseball took on the role of the "great uniter" during the Civil Rights Era and beyond. It is no coincidence that Jackie Robinson was a baseball player, even if he excelled in many other sports. Robinson and the Brooklyn (later Los Angeles) Dodgers symbolized what the postwar sport would seek to become: a model of integration. The hopes of the nation in a color-blind society found some of its strongest backers, ultimately, in the nation's favorite pastime. In other words, if it couldn't happen here, it couldn't happen at all.

With larger ballparks, and the corresponding decline in black leagues and black baseball playing fields, the role as great uniter became possible—but up to a point. It became increasingly untenable to segregate audiences on the basis

9. Nasaw, *Going Out*, p. 99.
10. Nasaw, *Going Out*, pp. 97–98.
11. Jane Addams, *The Spirit of Youth and the City Streets* (New York: The Macmillan Company 1909), p. 96.

of race, as was the norm in pre–World War II ballparks, and so the sections for blacks and whites could be joined together and even expanded. Larger ballparks were thus symbolic of the social largesse of the nation, which came to be reflected in virtually all spectator sports. As black athletes were increasingly courted and feted, whites patted themselves on the back for having achieved a home run in the highly publicized world of professional sports. The nation was doing very well, thank you, on racial integration.

Yet, in the rush to congratulate ourselves that baseball proved that the nation could in fact integrate, we need a collective moment of pause. The final barrier to equality—that among classes—could not and still has not been crossed: quite the contrary. The elite at ballparks enjoy prime seating in encased pavilions or "skyboxes," with access to club lounges and other benefits of membership—features by no means unique to baseball. One could indeed argue that if anything, baseball's new stadiums have enshrined that inequality for generations to come. You have to pay to play. Coast to coast, the high-flying elite remains fervently courted by ballpark owners, and there is no indication that this policy will change. How else could the owners hope to afford the perks they offer to the players, staff, and management?

We can take this point about class still further. Despite the dramatic upswing in the American economy over the past two decades, class difference in the United States is on the increase. The nation has achieved a radical disparity in wealth, in which only one percent of the population controls over twenty percent of the country's personal wealth.[12] The last time that the United States witnessed a similar situation was during the Gilded Age, and the baseball parks now readily reflect this change. As franchise owners increasingly tap into the elite financial base that supplements and even replaces the traditional fans who can no longer afford to attend the games, the nature of the game itself, and its place in American society and culture, must also change. While baseball is by no means the only sport in which we see such dramatic differences in the treatment of its customers, its visibility as the nation's favorite pastime does make the public display of these differences significant. And as wealthy companies take over ballparks as a means of promoting their image, the notion of the ballpark as encompassing a truly democratic spirit—that which Jane Addams reminded us of a century ago—readily diminishes.

With the country's retreat, arguably, from fully embraced equality in contemporary times, whether in terms of race or class, baseball stadiums and the audiences who fill them take on a particularly different meaning. The architectural nostalgia in the construction of newer ballparks, a reinvention of the "good old

12. Janet Hook, "Democrats Calculate Risk on Taxing the Rich," *Los Angeles Times*, November 2, 2007, p. A20.

days," paradoxically recalls an era that hardly had much to be proud of in terms of either racial or class treatment. Crowds were often unruly, largely male, and predominantly working-class. Today, middle- and upper-class families have taken their place, and skyrocketing ticket prices are necessary for affording skyrocketing players' salaries. Yet nostalgic we have nonetheless become, and as a study of ballparks illustrates, franchise owners are paying close attention.

The End of Utopia?

Klaus L. Berghahn

Russell Jacoby, *Picture Imperfect: Utopian Thought for an Anti-Utopian Age*. New York: Columbia University Press, 2005. Pp. xvii + 211.

Utopian imagination and the principle of hope have fallen on hard times. It has become almost a commonplace that utopian visions are obsolete. The present state of world affairs seems to paralyze utopian thinking. In an age of worldwide exploitation and destruction of nature (the greenhouse effect), epidemic diseases (AIDS), and Bush's "War on Terror," the future of mankind appears bleak and apocalyptic images dominate our imagination. Especially the collapse of communism in Eastern Europe, if that was supposed to be a utopia at all, has shattered all dreams of century-old social utopias. Utopia is draped in a mourning veil, and postmodernism, we are told, is ringing in the end of utopia. Would it not be wiser, under these anti-utopian circumstances, to say farewell to utopian thinking?

It is against this backdrop of recent criticism of utopian thinking and imagination that Russell Jacoby tries to rescue the concept of utopia and restore the power of utopian imagination. Already in his book *The End of Utopia: Politics and Culture in an Age of Apathy* (1999), he argued against the amnesia of postmodernism. With the keen eye of a cultural historian, his "reading the Zeitgeist" (9) uncovered the roots of this contemporary apathy in the 1950s, when intellectuals like Raymond Aron, Arthur Schlesinger, Judith Shklar, and many others declared "the end of the age of ideology," which Daniel Bell then summarized in his book *The End of Ideology* (1960). But Bell already sensed a shift in the political climate and the emergence of a "New Left."

For good reason. "In the early 1960s history was speeding up and radicalism found a new life" (5). Ideology returned with vengeance. The Civil Rights Movement, Black Power, protests against the war in Vietnam, and national liberation movements inspired a new radical thinking on the Left. It found its echo in the 1968 student rebellions in Paris, Berlin, Berkeley, New York, and many other places.

According to Jacoby, all this lasted until 1989, which marked "a decisive shift in the Zeitgeist" (7). After the implosion of Communism in the Soviet Union and the bankruptcy of "the real existing Socialism" in the GDR, the opponents of all social utopias experienced a real sense of *Schadenfreude*, smugly announcing "the end of the utopian age" (Fest). Many leftist intellectuals who had relied on their utopian capital lapsed into perplexed melancholy, or even silence, as if their utopian ideas had crumbled around them. Others rediscovered liberalism or became neo-conservative turncoats. Jacoby cites many examples of this drifting away from utopian thinking. His point is that "everywhere the left becomes practical, pragmatic, and liberal" (15). Socialism has become more "a normative ideal than a historical force" (Kellner). What is left of socialism for most of these neo-liberals is a commitment to a welfare state. And yet, something is missing: "The world stripped of anticipation turns cold and grey" (181).

It should, however, be noted that signs of dolefulness about utopian thinking were already visible long before the shock of 1989. The student rebellions met staunch resistance from the state (*Berufsverbot* in Germany for leftist students and teachers), or drifted into desperate terrorism. In 1974, Ernst Bloch already warned against a "Farewell to Utopia," which would lead to resignation and the abandonment "of each and every serious social movement." After Bloch's death, in 1977, his philosophy of hope was discarded and is now almost forgotten. It did not seem to fit into the new era of postmodernism, as it was proclaimed by Jean-François Lyotard. His sober inventory of the epoch, *La condition postmoderne* (1979), was nothing less than a radical break with the recent past, and it attacked everything that had for decades belonged to the intellectual capital of the European Left. He settled his account with two great narratives of the European tradition, *récits*, as he called them: the epistemological explanations of the subject and historical-philosophical narratives in the tradition of German Idealism; and the "myth" of the liberation of humanity from the shackles of capitalism. Important concepts that had been the basis of every leftist ideology fell victim to this clear-cutting: the ability of the autonomous subject to construe reality as a totality, historic-philosophical constructs and belief in progress, the concepts of class struggle and surplus theory. In short, Marxism with its utopian tendencies and latencies became obsolete.

In his latest book, *Picture Imperfect: Utopian Thought for an Anti-Utopian Age*, Jacoby seeks "to outline the history of the modern anti-utopian animus" (xiii). He knows all too well that anyone who defends utopian thought and imagination today will be judged as "foolhardy dreamers at best or murderous totalitarians at worst" (ix). He is not so much concerned with the common prejudice that all utopians were daydreamers as with the much harsher judgment that utopian thought leads to totalitarianism. The latter charge is a product of the Cold War, when western intellectuals equated Nazism with Communism, Hitler with Stalin, and warned against the modern specter of totalitarianism. Simpleminded readers and teachers of the great dystopian novels by Zamyatin, Huxley, and Orwell projected the danger of totalitarianism onto the horizon and instructed their pupils accordingly. Jacoby is more concerned with leading intellectuals of the twentieth century, such as Karl Popper, Isaiah Berlin, and Hannah Arendt. (He could have added Ayn Rand's libertarian circle, for which any form of collectivism smacked of communism/totalitarianism and to which such luminaries as Milton Friedman and Alan Greenspan belonged.) Their influential writings since the 1950s, which blackened all utopian thought, earn Jacoby's ire and criticism.

One should not overlook, however, that utopian thought has been scorned throughout the ages. Utopias as blueprints for society, even if they only existed on paper, have always been ridiculed and warned against. Soon after Thomas More had endowed the genre with its name, utopia was used in the political rhetoric of England to denote an unrealizable constitutional design. After the French Revolution, all revolutionaries were vilified as fanatics and utopists. Ever since the time when early socialists (Fourier, Saint-Simon, Owen) pushed for a realization of their utopias, utopianism has become a political slogan that has been used mostly to combat communist theories. Out of the fictional genre developed—by the way of an abstract concept—a political weapon, which conservatives could easily use for denouncing critics of society as irresponsible or dangerous. Even Marx and Engels took leave of utopia in 1882. They wanted neither to be considered utopist, nor did they want socialism to be understood as a utopia. They therefore distanced themselves from the early socialists whom they only allowed to be recognized at best as venerable forerunners of socialism. In his 1882 pamphlet "Die Entwicklung des Sozialismus von der Utopie zur Wissenschaft" ("The Development of Socialism from Utopia to Science"), Engels criticized the abstract social utopias of the early socialists as irrational, fantastic brainchildren of intellectuals who developed societal ideas without heeding the connection between theory and practice. Always vituperated by conservative opponents and now also criticized by Marxists, utopia had already fallen in a state of crisis at the turn of the twentieth century. After the October Revolution, and even more so after the end of the Second World War, opponents of utopia raised their warning voices. With the Cold War as a backdrop, they equated utopianism with communism, showing the common denominator of both to be totalitarianism.

This is where Jacoby comes in, by demonstrating how wrong-headed this equation is. Before he adds his caveat, however, he outlines the premises of his understanding of utopian thinking. "To save the spirit, but not the letter of utopianism" (xiv) becomes the motto of his book. He distinguishes between "the blueprint tradition and the iconoclastic tradition" (xiv). The traditional utopias from More to Bellamy and B. F. Skinner have mapped out the future society in much detail, which demonstrates the authors' power of imagination; but they have also built "castles in the sky" (Mumford). This blueprint tradition has exhausted itself over the centuries.

The iconoclastic utopians also dream of a peaceful and just society, but they do not project their images of a better world onto a distant horizon. True to their name, they break images—or more precisely, they "explicitly or implicitly observe the biblical prohibition on graven images of the deity" (xv) and avoid visualizing a future ideal society. In passing, Jacoby also invokes another Jewish tradition, Messianism, which is characterized by an end of all conflicts and by final universal peace and justice (Micah 4:3–5). Messianism is indeed important for the understanding of such utopian thinkers as Scholem, Benjamin, Bloch, and even Adorno (34f.). But leaving aside these biblical allusions to utopian thinking, as important as they might be, utopian thought of the twentieth century is of a different, secularized ilk: it is foremost a criticism of the existing social and political order and begets, through the negation of the negation, a utopian vanishing point.

What would utopia be without its opponents—past and present? A harmless illusion of a blissful life in *Schlaraffia* (the German term for utopia in the eighteenth century), Shangri-la or a Cloud-Cuckoo-Land. The critics of utopia were the first to legitimize utopian thinking as a critical intellectual intervention. They pointed out that utopian thinking was a thorn in the side of any moribund society, and they warned against utopian thought, which is above all a radical critique of the existing social order.

Of the many opponents of utopia, Jacoby has selected three of the most influential thinkers of the second half of the twentieth century: Karl Popper (1902–94), Hannah Arendt (1906–75), and Isaiah Berlin (1909–97). But first he refutes all those who can think of utopia only in terms of violence and oppression, bundled in the polemical slogan "totalitarianism." By presenting utopia as a place of happiness, friendliness, and peace, he tries to contradict those who only see it as order without freedom. The classical examples of utopian narratives, which he cites, such as Aristophanes, Lucian, and even Rabelais, are peppered with humor, satire, and irony at the cost of established authorities. Here Jacoby's learnedness often carries him away, which might delight the reader, but it also distracts a bit from the main argument. Yet this introduction has its purpose.

For even More, who inaugurated the genre, became a staunch enemy of the Reformation, Luther, Müntzer, and the Anabaptists, whom he pursued and persecuted mercilessly. Or as Jacoby summarized it: "More was battling what he saw as his own illegitimate offspring—utopianism gone amuck" (50). Can the seeds of anti-utopianism already be detected in the contradiction between More's utopian fiction and his anti-utopian political practice, as suggested by Norman Cohn in his book *The Pursuit of the Millennium* (1957), and later by many others, among them More's biographer Jasper Ridley (*The Statesman and Fanatic*, 1982)?

This intriguing question was answered affirmatively in the 1950s, when a liberal anti-utopian consensus, under the auspices of the Cold War, took shape. The three intellectuals mentioned above not only complemented each other, but they also shared important biographical similarities: they belonged to a generation that experienced Nazism and Stalinism first hand; as persecuted Jews, they fled their countries of origin; and, to different degrees, they "came from the left" (51).

Popper, who during his youth in Vienna was an "emphatic leftist" (53) and supported Austro-Marxism as the backbone of the opposition to fascism, became the most influential figure of this group. During his exile in New Zealand (1937–45), he wrote *The Open Society and Its Enemies* (1945), in which he equated Marxism with utopianism and attacked them as the enemies of an open, liberal society. He establishes a stiff binary opposition "between democracy and piecemeal engineering, on one side, and totalitarianism and utopian engineering, on the other" (55). Both are committed to the improvement of society, but while the piecemeal engineer is rational, practical, and even modest in his proposals, the utopian thinker is radical, far-reaching, and violent. In his 1947 lecture "Utopia and Violence," he explicitly makes the point that a utopian transformation of society leads to violence and dictatorship, and he leaves no doubt that he means Marxism when speaking about utopian planning.

While Jacoby handles Popper critically, but evenhandedly, he covers "Master" or "Professor" Berlin's concept of "negative freedom" with sharp irony (55). He treats him, so to speak, from the outside: "Undoubtedly Berlin's impact hails partly from his charm, demeanor, and social skills." This also colored his style, which Jacoby characterizes as "conversational, readable—and diffuse" (62). Berlin avoided controversies with contemporary political philosophers and historians, preempted criticism simply by humility, and shied away from taking a stand on any major political issue of his time. A staunch liberal, Berlin defended individual freedom and pluralistic society against any utopian system, be it fascistic or communist; but most of all, he was, as he saw himself, a "deliberate anti-Marxist." In spite of Berlin's fame, Jacoby presents him as an intellectual lightweight compared to Kant, Constant, Mills, and contemporary thinkers, whom Berlin often quoted—mostly out of context.

In contrast to Berlin, Arendt was immoderate, sharp-witted, and judgmental, which often lead to bitter controversies—even with friends. *The Origins of Totalitarianism* (1951) made her famous, and after *Eichmann in Jerusalem* (1963) she became a pariah, at least in Jewish circles. The success of *The Origins of Totalitarianism* was at the time largely based on her frontal attack of communism as a totalitarian system, but one should not forget that the first part of the book, her analysis of modern anti-Semitism and Nazi ideology, situated the Jews at the center of events, which made it particularly powerful for her Jewish readers. The coherence of the book's three parts may be problematic and the "origins of totalitarianism" can be considered at best elements or phenomena of it, and yet its polemical intention cannot be overlooked. While she started out to write about Nazi ideology, the central arguments of the chapter "Ideology and Terror" are predominantly directed at Marxism/Stalinism. The mixture of ideology, however vaguely defined, and state terror led under Nazism and Stalinism to "absolute evil," which cannot be understood or explained in theological or philosophical terms.

At the Eichmann trial in Jerusalem she saw herself confronted with ordinary, bureaucratic evil, which did not fit her mold of "ideology" and the resulting "absolute evil," as she had presented it in *Origins*. This shift in her position, which she admitted only privately in letters to friends, did not lead to a public disavowal of her earlier statements, but nevertheless "the pillars of her totalitarianism theory buckled" (79). Yet, "for countless readers the message of *Origins*, which targets an evil utopian ideology, repealed as it is by *Eichmann in Jerusalem*, retained its validity" (81).

One could still argue about whether all three political philosophers were equally committed to Marxism or socialism before they turned against it; or whether their attacks on communism were at the same time directed with the same vehemence against iconoclastic utopian thinking. But that they advanced their totalitarianism theory during the Cold War with great success is without doubt. Jacoby's point here is not so much to defend Marxism, but to demonstrate that "Marxism does not exhaust utopianism, and to damn Marxism is not necessarily to damn utopian thought" (82), as the continuation of his argument proves.

Of course, one can easily defend utopia against the massive onslaught of totalitarian blame by pointing out its human qualities, tolerance, and peacefulness; but one should not overlook its dialectic of order and freedom. What is even more important is the question of whether and where these utopian blueprints of a better world were ever accomplished on a large scale. Certainly not in the United States, the "graveyard of Utopias" (Bloch), and bureaucratic communism, as it was practiced in Stalin's Soviet Union or Mao's China, was not a utopia, as Jacoby points out repeatedly.

Perhaps, one could consider Theodor Herzl's *Altneuland* (*Old-New-Land*, 1902) as a blueprint for the State of Israel? Hardly, as Jacoby convincingly argues. Although Herzl's utopianism was triggered by the prevalent anti-Semitism in Europe, especially in France and Austria, his "New Society" in Palestine lacks any Jewish identity. This cooperative society, neither capitalist nor socialist, is still entangled in the contradictions of its time and represents, like Bellamy's *Looking Backward* (1888), a castle-in-the-air. But what many critics already objected to at the time was the lack of anything specifically Jewish, be it religion, language, tradition, or spirituality. Nobody more so than Ahad Ha'am (pen name for Asher Ginzburg) in his slashing review of *Altneuland* in 1903. He was, as Jacoby explains, a leading exponent of Eastern Europe's "cultural" Zionism. Herzl's Zionism centered on state building, Ha'am's on a cultural renaissance of Judaism. Jacoby avoids, however, the fallacy of pitting Eastern against Western Zionism; both are for him representatives of Jewish utopianism. Herzl still represents the blueprint tradition of utopian thinking, Ha'am utopian iconoclasm. This is for Jacoby the springboard to "follow the threads of [Jewish] iconoclastic utopianism" (91) from the turn of the century to the Weimar Republic, in which he is mostly interested.

Martin Buber, a leading Zionist and interpreter of Hasidism, opposed, like Ha'am, Herzl's vision of a secular Palestine that lacked Jewish culture, religiosity, and spirituality. His circle of friends in Prague's New Society before World War I, among them Franz Kafka and Max Brod, did much to recover the spirituality of Judaism and its mystical undercurrents. Whether one should call their intellectual activities already "iconoclastic utopianism" (93) or whether they tried "to shake the world off its hinges" (101), as Gershom Scholem declared sixty years later, is rather doubtful. Only Buber's late work *Paths to Utopia* (1946), in which he surveyed utopian models, is a major contribution to utopian thinking. In it, he criticized the technical fantasies of blueprint utopias, which so easily turn into closed systems. Instead he favored a "rebirth of the commune," where neighborliness and human relations are cultivated. As a model for such a communal experiment, the *kibbuzim* in Israel received his praise.

Buber's spiritual utopianism was nourished by his circle of friends, especially by the almost forgotten Gustav Landauer. This anarchist utopian, a writer and political activist before World War I, "drank from the well of Jewish messianism and utopianism," as Jacoby puts it (97). He too mistrusted utopian plans of a new state, and rather hoped for a cultural revolution, in which "beauty, love and dignity" lead mankind out of contemporary slavery. The concepts of *Gemeinschaft* (community) and *Geist* (spirit) united the friends in their renewal of a spiritual Jewish utopianism. Why Landauer distanced himself from Bloch's *Spirit of Utopia* (1918), which breezes the same "revolutionary Romanticism" (Bloch) as Landauer's, is not made clear by Jacoby. Perhaps Bloch's expressionist spirituality contradicted Landauer's efforts to transform reality through culture by politicizing *Geist*. His opposition to Marxism is of a different ilk. He mistrusted political organizations, which promised a better society and state at the cost of individual freedom and creativity. Marxists were for him "cold, hollow, spiritless" activists, while the anarchists have a "poetic vision": creativity, enthusiasm, harmony, and solidarity (101). In spite his mental reservations, he joined the Munich revolution of 1918 as its commissar for "Public Instruction" (110). Although he withdrew from the revolutionary government in protest over its communist leadership and methods, he was murdered as one of the instigators and orators of the revolution.

Fritz Mauthner, a Czech journalist and scholar, fits into Jacoby's schema of iconoclastic utopianism like a linguist into political philosophy—that is, rather asymmetrically. He certainly was one of the leading Jewish intellectuals of his generation, but any form of utopianism would have been too grandiose an abstraction for his skepticism toward language—he would have even called it a pseudo-concept. He was a lifelong friend of the twenty-years-older Landauer, who shared his skepticism of language to the point that he wrote to him: "The critique of language belongs inseparably to what I call anarchism and socialism" (107). Here their interests overlap, but for Landauer, who considered himself more practical and political than his friend, this criticism of language has to lead to action for a better world. Perhaps, this chapter on Mauthner, as interesting as it is in itself, is for Jacoby just a transition to the next one, where he deals with "A Longing That Cannot Be Uttered" (113ff.).

In this chapter, which seems to be central to his argument, he concentrates on the prohibition against "graven images," which is laid down in the Second Commandment and repeatedly mentioned by the prophets. It severely restricted Jewish visual arts and also limited any description of the Messianic Age. As Jacoby alluded to earlier (xv), the iconoclastic utopians avoided the visualization of their utopia. Therefore, the question arises: "How did the prohibition of graven images affect Jewish utopianism?" (119). His first answer is that God can only be described negatively. When Moses asked God his name, He answered: "I am that I am" (Exod. 3:13). He for whom no word or image is sufficient to describe Him, as Leo Baeck explained (124).

All this resonates, according to Jacoby, in the writings of "Weimar utopian Jews," such as Scholem, Bloch, Adorno, and Benjamin, and permeated their "ethos of silence" (127ff.). This "ethos of silence" has become rather fashionable recently, although Jacoby does not buy into it. He pursues his line of thinking about the unspeakable from Mauthner to Wittgenstein. One should, however, not restrict this discourse of silence too much by the prohibition of graven images, as Jacoby does, but keep in mind that it also structured the discourse on the limits of the representations of the Holocaust after 1960. And yet, Jacoby further pursues his line of thinking about Jewish theology from mysticism to the secrets of the oral tradition, although he knows only too well that this "goes far beyond the scope of this chapter" (131). What Jacoby writes about the prevalence of the ear over the eye in Jewish tradition is worthwhile reading for a perplexed non-Jew, but it distracts from the main argument about iconoclastic utopianism. Or doesn't it? "Jews keep their ears, not their eyes, on the future" (137); they do not envision the future, they long for it. While the pious Jew may be waiting for the opening of the gate through which the Messiah will enter, for the Jewish philosophers of the Weimar Republic and of the Frankfurt School it meant criticizing the existing order of society—and longing for a better one.

In this chapter, the erudition of Jacoby sometimes gets the better of him, until he finally summarizes his main thesis: "The Jewish iconoclastic utopians longed for the future but verged on mysticism and silence about it" (141). Nevertheless, they lived in the present and attended to the here and now with a critical eye. They do not need blueprints of a better world, and yet they project a future that is peaceful, harmonious, and enjoyable. For this hopeful vision, Jacoby loves to quote Heinrich Heine: "Yes—it will be a fine day, . . . when the sun of freedom warms the world" (143). For Jacoby "clues, fragments, and whispers sustain this hope." But today, disillusionment drains the power of utopian imagination, and this means "a journey without compass" (143).

What Jacoby bemoans most is "an incremental impoverishment of what might be called Western imagination" (5). This is one of the reasons for the contemporary fate of utopian thought, and in one of his historical detours he offers a whole array of possibilities for how "imagination nourishes utopianism" (22). In his introduction Jacoby reflects for a moment also on Bloch's *Spirit of Utopia*, which does not describe the future but circumscribes it by invoking the utopian spirit in art, music, and poetry (xv, 34, 99). He should have followed these traces of utopian thinking more closely, or he should have reflected more on Bloch's *Principle of Hope* (1955–59). Then he would have discovered that the power of utopian thinking and imagination permeates all aspects of life.

In a lengthy footnote (164–66n125), Jacoby reflects on his ambivalence toward Bloch. He is for him the archetypical iconoclast, and yet he has some difficulties with him: For a long period of his life, Bloch was an orthodox Marxist and a defender of the Moscow trials, and for shorter period he was a "champion of the GDR," which he left in 1961. One should add that he was also a Marxist anti-fascist during the Second World War, which at least partially justifies his partisanship, or as he jokingly confessed to his publisher: "Heidegger erred with Hitler, I with Stalin." Yes, he edited and changed many of his texts for the final edition of his works, but this was quite normal for Bloch, since he, like Brecht, considered his texts to be a work in progress. Be it as it may, it is a bit far-fetched to construct a symmetry between Bloch's biography and his oeuvre, since his philosophy of hope often contradicts the contingencies of his life, and he as often changed course during his long life without compromising his utopian thinking.

If there existed only a world of facts and information governed by technocrats, how boring it would be. But we are endowed with the power of imagination to anticipate what has not yet been. The utopian impulse becomes most visible during productive moments, when the human mind is not satisfied with the world as it is; then it explores possibilities, envisions new concepts, and projects itself onto the future. Each creative thought, be it in technology, the sciences, or the arts, transcends reality and opens new perspectives on the world. Never to forget, however, that utopian thinking is triggered by want, hunger, and oppression in this world, and its criticism of the existing social order aims at a better world that cannot yet be described or reached. Utopian thinking is an open-ended process, a regulative idea for mankind.

In the epilogue of his essayistic book, Jacoby becomes a political activist who asks the pertinent questions in an anti-utopian age. How can one still pursue utopian thinking in an age of terror, worldwide exploitation and pollution of our planet, and a growing gap between the rich and poor nations? When even the richest nation faces a defective social order and even reformist proponents of universal health care are ridiculed as utopists, how can iconoclastic utopianism still be the advocate of hope? The answer to these questions is not that a blueprint for the future will save humanity, but first and foremost that utopian thinking is criticism of the status quo, a negation of any false order. Or, as Adorno once argued in a disputation with Bloch: "Insofar as we do not know what the correct thing would be, we know exactly what the false thing is" (147). Jacoby rightly calls this "practical, intuitive, and political," for "without a concrete condition to negate, utopian impulses seem vague" (147). Utopian thinking is situated against oppression, injustice, and indifference, and to have any impact it requires the audacity of hope.

Jacoby wanted to bring "an anarchic breeze into the house of Utopia (31). What he has accomplished are timely reflections on an unfashionable genre and a resurrection of the spirit of utopia; or, as he stated in the beginning: "To save the spirit, but not the letter of utopianism" (xiv). For this spirit, often declared obsolete or even dead, is grounded in what Bloch called the "principle of hope." Hope is a human propensity, and utopian thinking is its strongest expression. If it could be repressed or even forgotten, it would not have been part of the human experience or a factor in human history.

"Can hope be disappointed?" This question was posed by Bloch in his 1961 inaugural address, at age 76, in Tübingen, after leaving East Germany. Yes, of course, he answered. Naïve optimism, wishful thinking, and daydreaming are easily disappointed; and even well-grounded hope can be frustrated by the contingencies of history. When we speak of hope, there are no certainties, only possibilities, latencies, and tendencies that have to be explored. Hope is not discouraged by setbacks; it only becomes wiser and corrects its course.

Jacoby's book is such a correction of current misconceptions about utopian thinking. It has opened a long-closed window to the world of utopian thought, and its "anarchic breeze" should encourage readers to follow Jacoby's utopian project. After all, such is the temptation of hope.

The Permanent State of Exception and the Dismantling of the Law

François Debrix

Jean-Claude Paye, *Global War on Liberty*. Trans. James H. Membrez. New York: Telos Press Publishing, 2007. Pp. 261.

> The state of emergency exists for the long term. It emerges as a new type of political system, dedicated to defending democracy and human rights.... [T]he citizen must be willing to renounce his/her concrete freedoms for a lengthy period of time in order to maintain a self-proclaimed and abstract democratic order. (2)

Belgian sociologist Jean-Claude Paye has collected several of his recent essays about the suspension of the rule of law, the emergence of a permanent state of exception, abuses of authority, and the generalized condition of restriction of freedom in Western societies since 9/11 in a single volume, *La fin de l'état de droit*,[1] now translated, updated, and published by Telos Press under the title *Global War on Liberty*. Paye's essays over the past five to six years have positioned him as one of the leading critical voices of the post-9/11 era. His critique of the so-called democratic state—from the United States to Europe—and of the transformation of liberal systems of constitutional governance into police, military, and security orders actually had been initiated before 9/11.[2] Unfortunately, most social, political, and legal theorists (particularly in the English-speaking world) paid little attention to Paye's incisive reflections prior to the terrorist attacks in the United States. The recent translation of some of his texts into English has given Paye's scholarship the visibility it deserves. With the publication of *Global War on Liberty*, Paye finds a place among the critical theorists who must be read if one is to make sense of, carefully reflect upon, and devise challenges to the contemporary condition of state abuse, imperial domination, and proliferation of daily insecurities.

1. Jean-Claude Paye, *La fin de l'état de droit* (Paris: La Dispute, 2004).
2. Jean-Claude Paye, *Vers un état policier en Belgique?* (Brussels: EPO Publishers, 2000).

To be sure, a lot has been written about this post-9/11 generalized state of exception and about its many social and cultural effects. New anti-terrorism laws in the United States, Great Britain, and the European Union, the placing of certain groups of individuals outside the law (terrorists, enemy combatants, suspect airline passengers), the creation of exceptional procedures of containment, detention, and interrogation by government agencies, an ongoing and intensified regime of police surveillance inside Western societies, and the launching by the American state of a global war against terror have been and continue to be the object of various publications, essays, journal articles, or newspaper editorials. Several of these interventions have sought to apply political theoretical insights derived from the thought of philosophers like Carl Schmitt, Hannah Arendt, Michel Foucault, or Gilles Deleuze in order to make sense of "our" current history.[3] Others have chosen to take advantage of recent events or policies in order to figure out how contemporary practices can speak to existing theory.[4] In a way, Paye's *Global War on Liberty* seeks to achieve similar objectives. The volume does contain theoretical reflections derived from Schmitt and Agamben on recent measures and practices. It also offers several empirical chapters that detail minute aspects of anti-terrorist laws in various Western countries. Thus, Paye's *Global War on Liberty* could be read (far too superficially, however) as yet another text on the politics of domestic and international securitization that accompanies the implementation by governments of measures of protection against terrorism.

But such a reading of Paye's work would miss what I think is the key contribution of *Global War on Liberty* to contemporary discussions on the state of the law, society, and political order. *Global War on Liberty* is not like any other critical study that seeks to take stock of the current condition of state control and its disastrous outcomes for democratic possibilities. It is not so because its mode of argumentation precisely consists of going beyond the point where many of those

3. See, for example, Julian Reid, "Deleuze's War Machine: Nomadism against the State," *Millennium: Journal of International Studies* 32, no. 1 (2003): 57–85; Michael Hardt and Antonio Negri, *Multitude: War and Democracy in the Age of Empire* (New York: Penguin, 2004); François Debrix, *Tabloid Terror: War, Culture, and Geopolitics* (New York: Routledge, 2007); Michael Dillon, "Governing Terror: The State of Emergency of Biopolitical Emergence," *International Political Sociology* 1, no. 1 (2007): 7–28; and Derek Gregory, "Vanishing Points: Law, Violence, and Exception in the Global War Prison," in Derek Gregory and Allan Pred, eds., *Violent Geographies: Fear, Terror, and Political Violence* (New York: Routledge, 2007), pp. 205–36.

4. See, for example, Alain Badiou, *Infinite Thought: Truth and the Return of Philosophy*, trans. and ed. Oliver Feltham and Justin Clemens (London: Continuum, 2003); David Harvey, *The New Imperialism* (Oxford: Oxford UP, 2003); Judith Butler, *Precarious Life: The Powers of Mourning and Violence* (London: Verso, 2004); Slavoj Žižek, *Iraq: The Borrowed Kettle* (London: Verso, 2004); and Giorgio Agamben, *State of Exception*, trans. Kevin Attell (Chicago: Univ. of Chicago Press, 2005).

currently fashionable critical studies take us. Whereas many of these studies have left us with the realization that the state of exception in the making is in fact a new norm, a state of permanence (and, of course, such a critical insight is essential, but perhaps a bit obvious by now), Paye takes this particular realization as the very point of departure for his own reflection. The state of exception created by emergency laws and other extra-constitutional decisions and actions in Western societies is indeed a permanent condition, the starting point for new types of normalization practices and ways of thinking. Again, other critically inclined thinkers (Agamben, Badiou, Hardt and Negri, Harvey, and so on), in their own fashion, have said as much. But, in a way, this is all they have said. For them, the analysis need not go any further. By contrast, Paye believes that, after one has declared that exceptional measures are not just to be seen as cases of Schmittian sovereign decisionism anymore (which would be premised upon the ability to insert arbitrary but temporary measures to better restore the law eventually) but that they are the points of origin for a new modality of sovereign governance, one still has a lot of critical work to perform. One must still detail what the principles, structures, and rules of formation of this new form of government, this new political order as Paye puts it, are and how they operate. For Paye, this critical investigation into the beyond of the state of exception as a new permanent condition requires a prolonged, detailed, meticulous, and case-by-case examination. Here, grand theory is no longer sufficient, as Paye reveals that the devil is very much in the details of this developing post-constitutional domain of power, governance, surveillance, and control. Although Paye never spells this out, the implication here seems to be that, if there are to be resistances to this new regime of disciplinization and suppression of individual liberties, these challenges (or their proponents) had better be able to know what they are facing rather than assume that prior instruments of social and political critique will do the job against the newly implemented measures and policies.

At this critical juncture, past the point of no return of the contemporary state of exception, Paye also suggests that one cannot simply assume that a deep critique of the American post-9/11 system of regulation of terror/insecurity will suffice (with the related assumption that other national or regional cases of exceptional order will necessarily wish to replicate the U.S. paradigm). In fact, and this is another crucial insight offered by Paye, some European national models of "exceptionally permanent" social/political governance (the British and French models in particular) did come up with some of the new ideas, principles, and applications (about surveillance, police work, or summary detentions), now attributed to the United States, before the 9/11 attacks.[5] Thus, a meticulous excavation of the documents or statements that form the basis of this new social and political order must start with singular cases. It must consist of what, with Foucault's help,

5. See Paye, *Global War on Liberty*, pp. 87 and 170.

one might be tempted to call an "archeology" of the present.[6] This is precisely how Paye initiates his analysis, with a succession of closely studied national and regional cases, and with an emphasis placed on the texts of these new "laws," executive decisions, directives, or sometimes, simply, explanations provided for actions already undertaken by various governmental agencies (police, military, intelligence) outside of existing legal frameworks. Only subsequently, once the "archeological work" has been performed, can the critical analysis move from the particular insights to the more general principles that, Paye intimates, will have revealed themselves through the cumulative examination of the cases. It is only at that point in Paye's analysis, after the detailed situations have been considered in their singular aspects (but also always keeping in mind the larger context of the global war on terror), that grand theory is allowed to return. Nevertheless, as I will argue, when it does return toward the end of *Global War on Liberty*, Paye is not always successful in identifying a theoretical language that can speak to the new durable condition of exception.

Beyond the Suspension of the Law

Paye writes that "the rule of law becomes increasingly formal, not only because its content, the protection of private life and the defense of individual and public liberties, turns out to be very limited, but also by the practical possibility offered to the executive power to free itself completely from the last safeguards of legal order" (34). He adds: "The strengthening of the executive relative to the other powers makes possible the general and permanent suspension of the law. It is the instrument for setting up a state of exception" (34). For Paye, the state of legal/constitutional exception implemented in most Western democracies is not about a temporary suspension of the law, one that might guarantee a preserva-tion of existing democratic principles in countries like the United States, Great Britain, France, Belgium, Italy, or the European Union in general (the cases that Paye spends his time detailing in *Global War on Liberty*). More importantly, it is also more than a suppression of democratic legal and judicial systems, and of the individual rights that these normally guarantee, that would become a new rule of permanence, a new long-lasting condition of suspension of the rule of law, whereby politics could become the product of a succession of ad hoc deci-sions made by government officials and bureaucrats (as Agamben and others have intimated). Paye does mention that the generalized regime of suspension of the law in Western democracies allows states' executive powers to remove legislative and judicial prerogatives from the decision-making process, thus further enabling governments to monopolize all legal and constitutional powers (making the laws,

6. Michel Foucault, *The Archaeology of Knowledge*, trans. A. M. Sheridan Smith (New York: Pantheon, 1972).

implementing and enforcing the laws, and deciding on the judicial validity of the laws all at once). This could amount to a replacement of liberal democratic systems with totalitarian or dictatorial modes of political order. Paye does recognize that this often appears to be what the current system is about. And, on several occasions throughout the text, Paye feels compelled to refer to the new order in the making as a dictatorship or as a totalitarian system. But this conclusion is too hasty and incomplete. In fact, it cannot be substantiated by the analysis Paye himself conducts in *Global War on Liberty*.

Indeed, more than an insertion of totalitarian or dictatorial rule into Western democracies through the many instances of suspension of the law, what Paye's text reveals is that this suppression of the law gives way to the creation of a new normative system (one for which there may not be any appropriate political vocabulary yet). As Paye puts it, the generalized state of exception "breaks new ground by modifying the very form of the state" (34). Or, as he adds later on, "this morphing of the legal order is significant...[because] it lays the foundations of a new kind of political regime" (61). Today's permanent state of emergency/exceptionality ushers in a new legal system and, more importantly for Paye, it announces a new political order, one that reshuffles the logic of social action and scrambles the relationship between the state and the citizen. Paye's analysis demonstrates that the contemporary condition is *not just* a return to totalitarianism or dictatorship (his temptation to fall back onto those terms notwithstanding). Or, at the very least, what we commonly take to be totalitarianism will have to be reconsidered to match the contemporary circumstances.

What is crucial here, both in the new policies that have been adopted and in Paye's language, is the passage from the idea of the suspension or even dismantling of the law to the notion of a "morphing" (his own word) of the entire legal order. Indeed, the new permanent system of exceptional normativity that is being constructed in many Western countries facilitates summary decisions and arbitrary removals of individual rights and public freedoms by the sovereign ("he who decides on the exception," as Schmitt famously put it), or by various branches of the executive power. It enables a power of interpretation (of the political situation, the suspected risk or danger, or the meaning of the new laws) by governmental officers to become the only possible point of reference of the law for individuals living under such regimes, the always variable and contingent expression of rights and obligations for the citizen. (In this sense, it recalls Kafka's argument in *The Trial*). But, and this is what distinguishes Paye's original contribution from previous studies, what allows all law-making and law-interpreting prerogatives to be exclusively shifted toward the state's executive or the government is *not* the presence of the sovereign per se, its centrality or accumulation of constitutional powers. It is *not* the institution of an authority that now would reside entirely in the sovereign's decisionistic capacities. It is, rather, the crafting of a legal order that is permanently here, yet always in the making, even before the sovereign's decision on the exception is rendered. This new legal order does release an arbitrary decisionistic power of the state's executive. But this order is also prior to all the sovereign measures taken by this executive or government. This is the reason why, as Paye shows us in his volume, it really does not matter who occupies the position of power, which member of the government or executive command structure possesses a capacity of interpretation or action, and in which nation, country, or even region of the globe this new legal totalitarianism (if we must still call it totalitarianism) takes place. In fact, as Paye implies, it probably does not fundamentally matter whether a country has been attacked by terrorists or not, as this (morphed) model of legal and political order always operates at the level of potentiality, plausibility, and precaution (27, 33). Operating on the assumption that some catastrophe may take place at any moment in a given society, the newly established legal regime permanently triggers a sovereign's interpretation, decision, and subsequent action (often as a limitation of basic freedoms).

Procedure and Police Work

But what could form the basis, the structuring force, of this morphed legal order, of that normative substrate that, as Paye puts it, "legalizes the executive's self-proclaimed judicial powers" (61)? According to Paye, more than some (Schmittian) sovereign decisionism (which, as we have seen, is only a consequence of this model), two essential elements are needed to realize the transition to this local, national, or regional, yet all-encompassing and possibly transnational in some of its effects and objectives, legal order. The first basic component of this developing normative system is an emphasis on procedure over substance. Paye writes that "if the intervention of the law is increasingly present everywhere, it is expressed in the form of the procedure, so that it is possible to speak of a 'proceduralization' of social relations" (222). What the (new) laws and measures actually stipulate, who they will affect, how they will deprive individuals of rights or violate previous constitutional safeguards is secondary, probably irrelevant, as long as the process or chosen method of achieving a set (but generally vague) result—control, command, surveillance, security, victory—is respected. Of course, a law that bases itself on procedures, that is in fact nothing but a series of procedural stipulations, and that is made to constantly fluctuate as new techniques (of arrest, conviction, adjudication, internment, interrogation, coercion, defense, and military attack) are produced and taken to be the norm, deprives itself of any standard (moral, judicial, or institutional) against which it could be evaluated and that could keep it in check. Instead, a legal order that is strictly procedural makes and unmakes its own standards as it goes along, as it covers more and more political terrain, and as it regulates more and more social relations. Thus, according to this legal or rather procedural framework, if it appears that the law changes every time the state's executive or sovereign makes a new decision, it is in fact because the normative basis of the (new) system cannot accommodate anything other than a succession of constantly revised, fine-tuned, or transformed techniques and procedures. The vaguely formulated objectives of such procedural measures are incidental and come after the fact, once the rules are already in place. Thus, the sovereign's task is far more to find a way of connecting the new procedures to (the pretense of) a final purpose, to an overall justification, than it is to actually actively decide on the ultimate goal and, on that basis, invent appropriate laws. Put somewhat differently, the functional or formal fullness of the law (or its substantive emptiness) is for Paye what determines most normative, and further political and social, priorities in (seemingly) democratic states today. As Paye argues (but perhaps with too much emphasis on the autonomy of the government still): "The law is no longer what delimits the prerogatives of the government, but, on the contrary, what eliminates any barrier to its activity. The legal order becomes the symbolization of non-law" (100). Nevertheless, this so-called non-law, or rather this procedural order, forms the basis of the present condition of permanent exceptionality.

Transforming democratic legal orders into procedural ones does require some agency. If, as Paye intimates, sovereign decisionism is not the basis of the current system of exception but, rather, its consequence, and if a different (formal, functional, technical, and process-driven) normative order is the precondition for today's mode of totalitarian power over society, some agents or actors with a capacity to enforce procedures are still needed for the maintenance of the system. This is the point where a second fundamental element in the making of the new normative order emerges. Governmental institutions that previously were in charge of guaranteeing the respect of the rule of law and the preservation of the democratic social order now become endowed with an additional, more fundamental (to the functioning of the system) mission. Indeed, Paye asserts that the police and the military in Western societies become the two essential agencies of this contemporary regime of durable, possibly endless exception. The police and the military are agents who make possible the application of the new law as a purely procedural and formal normative structure (their arbitrary and summary actions make sure that procedure/process is followed). Consequently, they also enable the implementation of the sovereign executive's decisionistic force. As Paye repeatedly mentions, the police and the military embody the "pure violence" of the new legal system (87). In a sense, these two institutions—and more importantly, their agents (the police forces and the warriors)—operate in a purely (because procedurally limitless) sovereign fashion, and they do so even before the newly constituted powers of interpretation and decision of the state's executive can be instituted. In *Global War on Liberty*, Paye does not have much to say about the role of the military (despite the book's somewhat misleading translated title). But his sustained emphasis on the actions of the police is compelling. For example,

Paye notes that "[t]he weakening of the judiciary and its subordination to the police, an increasingly autonomous part of the executive, is a structural element in the extinction of the form of the rule of law" (182). Paye's careful examination of the growing autonomy and expansion of police operations throughout the Western world (surveillance, arrests, and collection of private information without warrants, cooperation with intelligence services, investigations and interventions without judicial approval outside existing national borders, sharing of data and resources between various national police forces beyond existing international treaties, and so on), most of which was already in place before 9/11, leads him to conclude that, "in the absence of any control, be it judicial, legislative, or executive, there is an increasing autonomization of police operations at the national, European (Europol), or world levels. This process places the police at the center of the structures of the national state" (183). By establishing procedures (often investigative, criminal, and punitive) that constitute the legal system, the police steers society toward new organizational frameworks and categories of life and living. It sets up formal and functional foundations of social and cultural existence whereby anyone in society, at any moment, can become (in fact, is always potentially) a subject of the anti-terror, anti-danger, anti-crime, and anti-dissent regulations that the government will implement (if nothing else, to provide some appearance of substance or justification to the police procedures). The police forces are thus crucial to the new legal system but, more importantly for Paye, to the new political order. The police function ensures the end of the social and assumes a "hegemonic function through [its] mobilization of the population in the implementation of security policies" (186). Once again with Foucault's assistance,[7] one could say that Paye makes us aware of the passage from biopolitical sovereignty to *bio-policed* normative orders. The power to make or produce life, to put to efficient uses the live forces of the nation, and to mobilize society around active disciplinary, coercive, criminal, and security procedures is now the primary (sovereign) task of the police (just as it is also the primary role of the military outside the state's borders, in the context of the war on terror). Again, the rest of the governmental functions, and in particular the power of interpretation of the head of the executive, are secondary. The sovereign and its decision on the exception are the fortunate beneficiaries of the normative groundwork of procedural biopolitical reorganization performed by the (bio)police. This is once again why, as I intimated above, totalitarianism and dictatorship can no longer help us to make sense of the current condition of legal exception and abuse of authority. In an age when the biopolice and its mastery over procedure are in charge of the "mobilization of the population" (as Paye puts it), the executive power, or

---

7. See Michel Foucault, *"Society Must Be Defended": Lectures at the Collège de France, 1975–1976* (New York: Picador, 2003).

In other news, Telos Press Publishing was recently awarded the First Prize Gold Medal in the Religion category for *Jihad and Jew-Hatred*, by Matthias Küntzel, in the prestigious Independent Publisher Book Awards. This award is conducted annually to honor the year's best independently published titles that exhibit the courage, innovation, and creativity to bring about change in the world of publishing. *Jihad and Jew-Hatred* is an important and timely book that makes a major contribution to our understanding of radical Islamism.

As a small independent press, Telos Press Publishing is committed to stimulating political and scholarly debate—no matter how provocative or unorthodox. We thank you for your ongoing support, and as always, we invite you to offer your feedback and ideas. Write to us at telospress@aol.com.

Best wishes,

Marie Piccone
Publisher

Russell Berman
Editor, *Telos*

Tim Luke
Bookline Editor

Telos Press

431 EAST 12TH STREET
NEW YORK, NY 10009
www.telospress.com

Tel: 212·228·6479 Fax: 212·228·6379
E-Mail: TelosPress@aol.com

Celebrating 40 years of exploring politics, philosophy, critical
theory, culture, and the arts

ISSN 0090-6514 (print) · 1940-495X (online)

PUBLISHER: Marie Piccone

EDITOR: Russell Berman, Walter A. Haas Professor in the
Humanities, Stanford University

REVIEW EDITOR: David Pan, Associate Professor of German,
University of California, Irvine

BOOKLINE EDITOR: Tim Luke, University Distinguished
Professor, Department of Political Science, Virginia
Polytechnic Institute and State University

MANAGING EDITOR: Robert Richardson

June 1, 2008

Dear *Telos* Reader,

As part of Telos Press's 40th Anniversary Celebration, we are offering a 20% discount on any book purchased at our website, www.telospress.com.

The newest addition to our collection, *Confronting the Crisis: Writings of Paul Piccone*, gathers together the best writings of *Telos*'s founding editor. Over the span of several decades, Piccone's incisive and often iconoclastic thinking made an important contribution to the political and social thought of the times. A new classic that belongs on any serious reader's bookshelf!